T
WW
WL
RO
RR

IAN McKELLEN

IAN McKELLEN
An Unauthorised Biography

Mark Barratt

Thames Wharf Studios
Rainville Road
London
W6 9HA

Typeset by TW Typesetting, Plymouth, devon
Printed and bound in Great Britain by CPD Wales

CONTENTS

ACKNOWLEDGEMENTS

I talked to a lot of people in the preparation of this book, a few of whom preferred to remain 'off the record'. I particularly enjoyed my visit to Lancashire and conversations with the people of Burnley, Wigan and Bolton, who were, without exception, friendly and encouraging to a wandering southerner.

My thanks to those who assisted my researches at the British Film Institute Library and the National Theatre archive; to Robert Witts and all at the Coventry Archives; Jim Howell of the Burnley & District Historical Society; Janet Birkett, Natasha Billington, Andrew Kirk and Jonathan Gray at the Theatre Museum; Old Boltonians Liaison Officer David Shaw; Karin Brown at the Shakespeare Centre Library in Stratford and Michael Paige at BBC Information & Archives.

Special thanks to David Allison, David Ashton, Geoffrey Banks, Daniel Barratt, Cicely Berry, Ralph Britton, Faith Brook, Harold Bullough, James Cairncross, Robert Chetwyn, Alan Cohen, Richard Digby Day, Marielaine Douglas, Frank Dunlop, Lucy Fleming, Jacqueline Fletcher, Nickolas Grace, Nigel Havers, Edith Macarthur, Margery Mason, Tim McInnerny, Frank Middlemass, Bill Moody, Ann Nightingale, Emily Richard, Ian Robinson, Michael Shipley, Patricia Taylor-Robinson, Zoë Wanamaker and Dorothy Watson.

Sir Ian McKellen himself didn't want to be involved, which made it harder in some ways, but meant I searched all the more diligently for the input of his fellow professionals. For those who want more of his own take on his life and career, I would recommend strongly his website at www.mckellen.com.

Finally thanks to Kirstie Addis at Virgin who had the idea in the first place and to my agent Caroline Montgomery for helping me get the gig. It's been a pleasure.

AUTHOR'S NOTE

In telling the story of Ian McKellen's life, I have tried to stick to the obvious chronology, except where it makes more sense not to. So McKellen as actor–manager is all in Chapter 4; McKellen as gay activist is in Chapter 7, and all discussion of television and film is in Chapter 9. The book looks at key jobs in detail and skips over some other plays and films more quickly.

Words have been borrowed from press interviews where they help to tell the story, but you won't find yards of theatre and film reviews reprinted. There's more emphasis on what friends and colleagues thought at the time, and what they think now.

INTRODUCTION

EXTERIOR. LEICESTER SQUARE, LONDON. EVENING

There are people screaming. A red carpet covers the worn London pavements for the evening. A battery of TV cameras whirrs. Autograph hunters' arms stretch, ever-hopeful. A 62-year-old man in a brown tweed suit steps out of a rented Mercedes saloon – London has run out of limos. Flashbulbs. But most of the lenses are pointed at a pretty young actress called Liv Tyler in a red dress. So who's the man in the suit, with the conservative collar and tie? He can't be a movie star, can he?

He speaks to someone in the crowd. The voice has a strong flavour of the north of England. Hardly a movie star's voice. But the sound – butterscotch and gravel – that's something distinctive, isn't it? And the milky blue eyes – humorous, intelligent, and just a little sad – you wouldn't forget those eyes. He signs some autographs, but he won't write the name of the character he's playing in the film. 'Gandalf isn't here,' he says. He writes: 'Ian McKellen'.

Like any good production of a play, this book aims to tell the story – the story of a boy from an untheatrical, middle-class, north-country background, who went from star of the school play to star of the British and American theatre, but who had to wait until he was close to drawing his pension to make it in movies. The story of a boy who lost his mother and found out he was gay when he was twelve years old, but didn't come out finally until he was 49.

The book is also an attempt to connect the man to his work, to look in detail at things that often seem to get forgotten in theatrical biographies: just what makes McKellen a good actor? How does he do his job? How has he changed in more than forty years as a professional? In what ways does what Ian McKellen is like make a difference to what Gandalf is like? Or Macbeth? Or Richard II? Or James Whale? Where do Ian the private man and McKellen the actor and gay activist intersect?

There are plenty of circles to square.

He's a vegetarian and a pacifist, but he's been a heavy smoker most of his life. He's flown back and forth across the Atlantic more times than he can remember, but he doesn't own a car. He's a knight of the British Empire with his picture hanging in the National Portrait Gallery, but he marched in London against the Iraq War. He's openly gay, but he won't talk about his private life. He's the leading classical actor of his generation, but he's best known for two immensely popular fantasy film franchises. He's 65, but he's got a tattoo of the Elvish character for nine on his upper arm. He founded a company which reclaimed power in the theatre for actors, but he turned down the chance to run both the Royal Shakespeare Company and the National Theatre. He's played leading roles in fifteen of Shakespeare's plays and won more than forty major acting awards, but he's also played a vampire in a Pet Shop Boys' video and turned up in an episode of *The Simpsons*.

Take a look backstage – maybe the answer to the man is there. Whether it's the star alone in Number One or the chorine jostling with twenty others in Number Fourteen, an actor's dressing room can tell you a lot about him. Some paper the place with cards and telegrams telling them they're going to be wonderful – everybody needs a little reassurance; some try to make the place safe by turning it into home with teddy bears and photos of kids and lovers. If they're in Number One, there are plenty who'll demand the place is redecorated to their specifications . . .

SCENE: BROADHURST THEATRE, NEW YORK. BACKSTAGE AFTER THE MATINEE OF THE DANCE OF DEATH. FIVE DAYS AFTER THE LONDON PREMIERE OF THE FELLOWSHIP OF THE RING.

The dressing room of Sir Ian McKellen is small. And bare. Mostly white. North-country puritan. Light bulbs around the mirror. A single theatrical caricature by Al Hirschfeld on the wall.

McKellen takes a shower. He settles down on a beige dressing-table chair, sips at a drink made from bananas and strawberries, and lights a Dunhill. He's on his way out to get something to eat before the evening show. It doesn't take long to get the make-up on and off these days.

And then we notice. No make-up box on the dressing table. Just one eye-liner. And there's a key.

No disguise.

1. THE ROAD FROM WIGAN PIER

There's a discreet blue plaque just next to the front door now. It reads:

Sir Ian McKellen.
Sir Ian, international actor on stage and screen, was born in this house, 25 Scott Park Road, Burnley, on 25 May 1939.

It was 8.30 p.m. to be precise, though the blue plaque doesn't mention that. But down at the bottom it does tell you the practicalities of just how these blue plaques get put up – 'Sponsored by Granada Television'. Standing at the end of the terrace on the corner of Albion Street, the house, with its turreted attic room and 'Aldersyde' etched with just a trace of pretension onto the stone gate post, stands out from the rest of the row like a star actor in a chorus line.

Burnley's an old Lancashire mill town with the industrial revolution in its bones. Some of its inhabitants can still remember what the place looked like 65 years ago when Ian McKellen was born. You came up over the green and brown fells that loom above the town, and all you could see were chimney stacks belching smoke and a great industrial smog lying across the valley. The smog's gone. But walk on down Scott Park Road and into Coalclough Lane, past the old Co-op, and the rows of two-up-two-down workers' cottages are still there, and so are the cobblestones.

But this is not quite a rags-to-riches tale. Some say Scott Park Road's gone down a bit since the McKellens lived there – there's graffiti and kids throwing things at passing traffic – but in the 30s and 40s, Scott Park Road was very much the 'nice' end of Burnley. Far enough up the hill to be out of the worst of the smoke, its dwellings were built for the nineteenth-century managerial classes. Theatre director Tyrone Guthrie lived just round the corner in Manchester Road during World War Two, when both the Old Vic and Sadler's Wells ballet relocated to Burnley. Star dancer Robert Helpman was a regular in the local fish and chip shop for a while. One resident remembers seeing Laurence Olivier and Vivien Leigh walking up Scott Park Road in March 1941 on their way to visit Guthrie. But by then the McKellen family had moved. In fact, they left in the very month war broke out. It would be another 25 years before Ian McKellen would meet Tyrone Guthrie. And by then he would be an actor on the brink of national fame.

Number 25 Scott Park Road is right opposite the entrance to the park itself. The McKellens didn't have much of a garden at the back, but Scott Park, with its elaborate wrought-iron gate, bandstand and duck ponds, was a fine place to walk the baby and for older sister Jean to run around. She was five when her brother, Ian Murray McKellen, first saw the light of day.

Murray was a family name. Ian's paternal grandfather, William Henry McKellen, registered his marriage to Alice B Murray at Barton-on-Irwell register office in Salford in 1904. The following year they had a son, Denis Murray McKellen. By 1939 Denis was married to Margery Lois Suttcliffe and working in the office of Burnley's borough engineer. He was 33 when his son, Ian, was born. Geoffrey Banks, who taught McKellen at Bolton School, remembers Denis McKellen as an imposing man of Scots-Irish descent, steeped in the Lancastrian nonconformist tradition – a pacifist, socialist, temperate tradition. The family ethic was: 'Never cheat. Always look after the underdog. Stand up and be counted. Try to make the world a better place.' Family tradition has it that, on return from their honeymoon, McKellen's grandparents knelt down on the stone-flagged floor of their house and prayed to God to bless their home.

But there was another side to this upright, stoic, Christian tradition. Emotion was held in check. Difficult subjects, such as sex, were not discussed. Awkward truths were swept under the carpet. McKellen's maternal grandmother died giving birth to Margery's younger sister, Dorothy. Grandpa Suttcliffe married again. An extraordinary family story relates how little Dorothy pointed to a photograph of her own mother one day and asked her stepmother who it was. 'Oh, that's a friend of your father's,' was all the answer she got.

There were preachers on both sides of the family. Grandpa Suttcliffe was a mild-mannered Congregationalist minister in the village of Romiley near Stockport. Grandpa McKellen was a barnstorming Baptist lay preacher in the same village. Fifty years on, Ian would recall memories of the old man's theatrical preaching, and put them to comic use as Amos Starkadder in the film of *Cold Comfort Farm*.

There was no acting tradition in the family, unless you count Margery's occasional forays into amateur dramatics. But as John Hurt, another actor with a church background, once put it in a *Sunday Times* interview, 'Religion and theatre: same business – different branch.' You only have look at the lineage of Laurence Olivier, Alec McCowan and Sybil Thorndike to see what he means.

Four months after the birth of his son, on the eve of the outbreak of World War Two, Denis McKellen got a new job: Borough Engineer in a town with a population of some 85,000. But it meant moving the family 25 miles south across the bleak uplands of the West Pennine Moors to the centre of the Lancashire coalfield – Wigan.

This was just two years after the publication of *The Road to Wigan Pier*, George Orwell's shocking account of conditions in the town. Orwell found Wigan Pier itself, the old loading jetty on the Leeds and Liverpool Canal, demolished. He also found the lives of the people demolished by mass unemployment. The war was about to change that, but in September 1939 Wigan was still the town Orwell had described, with its 'labyrinthine slums' and its 'monstrous scenery of slag-heaps, chimneys, piled scrap-iron [and] foul canals'. Roughly one in three of the population was on the dole. Around a thousand lived in shanty towns on waste ground along the canal in homes made from derelict buses with the wheels removed. Two thousand houses in the town were condemned as unfit for human habitation, but the Corporation couldn't demolish them because of a chronic housing shortage. Up on the 'Wigan Alps', the grey, smoking slag-heaps on the edge of town, starving people scrabbled in the dirt for scraps of coal through the bitter winter months.

Number 17 Parson's Walk, where the family of four took up residence, was a ten-year-old redbrick semi on the main bus route, about a mile from the centre of town. This was a world away from Orwell's Victorian slums. The new house was smaller than 25 Scott Park Road, but it was semi-detached, a clear step up the social ladder, and the neighbours were of the professional classes. A solicitor's plaque on the house next door announced the kind of people they had come to live among. When McKellen thinks of his childhood – and there would be another move before he finally left home – it is this house that he recalls.

There was no question of the McKellen children playing with the slum kids down on the 'flock mattress', a piece of rough, lumpy waste ground left behind in the middle of town after an old slag-heap subsided. At the back of 17 Parson's Walk were the grounds of Wigan Cricket Club, where Ian later scored for the Second Eleven. Directly across the road was the entrance to the park, just as in Bolton. Still, even in the middle class areas, you couldn't escape altogether what the industrial revolution had done to Lancashire. Wherever you lived in Wigan, you could only wear a shirt for one day. After that it was filthy, just from the air. If you hung your washing on the line, it was likely to come in dirtier than it went out.

Within weeks of the McKellens' arrival in Wigan, war broke out. Soon air-raid sirens were commonplace, and the glow of fires, burning after the latest raid on Manchester, could be seen in the sky. Margery McKellen put the baby to sleep under an iron table in the dining room for safety. In the event Wigan was spared the bombing, but Margery's precautions did not protect her young child from a more insidious threat.

Widespread vaccination against diphtheria began in Britain in 1941, but Ian Murray McKellen was not among the children to receive the vaccine, and in the following year he caught the disease. Diphtheria was a killer. In 1940 there had been 46,281 cases and 2,800 deaths. Beginning with a mild fever and a sore throat, in its milder forms the illness was gone in a week. But there could be complications, and between 5 and 10 per cent of sufferers, usually children, died. Ian was hospitalised and nursed in isolation and in due course got better, but some have speculated that diphtheria could have permanently affected his throat, helping to produce the highly distinctive vocal tones for which he is now famous.

Fully recovered and past his fourth birthday, the boy started school at Dicconson Street Wesleyan Primary in 1943. Residents on Dicconson Street say that the primary disappeared under the new dual carriageway some years ago, but, in the 40s, Ian's route to school took him straight across Mesnes (pronounced Mains) Park. Dominated by the old Gidlow Mill, said to be haunted by dead mill workers, the park was an oasis in Wigan's all-pervasive red brick. There was a duck pond and a bandstand, where a brass band played on summer Sundays, and Frederick's snack bar (established 1896) rose like a castle on its mound in the ornate pavilion above the formal flower beds. As they passed the statue of Sir Francis Sharpe-Powell, twice Wigan's MP in the nineteenth century, the kids liked to touch his foot for luck. Much of the statue had grown the green patina of age, but on that foot the bronze showed through. The children of Wigan still follow the same superstition, and sixty years on Sir Francis still sports one bronze-coloured shoe.

Before Sunday school, on Sunday mornings, the whole family would troop over to Hope Street Congregational Church for the service: religion was a serious business in the family. Denis and Margery McKellen also had another passion – the theatre.

Ian McKellen's very first experience of theatre was at Christmas 1942 when his parents took him and Jean to see *Peter Pan* at the Manchester Opera House. Not yet four years old and recently recovered from his bout of diphtheria, the show does not seem to have made an altogether favourable impression on young Ian, who was disappointed it wasn't a real crocodile and complained that he could see the wires. But it was the start of a regular habit of theatre-going. The McKellens became frequent attenders at Frank H Fortescue's repertory theatre, which cranked out a different play every week, Ben Travers farces a speciality. For more glamorous productions the family travelled to Manchester. Margery gave a tremendous build-up to the arrival of Ivor Novello in his Ruritanian romance, *King's Rhapsody*, which played four weeks at the Opera House in 1949. McKellen claims to have had his first erection watching Novello lean across a chaise longue with a glass of champagne.

At Dicconson Street Primary, McKellen's own performing never extended beyond the school reciting team, who appeared at nonconformist church socials around Wigan. But sister Jean was already doing Shakespeare at school, playing Bottom in Wigan High School's production of *A Midsummer Night's Dream*. Throughout her career as a schoolteacher and into her retirement, Jean would remain a keen amateur actor.

At the Saturday morning cinema club, the young McKellen was entranced by Robert Newton in *Treasure Island*, and suffered nightmares about the wicked witch on the broomstick in *The Wizard of Oz*. *Bambi* scared him to death. A couple of years after the war there was a memorable occasion during a holiday in Bournemouth on the south coast, when Denis took them to see Olivier's *Hamlet* on a Sunday afternoon. Cinemas hadn't been open on Sunday for long, and for the McKellens to be anywhere but church or Sunday school on the Lord's Day was most unusual. McKellen's favourite film, *Monsieur Hulot's Holiday*, dates from boyhood.

But Denis and Margery McKellen had little interest in films themselves. Part of the reason may have been the reputation cinemas enjoyed in Wigan. Through the Depression years of the 1930s, cinema owners kept the price of seats particularly low in the town. You could get any seat for four old pence and some matinees were as cheap as 2d. What this meant was that for a long time, and particularly in winter, the cinemas were full all day with unemployed people, willing to part with a few pence to keep warm. The memory of those days may well have left the middle classes of Wigan with a tendency to avoid their local 'flea-pit'.

But the young McKellen was not drawing his sense of theatre only from the stage and cinema. The sights and sounds of the streets of Wigan made an indelible impression on the boy. There were the grime-faced miners clumping down the road to work in their wooden clogs. In the market-place he would remember 'wonderful, romantic, gypsy-like men with long, greasy hair' peddling floor polish and wonder cleaners. When he wasn't dreaming of running away to join a fairground, the boy fantasised endlessly about joining those itinerant salesmen.

'I've never made much distinction between fairground barkers, peddlers selling stuff at Wigan market, preachers, actors, politicians on the stump – I once saw Aneurin Bevan in Bolton market square – because they're all performers,' he told John Walsh in 2003. There's something in those words of the man who would never go inside a church again after he left home. There's also something of the seasoned campaigner's disillusion with politicians. And there's also a nugget about McKellen the actor. Because there is a sense in which he grew up into a fairground barker of a performer, with that bravura, high-energy acting style, so derided by detractors as 'mannered', those endless years of touring highly theatrical productions the length and breadth of Britain, Europe and the USA, not to mention the tireless promotion of his latest film or play. In a sense Ian Murray McKellen did run away and join the fairground. It's just that, in his case, it's called the legitimate theatre.

Through the war the family struggled with rationing like the rest of the country. That meant a big shop on Saturday, after which Margery concocted a paste from butter and margarine, bulked out with a bit of top of the milk. In theory this was supposed to last all week. In practice it usually ran out on Thursday, after which it was dry bread only. As for meat, they had a roast for Saturday lunch, which reappeared cold on Sunday after church, and finally in a shepherd's pie on Monday.

When the war was over, foods that children born in 1939 had never seen began slowly to appear in the shops. Michael Shipley, a contemporary at Bolton School, remembers those years in Lancashire: 'There were things you didn't remember like lemons, bananas. You could go into a temperance bar or an ice cream parlour and have real ice cream. But, of course, rationing on sweets lasted for years. So you went down to the shop and the man would hand you over the scissors and you had to cut your coupon in quarters.' In Wigan, sweets meant the town's most celebrated product (after George Formby and Rugby League) – Uncle Joe's Mint Balls. Manufactured only in Wigan and a favourite with the local kids for over a hundred years, how could any product die with a slogan like theirs?

Uncle Joe's Mintballs keep you all aglow.
Give them to your granny, and watch the bugger go.

The McKellen family were prospering. By 1948 they had one of the new television sets – still quite an unusual possession – on which to watch the Olympics. Holidays were more modest. Grandpa McKellen was chairman of the local branch of Christian Endeavour which ran inexpensive holiday homes for Christians – plenty of prayers and Bible readings, but no alcohol and no cards on Sundays. So most summer holidays the family travelled to Beechwood Court on the lower slopes of Conwy Mountain in north Wales.

Once the country home of an Oldham magnate, you could walk straight out of Beechwood Court onto the mountainside. With his passion for rock-climbing, it suited Denis perfectly. His son liked the wild scenery, better even than the moors around Wigan where the family went walking regularly, but Denis never taught his son to climb. Not until he was faced with the awe-inspiring scenery of New Zealand on location for *The Lord of the Rings* more than fifty years later, did McKellen say he regretted this, but his father's failure to involve his son in such an obvious area for male bonding suggests a certain distance already between the two.

During the war a Mrs Levicks and her two children, evacuees from London, had stayed with the McKellens at 17 Parson's Walk. After the war a German soldier from the local prisoner-of-war camp spent Christmas Day with them. As people who took their religion very seriously, it was the kind of thing Denis and Margery regarded as no more than their Christian duty. The Bulloughs lived next door at number fifteen. Still in the same house sixty years on, they remember the McKellens as good neighbours. Now retired, Harold Bullough worked as a solicitor in Wigan all his life. It is a measure of how important the place remains to Ian McKellen that he visits the Bulloughs every time he is in the area.

In pride of place on the mantelpiece Harold Bullough has a photograph of McKellen taken in the summer of 2003 in Mesnes Park across the road. It looks like an extended family group – an old couple, a smiling actor in late middle age, a young couple, a baby. In fact the couple with the child are the current owners of the McKellens' old house – an alternative or replacement family.

Ian McKellen's career as an actor can be seen as a continual search for an alternative or replacement family – an instant family of rogues and vagabonds on tour, a tight and protective group of theatrical friends, even a bunch of very diverse actors dumped in New Zealand for a year to make a fantasy film. The reason for that prolonged search begins in Wigan in 1949, because a different kind of bombshell was about to drop into the childhood of Ian Murray McKellen. And not the kind of bombshell that an iron table in the kitchen can protect you from.

He was ten years old when his mother went into hospital. Nobody said what was wrong. Eventually there was much rejoicing when Margery came home. She got tired easily and had a bed downstairs to save her going up and down all the time. It was clear she was weak, but the ten-year-old McKellen thought she was just recovering. His father knew differently.

Life went on. The old grass tennis courts in Mesnes Park had been ploughed up during the war, as part of the government's 'dig for victory' campaign, encouraging people to grow their own food. Denis and other members of the Corporation formed a committee to create a rose garden on the plot. The result was opened with due civic pomp in August 1949. Fifty-one years later, when the garden was restored, Ian McKellen returned to reopen his father's old project. It is another measure of his feeling for the place.

Margery kept to her downstairs bed. She did not get better. Before long Ian was moving on to Wigan Grammar School. The family celebrated the day when Denis's salary broke the £1,000-a-year barrier. Then there was more success. Denis continued his slow and steady progress up the career ladder with a new job as surveyor and Borough Engineer in Bolton in charge of everything from sewers to lighting. The family moved the ten miles east. But this time not to the grimy centre of town but to a detached house on the edge of Barrow Bridge, just north of Bolton. Number 34 Barrow Bridge Road was in the land of leafy success with the picturesque model village of Barrow Bridge just up the road, James Cosgrove, director of Edbro engineering works, living next door with his wife and two girls, and the open moors rising above a lake at the back. And, of course, as always in a McKellen house, a park straight across the road. No smoke, no traffic roaring past the house, still just a short journey into the centre for Denis and a place for Ian at one of Lancashire's most prestigious grammar schools, Bolton School.

Then it all fell apart. In the summer holiday of 1951 Ian went with the rest of his second-year class mates to the school camp at Saundersfoot in South Wales. He was twelve. While he was there family friends arrived unexpectedly. His mother had died of breast cancer, aged 45. They asked if he wanted to go to the funeral. He said no. It remained a regret.

McKellen feels he didn't deal with his mother's death. He remembers crying uncontrollably at the death of Princess Diana in 1997 and, even at the time, he felt it was somehow a substitute for mourning the death of his own mother. The one positive thing he takes from losing his mother at such an early age is that his only memories of her are good ones – there was none of the inevitable strife of adolescence. And he had one other thing to hold on to: just before she died, Margery told her sister, McKellen's aunt, that it would be a good thing if he became an actor, because it was something he would really enjoy.

That autumn Jean left for university. Father and son were left alone together. It was a difficult time during which Margery's death was never discussed. At home Ian became increasingly sullen and withdrawn. Geoffrey Banks at Bolton School thinks McKellen and his father were never on the same wavelength. 'Let's not pretend,' he says, 'there was too much of a rapport between him and his father. His father was an engineer and I don't really think he understood Ian too well. He came to parents' evening and he took an interest in Ian's work but his understanding of it was limited.'

Yet there was more to Denis McKellen than this suggests. After all, he had played a part in introducing his son to theatre. He was also something of a pianist, sending the melodies of Chopin, Liszt and Tchaikovsky filtering up through the floorboards from the lounge to Ian's bedroom above. With his oversized hands, Denis struggled to avoid getting his fingers stuck between the keys of the upright piano. One look at Ian's hands, and you can see where he gets them from. So, though it was his mother who told Ian the story of Gracie Fields being discovered singing in a Rochdale cotton mill and encouraged him to buy her famous recording of 'Sally', the first record he ever bought, it was his father who actually played the music. Unlike the rock climbing, Denis did encourage his boy to play the piano. In the *Sunday Correspondent* in April 1990 McKellen identified his failure to persevere with piano lessons as his greatest regret. His greatest fear, he said, was loneliness.

With Margery gone, Denis McKellen hired a housekeeper. Then, when Ian was fourteen, his father approached him somewhat tentatively with a question. How would he feel about him marrying a woman named Gladys? 'That'll be fine. Can we have a dog as well?' was the boy's reply. So he got a stepmother and a corgi on the same day. They called the dog Glyn.

Gladys was a Quaker, and the couple were married at the Friends' Meeting House in Liverpool in 1954. There is no formal ceremony at a Quaker wedding but, as at all Quaker services, people get up as and when they feel like it and speak. Ian remembers family friends talking quite naturally about his mother. There was no attempt to forget about her. This approach to what can be a difficult relationship seemed to pay off, because stepson and stepmother soon grew close. Now in her late

90s, Gladys still lives in the north-west of England near Morecambe Bay and McKellen is a frequent visitor.

Meanwhile, with life at home disrupted by tragedy, McKellen the actor was beginning to surface at Bolton School. Created through a bequest from the Lancashire soap magnate Lord Leverhulme, Bolton School, with its boys' and girls' 'divisions' separated by a green quadrangle, was still only half finished when McKellen joined in 1951. Building work had been held up by the First World War and interrupted by the Second World War, but the great red sandstone castle of a school already dominated the Chorley New Road in the affluent northern suburbs of Bolton. The school was a direct grant grammar school, which meant that pupils whose parents could afford to were paying, while others, including Ian Murray McKellen, received varying degrees of financial assistance from the local authority.

Amidst the building work, some enterprising teachers with an enthusiasm for theatre under the leadership of Latin master George Sawtell had taken possession of one of the Edwardian houses on the site, which had not yet been demolished, and created a small theatre. The Hopefield Miniature Theatre, really no more than a raised platform in a damp room, would become a haven for the resolutely unsporty McKellen in what was, according to fellow pupil Michael Shipley, still 'essentially a sporty school'. At school dinner times, after school, even during the holidays, a group of boys would be down at Hopefield, building scenery, writing and directing. Ian McKellen was always among them.

Geoffrey Banks, an ex-pupil of Bolton School, had been teaching at the school for four years when McKellen arrived. Not long out of the army, he was dismayed by some of his older colleagues, still hanging on from the war years. There was the classics teacher with a smallholding near Warrington, who turned up every day with two dustbins in the back of his car to scrape up leavings from school lunch and take them home to feed the pigs. There was another teacher whose teeth used to fall out when he laughed and whose favourite phrase was, 'I confess I'm completely baffled by the situation.'

The headmaster, F R Poskitt, had his own methods of addressing the staffing difficulties. Michael Shipley, three years ahead of McKellen at the school, became friendly with 'F R P' later: 'I remember him telling me once that he always got bachelors when he took on new staff after the war, because if they came to Bolton with their wives they'd turn round and go straight back south again – the wives would never put up with the immediate vision of industrial Lancashire. So he always went for bachelors, because he hoped they'd meet local girls and then settle down.'

A professional actor himself, combining mainly radio work with teaching throughout a long career, Geoffrey Banks remembers the impact of McKellen's first performance in the school. Extracts from a range of plays were being put on in the Easter term at Hopefield as usual, and McKellen had been cast as Malvolio in the box hedge scene from *Twelfth Night*. 'I'd directed one of the other pieces,' Banks relates, 'and I was busy behind the scenes doing make-up, so I never actually got to see it. But my wife was there, and when I came out afterwards, she was raving about this boy. She went on and on about his command of the stage in that tiny space, the use of the hands and gestures, the eyes. And he was only thirteen. I was a bit miffed at the time because she never mentioned my play at all.'

Geoffrey Banks didn't teach the young McKellen until the sixth form, when the star of the English class found himself having to re-sit a French exam due to a dodgy command of grammar. With his father's jug ears and hooter of a nose, Ian was no Adonis, but Banks, like his wife, was struck by his pupil's piercing blue eyes, the feature that theatre critic Kenneth Tynan always said is an actor's most important weapon. 'You look 'em in the eyes, you know,' says Banks with a smile, 'otherwise you're not much of a teacher, and I was struck by McKellen's eyes – enormous humour – potential for it. He never actually cracked out into huge gales of laughter but the potential for it was there. He was quiet in the lessons,' he goes on. 'But when it was a question of the literature he shone. Boys usually have to be persuaded kicking and screaming that literature was not written by a lot of old grey-beards purely for the purpose of exam questions, but he was onto that immediately. He knew that.' That understanding of literary effects, combined with an actor's instinct for the theatrical, would make McKellen into a star of the classical stage in little more than a decade.

George Sawtell at the Hopefield Theatre was an ex-Royal Marine with a short temper who, according to one colleague, was disliked by many of the boys. The man behind the main school plays, Frank Greene, was his complete opposite. A modest, self-effacing man nicknamed 'Charley' by the boys, Greene would never allow his name to appear on the programmes for the plays: 'The boys deserve the credit – not me,' he would say. He sat in rehearsal halfway back in the great, echoing school hall, allowing the boys to do most of the work onstage. Only when he could not hear would he intervene.

McKellen has found two kinds of director in the professional theatre too. On the one hand there is the martinet who directs as though for a military operation; on the other there is the director who establishes a creative working atmosphere in which to rehearse, and allows his cast to 'play'. Like most actors, he developed a marked preference for the latter variety.

The hall in which McKellen appeared in a succession of school plays is a model for the big theatres in which he would dazzle audiences with bravura acting displays in the years of touring to come. Over a hundred feet long, wood-panelled with mullioned windows and a great hammer-beamed roof, like everything in Leverhulme's grand design it was modelled on a Tudor castle. It sat up to 900. The whole school, plus parents and visitors could be packed in on the ladder-backed, rush-bottomed chairs made specially for the school by a local Crafts Movement firm. Those chairs were capable of generating a fearsome noise of creaking and bottom shifting. Add to that the vast roof space and the sheer size of the auditorium, and you have a challenge which must have proved insuperable to many schoolboy actors. Irving Wardle, later theatre critic of *The Times*, played Hamlet there in 1947 with Leslie Halliwell of *Halliwell's Film Guide* fame as Claudius. The experience decided Wardle that he was not cut out to be an actor.

McKellen, on the other hand, thrived on it. 'It was the voice which even then was very powerful,' remembers Geoffrey Banks, 'but it was also the attack and the energy which amateurs lack so often. And the sheer command of the text.'

McKellen appeared in a string of plays. Some were surprisingly obscure, like *The Honourable History of Friar Bungay and Friar Bacon*, a comedy by Shakespeare's contemporary Robert Greene, in which McKellen appeared in drag as Margaret. Some were more obvious, like *Henry V*, which was one of his schoolboy *tours de force*.

School legend has Frank Greene walking backwards down the aisle of the hall, checking McKellen's audibility during one rehearsal. 'I can still hear you . . . I can still hear you . . .' Out of the double doors at the back. 'I can still hear you . . .' Down the corridor. Still as clear as a bell.

One review in the *Boltonian* is worth quoting. The reviews were usually written by returning old boys, so they weren't quite the usual 'everything was marvellous' guff. This is what R Clive Willis had to say about McKellen's *Henry V* in the spring term of 1957 (McKellen had played Prince Hal in *Henry IV, Part* 2 the previous year): 'There was, of course, an outstanding performance. Prince Hal and I M McKellen seem to have matured together, *pari passu*. His conviction and poise, timing, modulation, gesture and demeanour were rarely at fault. If the pointing of some lines appeared rather odd, let me not cavil: his originality was like a breath of fresh air. Youthfully majestic, he always dominated the stage.'

It's an extraordinarily accurate foretaste of McKellen reviews to come. And there would be plenty in the future that, while noting that ability to dominate a stage (and an audience) and to breathe new life into familiar texts, would cavil in spades about 'the pointing of some lines' appearing 'odd'.

McKellen learned to act by doing. He also learned by watching. During Bolton Wakes Week, when most of the town shut down, the fifth and sixth forms headed for Stratford-upon-Avon, where they spent the week under canvas near Tiddington, a mile and a half upriver from the Shakespeare Memorial Theatre. 'We camped in a field by the river,' remembers Michael Shipley, 'and hired several punts. We took our bicycles down in the train. I remember we used to set off at five o'clock in the morning to get to Stratford. You could stand at the back for two and six.'

McKellen himself was bowled over by Alec Clunes's ape-like Caliban in Peter Brook's 1957 production of *The Tempest* with John Gielgud as Prospero. He queued for tickets to see the matinee of Olivier's legendary Coriolanus, cycled back to camp for tea, then back to Stratford to see it again in the evening. He saw Olivier and Vivien Leigh in *Twelfth Night* and *Macbeth*. He saw Peggy Ashcroft as Imogen and Rosalind, and returned to Bolton in despair of ever attaining such heights himself. He learned to discern what he admired and what he didn't in discussion around the campfire with masters and other boys. He was particularly critical of Paul Robeson as Othello, who he thought sounded like a wounded elephant.

In the 1950s in Bolton you didn't need to go as far afield as Stratford to see theatre. At the Hippodrome Theatre in Deansgate, long since demolished, The Lawrence Williamson Repertory Players claimed to be the longest-running weekly rep in existence. Spoiled by his experiences at the Shakespeare Memorial Theatre, McKellen took to marking each actor's performance harshly out of ten on his programme. Elsewhere, major theatre was still making the journey north. In November 1955 he saw Gielgud's Lear at the Manchester Opera House, directed by George Devine and designed in the Japanese manner by Isamu Noguchi. A woman in front giggled when Gielgud fed toasted cheese to an invisible mouse, and McKellen hit her on the hat. Gielgud himself might have had more sympathy for the giggler – he thought the actors disappeared amidst the grandeur of Noguchi's designs. At the Bolton Odeon in 1958 he saw Olivier's film of *Richard III*. Within ten years critics were comparing him him to Olivier, but McKellen doesn't think of the great Shakespearians as the primary influence on him as an actor, let alone the hurried professionals of weekly rep. He places that in a surprising and revealing place. Denis McKellen was friends with the manager of the old Bolton Grand, and by special permission the young Ian McKellen was allowed to hang around backstage to his heart's content. This was not 'legitimate' theatre. This was Music Hall. In an interview with the *Illustrated London News* in January 1970, when he was 31 years old, McKellen could still reel off the names of the performers he watched and admired from the wings of the Bolton Grand: Issy Bonn, Suzette Tarry, the Western Brothers, Bob and Alf Pearson, Gladys Morgan, Albert Modley, Hylda Baker, the Maple Leaf Four. Even his schoolboy slang seemed to come back to him: 'I used to see theatricals coming through the stage door reeking of Guinness and fairly drably dressed and then putting on their shining suits, going out and doing something rather smashing.'

What he found particularly 'smashing' was the transformation in these old troupers at the moment they stepped out of the wings onto the stage and the illusion of total spontaneity the music hall artistes could create. They were quick on their feet, able to adapt in an instant to a heckler. Above all they knew how to handle an audience, to hold them in their hand, manipulate their responses. The performance he remembered most clearly was the Irish tenor Josef Locke – first house, Thursday afternoon, 5 March 1953. McKellen was just short of his fourteenth birthday. Already a radio star, Locke with his moon-like face and pencil-thin moustache held the audience spellbound with an hour of 'I'll Take You Home Again Kathleen', 'Dear Old Donegal' and the like. In between songs he chatted to the audience as if they were old friends, dropping in the odd risqué sequence about encounters with Irish colleens. He finished with one of his signature tunes, Romberg's 'Goodbye'. Of course, the audience didn't want to let him go. Eventually the stage manager in white tie and tails appeared from the wings and ushered Locke, apparently much against the singer's wishes, from the stage. It was a moment of pure theatre, not unlike the ending of a James Brown concert in the 1960s. 'If I have to identify it,' McKellen concluded in the same interview, 'that was the night when I became irresistibly fascinated by the lure of the theatre.'

McKellen and his acting friends at school, who included David Hargreaves, later head of the Qualifications and Curriculum Authority but then known to his school chums as Happy Hargreaves, were soon looking for further outlets for their talents. They found one at the Bolton Little Theatre on the corner of Hanover Street near the gasworks. Created out of a disused foundry in the depths of the old industrial engineering district of Bolton, the Little Theatre was no glittering palace of art. 'The whole place was filthy from the burning to create the gas, and the smell was quite overpowering,' remembers Michael Shipley. In these unpromising surroundings, boys and masters from Bolton School, as well as other keen amateur actors, worked together. It put pupils and teachers onto quite a different footing. 'It would be Mr Sawtell at school and then George at the theatre,' Shipley goes on.

Geoffrey Banks's wife, Elizabeth, remembers playing Olivia to McKellen's Sebastian in a Little Theatre production of *Twelfth Night* in May 1958. McKellen was nineteen, and just out of Bolton School. Through rehearsals he didn't seem to be doing much. Then at the dress rehearsal he suddenly 'let loose with all barrels, and began really to pay court to me with the eyes, and I went weak at the knees'.

The story says something about the difference between a keen amateur and a young man who already had some of the focused energy of the professional. But it is interesting in more personal terms too, because by the age of nineteen, when McKellen was making Elizabeth Cunningham, as she then was, go weak at the knees at Bolton Little Theatre, he had already known for seven years – from the year his mother died – that he was gay.

He remembers being very drawn to a girl when he was six years old – the usual time for 'doctors and nurses' – and then again at eighteen, when he came his closest to having sex with a woman. He's said that he loves being touched by women and touching them, and claims to have been asked many times by women to let them persuade him of the joys of heterosexuality. He has always politely declined. It all goes back to the twelve-year-old boy in the cinema, watching a love scene between a man and a woman. 'I could feel the heat rising in the cinema,' he told Christian Tyler of the *Financial Times*, 'and I was getting cooler.'

Bolton School did not consider it part of their job to teach the facts of life. At home things were no different – in a house where emotions at the death of a wife and mother were suppressed, it seems hardly likely that sexuality could be discussed. And as for homosexuality . . . This was the 1950s and homosexuality was still illegal. No less a personage than John Gielgud was arrested for cottaging in 1953. It was not a time when such subjects were openly discussed. Boys at school, of course, policed each other's sexuality ruthlessly, as they still do now, by throwing accusations of being 'queer' at each other. But, despite feeling ashamed deep down of not being 'normal', all the time McKellen was becoming more and more certain that he was one of 'them'.

Not that he did anything about it. Shy and diffident, he knew no one else in Bolton whom he suspected might feel the same way. Around that time a sex-change, complete with 'before-and-after' photographs, received sensational coverage in the newspapers. Lonely and isolated in his certainty that there was something wrong with him, McKellen wondered if he was changing sex. Would he begin to grow breasts?

Yet at the same time that he carried within him what he saw as a terrible and inexplicable secret, on the outside I M McKellen continued a triumphant progress through Bolton School. Standing tall at the bus stop in the morning, or striding across Moss Bank Park with the family corgi, Pat and Dorothy Cosgrove, the girls next door on Barrow Bridge Road, were much too frightened to talk to him. Star of the school plays, chairman of the Geographical Society, secretary of the Literary and Debating Society, already contributing short pieces to the Chit-Chat column in the *Bolton Evening News* at 7/6d a time and appointed School Captain in his final year, he was a star at school. He worked hard, he was never in trouble and he certainly never provoked a whisper of comment about his sexuality. And however certain he later said he was of his homosexuality at this age, in a florid piece he wrote for the *Bolton Evening News* just after leaving school, McKellen commented on his awareness of growing up: 'I realise with a shock that as I shall outlive my father so will my son me.' In his public persona at least he was still assuming that he would have children.

This beginning of a kind of double life was reflected in his changing accent. Bolton School encouraged its pupils to try to lose their flat, Lancastrian vowels, which McKellen proceeded to do. But at home he reverted to his original voice.

Meanwhile his school career was about to reach its climax: he had been invited for interview at St Catherine's College, Cambridge. Then a letter dropped onto the mat at 34 Barrow Bridge Road. He was being called up for National Service. With two pacifist grandfathers and a father who had been a conscientious objector, the decision didn't take long. McKellen was on the point of signing the papers as a conscientious objector himself, when the news came through – his National Service could be deferred until after university.

In the event, by the time he left Cambridge, National Service had been abandoned, but he has no doubt about what he would have done. His opposition to war remains to this day unequivocal and absolute. Even when the spectre of Adolf Hitler is raised, he still insists that World War Two is not the special case it is often made out to be. 'I would have been an appeaser,' he told Fiona Maddocks in February 2003.

At St Catherine's he was interviewed by the Anglo-Irish, W B Yeats scholar, Tom Henn. Dressed in his customary tweeds, with a pipe and a couple of spaniels stretched out on the carpet, Henn, an ex-military man, scanned through F R Poskitt's glowing reference. The school had advised McKellen to apply to St Catherine's, because they knew it was a college with a strong theatrical tradition. Peter Hall had recently left. 'I see you've done *Henry V*,' said Henn. 'Let's hear a bit.'

McKellen stood up without hesitation, leaped onto his chair and delivered, 'Once more unto the breach, dear friends . . .' Whether it was this that tipped the balance or not, he was awarded an open exhibition, Cambridge's second highest scholarship, to study English at St Catherine's College.

In interviews in later years McKellen would differ in his attitude to his three years at Cambridge. One moment he would be remembering it with enormous pleasure. The next he would describe himself as alienated from the whole place, and tell stories of ex-public school boys who mocked his northern accent and the agony of self-consciousness he felt going to parties. Ten years after leaving he told one acting colleague that Cambridge had been awful. In 1999 he told the *Sunday Times*, 'I found I could only be confident when acting, because it's a wilful escape from life.'

But for now, acting was what he did. In his three years at Cambridge, McKellen appeared in a total of 21 different productions for the Amateur Dramatic Club (ADC) and the Marlowe Society, most prestigious of Cambridge's many dramatic societies.

He was in powerful company. Among the people McKellen acted with at Cambridge were Trevor Nunn, Corin Redgrave, Derek Jacobi, Toby Robertson, Clive Swift, Richard Cottrell and the novelist Margaret Drabble. While over at the Cambridge Footlights, British comedy's greatest forcing ground, were Peter Cook, David Frost, John Fortune, John Bird, Eleanor Bron, John Cleese, Graham Chapman and Tim Brooke-Taylor. Peter Hall had just left. Asked what he thought had produced so many future stars at Cambridge at the same time, Peter Cook responded typically: 'Just put it all down to rationing!'

Of all the future luminaries McKellen met and worked with at Cambridge, by far the most important for McKellen's future career would be Trevor Nunn. Another grammar school lad from the provinces – Ipswich in his case – Nunn was a would-be footballer and pop star and one half of a drag act before developing into the leading theatre director of his generation. He directed his first *Hamlet* at the age of seventeen, and put Cleese, Chapman and Tim Brooke-Taylor on stage together for the first time in the Footlights Review of 1962.

Some of the shows these young actors and directors produced took them way beyond the usual confines of student drama. Richard Cottrell's first play, *Deutsches Haus*, starring McKellen and Margaret Drabble, made its way to the Arts Theatre in London. A musical version of *Love's Labour's Lost*, devised by Corin Redgrave and John Fortune, directed by John Tydeman (later Head of BBC Radio Drama) and transposed to England just before the First World War, came to the Lyric, Hammersmith, and got a rave review in *The Times*. McKellen even made it to Stratford in 1960 in a production of *Doctor Faustus*, which played in the gardens outside the Memorial Theatre, while a young Peter O'Toole drew the crowds inside for his Shylock. McKellen remembered mainly the punters jeering at them from the river, the biting gnats and the sparse audience.

But perhaps what is most interesting in the bewildering array of roles in which McKellen shone at Cambridge is that many of the most successful were of old men. He was a decrepit Holofernes in *Love's Labour's Lost*, complete with false nose and mortar board. He was an ancient, epicene Pope in *Doctor Faustus*, with Trevor Nunn dancing attendance as his cheeky acolyte. He was padded and bearded as Sir Toby Belch and, in his first year at the university in the part which made him a Cambridge legend, he was a mad old Justice Shallow in the Marlowe Society's production of *Henry IV Parts 1 and 2*, conflated with typical insouciance by the director John Barton, then a young don at King's College. By tradition the Marlowe Society didn't credit its actors in the programme, so the *News Chronicle* on 11 March 1959 headlined its review: 'Here's a brilliant Justice – but who is he?' Beneath this headline Alan Dent noted the contributions of Derek Jacobi as Prince Hal and Clive Swift as Falstaff, and then wrote, 'Infinitely the best performance though, is that of Justice Shallow who is genuinely ancient, wheezy, full of sudden changes and chortles and sadnesses . . . one would like to know the name of this Shallow because it might obviously become a name to remember.'

Outside the stage door of the Arts Theatre on the day the review came out, Richard Cottrell stopped McKellen. 'That'll be very useful in getting you your first job,' he said.

It was not that McKellen had never thought of being a professional actor before. Walking to school he had fantasised modest answers for future interviewers. Whenever the grown-ups asked what he planned to do with his life, he said he wanted to be an actor. But they always laughed and he laughed too. They didn't believe it, and neither did he. That review made him think for the first time that maybe – just maybe – he might actually be good enough.

'It was like being told you were beautiful, when you always thought you had big ears,' McKellen told *Woman's Journal* in May 1976. Perhaps there is more behind the remark than the unwitting revelation that the young man had always been embarrassed by the size of his ears – particularly the right one which sticks out. That equation of praise for his acting with sexual admiration says something about the secret he was concealing at Cambridge and indeed still in 1976. Boyish and unassuming, affecting a briar pipe for a while and dressed in the short brown duffle coat Trevor Nunn recalls so vividly, despite finally losing his virginity there at the age of 22, McKellen at Cambridge was still nowhere near coming to terms with his own sexual nature.

Which brings the story back to his odd description of university (and of acting) – 'I found I could only be confident when acting, because it's a wilful escape from life.' In parts more obviously suited to his age, like Posthumus or Beliayev, Kolya's tutor in Turgenev's *A Month in the Country*, McKellen found his own acting self-conscious, embarrassed and embarrassing. But behind a mask of make-up and a characterisation, which in Shallow's case he says was copied entirely from John Barton's demonstrations, he was liberated, he could escape. So acting was an escape from himself. That may seem a perfectly obvious statement; after all, isn't that what acting is – a pretence, a disguising of the true self behind a mask? But for McKellen it would be another thirty years before he could reconcile himself to what was for him the truth about acting, which is that to act is not fundamentally to pretend but, as he put it in a piece for *People*, a collection of essays and poems edited by Susan Hill in 1983, 'to release and reveal my inner life'. And that, of course, was written still six years before he finally came out publicly as a gay man.

Amidst all the acting, like most sensible undergraduates, McKellen found little time for academic work, and at the end of his second year his exhibition to the university was withdrawn – although he seems to have done more work than some. Some years later Geoffrey Banks, McKellen's old teacher from Bolton School, confronted David Frost when he came to do a guest spot on Granada TV's *What the Papers Say*.

'I taught this young man who reckons he got you through your degree on his notes.'

'What? Who's that?' came the startled reply.

'Ian McKellen.'

'My God, you're right,' said Frost.

But that is not to say that academic Cambridge was unimportant in its influence on McKellen. In fact it's arguable that the twin, though distinctly ill-matched pillars of the intensely serious F R Leavis at Downing and the flamboyant George 'Dadie' Rylands at

King's supported the entire edifice of British classical theatre for a generation.

Ian Robinson, a contemporary of McKellen, who studied under Leavis at Downing and later worked alongside the great man, paints a vivid portrait of the eccentric Frank Raymond Leavis: 'He was a small man, very thin and wiry (I have heard him boast that he never weighed eight stone in his life), usually dressed in nondescript grey flannel trousers and floppy, chocolate-coloured corduroy jacket, in winter under a snuff-coloured overcoat, but all year round with very wide-open shirt. He got about Cambridge on a big-framed old bicycle, on which he would bank round the corners of the court by the hall in Downing in a manner that sometimes made me wonder whether he would have to be picked up if the bike skidded badly on the loose gravel, but he always stayed on. The first glimpse I ever had of him was on a wet day in a cycling cape and sou'wester I remember, rightly or not, as being bright yellow, in which, his bony limbs sticking out and his beautiful thin face peering from under the peak, he looked a little like a bandit in a farcical review.'

Not that Leavis had much time for theatre, whether of the farcical review or Shakespearian variety. He hated the artificial forcefulness of speech which he thought marred the delivery of classical text in the theatre. And for Leavis the text was everything.

Up to twelve students at a time attended supervisions, as seminars were called at Cambridge, in Leavis's rooms on 'E' staircase at Downing. Students from other colleges could get permission to attend, and despite the fact that Leavis had a tendency to refer to McKellen's own tutor, Tom Henn, as 'the great booby', McKellen was one of them. And there the great man would, as Robinson recalls, 'worry away at a passage of Dickens or Eliot, endlessly coming back to the same questions until he was satisfied or exhausted'.

What Leavis taught was the essential moral seriousness of literature, that it was the function of all art to make people better people and the world a better place. How could such a message not strike a chord with a boy brought up in the muscular Christianity of Denis and Margery McKellen? Practical criticism was at the heart of Leavis's method, the detailed analysis of a passage of text, a meticulous investigation of meanings and ambiguities. And it was precisely this insistence on meaning in Shakespeare's plays, as opposed to the music of the verse which had been the prime consideration of an earlier generation epitomised in the mellifluous tones of Sir John Gielgud, that would form the intellectual backbone of the Royal Shakespeare Company and the

National Theatre under Peter Hall and Trevor Nunn. It would also be the underpinning of all the classical acting of Ian McKellen. And it was Leavis's message that art was a morally serious, worthwhile and important business, which would encourage a generation to commit their working lives to the theatre.

On the other hand there was Dadie Rylands: educated at Eton, fellow of King's College, Director of Studies in English, friend of Leonard and Virginia Woolf and all the stars of the London theatre – John Gielgud, Peggy Ashcroft and the all-powerful Hugh 'Binkie' Beaumont without whom little moved on the West End stage.

Leavis had what Ian Robinson calls 'a peculiar generic hostility to King's'. He looked down on Maynard Keynes, fellow and bursar of the college and the most influential economist of the period, as a stock-market manipulator. He also made glancing reference to King's College's homosexual tradition – Keynes and Rylands were both homosexuals – though for a man of his time, born in 1895, Leavis was not essentially hostile to homosexuals.

Rylands directed McKellen as Posthumus in *Cymbeline*, a performance the young actor was unhappy with, but his influence was felt more widely at the Marlowe Society and before long, via his protégé John Barton, at the RSC too. Founded in 1907 by poet Rupert Brooke's brother Justin, the Marlowe Society rediscovered forgotten Elizabethan and Jacobean plays like Marlowe's *Edward II*, Webster's *The White Devil* and Middleton's *The Duchess of Malfi*. Exactly such a re-examination of rarely performed Jacobethan plays would be integral to the RSC's success in the 1960s and 70s. The Marlowe Society was also part of the movement, begun by William Poel in the 1890s, to strip away the Victorian decoration which had turned the plays of Shakespeare into ponderous vehicles for the star actor managers of the period. The aim was to do away with the kind of ludicrously over-realistic settings which had seen real rabbits hopping across the stage in Herbert Beerbohm Tree's 1900 production of *A Midsummer Night's Dream*, to consign to history the operatic style of Victorian performance and to establish a much faster, more colloquial style of speaking Shakespearian verse.

Joining the Marlowe Society as an undergraduate in 1921, Rylands 'received the wisdom' direct from Poel, and passed it on to his students, including, of course, Barton, Hall, Nunn and McKellen. In 1982 McKellen himself put into practical actor's terms what the whole philosophy meant in one of the workshops which went to make up the Channel 4 series *Playing Shakespeare*, turned by John Barton into a book of the same name in 1984. After eleven sessions, in which he attempted to distil his wisdom through discussion and rehearsal with a range of star RSC actors, Barton was still worrying over how he could communicate to his actors what he wanted in terms of verse speaking. McKellen suggested, 'What about just saying to them as somebody said in *Alice in Wonderland*: "Look after the sense and the sounds will look after themselves?" ' It's a simplification, but it's more or less the method McKellen went on to use to create some of the greatest Shakespearian performances of the second half of the twentieth century.

So, with three years experience of working with some of the most brilliant young actors and directors in the country, steeped in the radical Shakespearian tradition of the Marlowe Society, stimulated by the intellectual rigour of Leavis and armed with a modest 2:2 for his pains, McKellen emerged from Cambridge University in June 1960. Then came the dreaded question all graduates face: what next?

2. LEARNING THE JOB

Publishers have been after Ian McKellen to write his autobiography for years. No one has yet persuaded him, but in 1979 he told the *Evening Standard*, 'If I were to settle down and write a book, I would try and answer the question "why did I become an actor?" '

So why did Ian McKellen become an actor? It's not that he didn't consider other possibilities. There was teaching – Jean had gone that way. There was journalism. But the editor of the *Bolton Evening News*, who had accepted those schoolboy contributions, told him he got as many applications for jobs in a week as he could fill in a year. He even thought about becoming a chef, and friends will still tell you he's a brilliant cook. So what was so appealing about the theatre to the 22-year-old McKellen? Despite not writing that autobiography, it's a subject he has pondered a good deal over the years.

On one level he came to believe he took up acting simply because he craved the pat on the head. But surely we all want to be wanted. The truth seems to be tied up more closely with his homosexuality.

A disproportionate number of actors are gay. McKellen thinks that's because society discourages gay people from expressing their feelings honestly in everyday life, whereas on stage they can be open emotionally while playing another character. 'It's a fact of one's life that one had to be secret about,' he told Robert Hewison of the *Sunday Times* in January 1991. 'It's why gays would be good at being spies, why the royal family often employs them, why so many are actors. It's because we've spent our lives hiding the truth.'

But that doesn't explain why so many designers, directors, choreographers and stage managers are also gay. They don't get to be somebody different on stage. Perhaps the truth is simpler. Perhaps it's more because the theatre is somewhere where homosexuals are accepted, where, as McKellen put it to Lynda Lee-Potter in a *Daily Mail* interview, 'To be gay [is] not extraordinary or a difficulty.' Though his homosexuality would remain a secret from the public, at least at work he could be open about his nature. 'If I'd become a teacher, it would have had to be hidden,' he added in the same interview.

So, having made his decision, McKellen wrote a string of letters to the repertory companies and began to do the rounds of auditions. Back in Bolton before one interview he called in to see his old school teacher Geoffrey Banks. On a visit to Cambridge, Banks had seen McKellen as

Warwick in the Marlowe Society's production of *The Lark*, Jean Anouilh's take on the Joan of Arc story. Banks had been stunned by the jump in standard in his ex-pupil's acting. But Banks the professional did still have a suggestion to make to the young actor. 'He was a bit dropped-on,' says Banks, 'when I tentatively broached the subject of accent and that really the one obtrusive sound was the Lancashire pronunciation of "one" which with Ian at that stage even after Cambridge still came out as "wOn". His head went down for a moment but he didn't say anything. He accepted it, and the next time I heard him on stage it had disappeared.'

The next time he heard him was on the professional stage. Offers had come from the Derby Playhouse and Hornchurch, but McKellen took the job that paid best – £8 12s a week at the Belgrade Theatre, Coventry. Originally contracted just for the part of Sir Thomas More's son-in law, William Roper, in *A Man For All Seasons*, he stayed for ten months.

The Belgrade Theatre was the first building block in the brave new post-war world of regional theatre. On opening night in March 1958 all the London luminaries descended on Coventry, still in the process of reconstructing itself after the ferocious German bombing of World War Two. Kenneth Tynan hailed the construction of the theatre as one of the great decisions in the history of local government. Across Britain towns and cities would follow suit, so that by 1970 twenty new theatres had been constructed, fifteen of them specifically for repertory.

The problem in Coventry was that the building had cost the city council £220,000, so the Belgrade was saddled with a whacking mortgage to pay off. Then, in its second year the theatre lost its director, Bryan Bailey, killed in a car crash. There was a near disastrous gap with visiting directors setting up ad hoc companies before Anthony Richardson, not to be confused with his namesake Tony Richardson the film director, arrived from the Queen's Theatre, Hornchurch to take over.

'What we want and what Coventry vitally needs is a theatre with the aspect of Dublin's Abbey,' announced Richardson in the *Coventry Evening Telegraph*. That suggested exciting new work and longer rehearsal periods. What they got and what Coventry seemed to want was bucketfuls of Agatha Christie. Arnold Wesker's *The Kitchen*, directed by a young John Dexter, had premiered in June 1961, before McKellen arrived at the Belgrade, to general incomprehension and fury over the lack of an interval. *The Caretaker* would do a week to a mixed reception in September. But McKellen wouldn't be in that one either. What he did was a series of good old rep stand-bys – plays that had just finished their

West End run, plays that might make it to a West End run, the lightest end of Bernard Shaw and schools Shakespeare.

The local press scoffed. While Frank Hauser, director at the Oxford Playhouse, was planning the first complete production of Aeschylus' *Oresteia* for 56 years, Coventry was getting *When We are Married* and *You Never Can Tell*. But you could hardly blame Richardson. Shaw just about survived, but only Christie really drew an audience. Richardson's assistant, Brian Bell, tried subverting *Black Coffee*, one of Hercule Poirot's finest hours, with some tricksy effects borrowed from the cinema, involving the title and credits on a screen and sudden spotlights on individual characters. The audience didn't seem to notice. The show did the best week's business in Coventry for fourteen years.

McKellen has told the story of his first day of rehearsal at the Belgrade. The *Bolton Evening News* had proudly announced the date of their local boy joining the company – 22 August 1961. In awe of the professional actors with whom he was about to work, amazed that he was actually to be paid for doing what he wanted to do most in all the world, McKellen arrived for his first day's work in the professional theatre. The stage manager passed out copies of the script. It was the French's acting edition. 'OK,' announced director David Forder, 'the play's *A Man For All Seasons*. In your scripts you'll find the moves they did in the West End production. What was good enough for Paul Scofield for over a year will do us very nicely for a couple of weeks.' What they would have made of such a speech at the Abbey Theatre, Dublin, one does not know. But it was not an auspicious beginning. McKellen had already been directed by Trevor Nunn, John Barton, Corin Redgrave and Dadie Rylands. Such poverty of ambition could hardly impress.

But whatever his reservations about artistic standards at the Belgrade, McKellen threw himself into the work with a fury. Living in cheap digs on Corporation Street and eating food sold cheap to the actors by the local Co-op, he felt himself embraced, first by the company of actors with cheerful after-hours lock-ins at the Belgrade's local, and before long by the Coventry audience. 'That's why actors often look back on rep as the happiest days of their lives,' he told Nicholas de Jongh many years later. 'People know who you are and are glad you're there.' The local papers' reviews of young actors in Coventry for an extended season would often sound more like school reports – 'seems to progress in giant strides with every major role'; 'performs with the assurance we have come to expect'.

Not that McKellen's progress was by any means sure or steady at this stage. His fellow actors thought him quiet, noted his willingness to work hard, but saw little sign of the inventiveness which would later be a trademark of his work on stage. But before long some of the other younger members of the company grew jealous, as the season seemed to be being shaped around McKellen.

His first crack at a major role came in January 1962 as Konstantin in Chekhov's *The Seagull*. It was a disaster. Gareth Lloyd Evans of the *Guardian* wrote the kind of personally critical review young actors find particularly hard to cope with. 'The biggest disappointment is Ian McKellen's Konstantin. This young actor of much promise in voice and intelligent interpretation seems determined to invite disaster with his legs and arms. So often they seemed to be playing one part and the rest of him another.'

McKellen himself felt equally ill at ease in his first professional shot at Shakespeare – Claudio in *Much Ado About Nothing*. Reacting against his disastrous Konstantin, he tried underplaying. But just as he had at Cambridge with Posthumus and Kolya in *A Month in the Country*, he felt exposed and self-conscious in a juvenile role.

The rep apprenticeship meant that young actors had a chance to test themselves in a range of parts, to fail perhaps, but then two weeks later be on to something new, both they and the audience having forgotten they'd fallen on their face in the last one. The danger of rep was that bad plays and short rehearsal periods taught lazy acting habits which were never unlearned. Patrick Stewart, another actor who started out in rep before going on to find fame as Captain Picard in *Star Trek: The Next Generation*, thinks he and McKellen were lucky to have had the experience of playing such a multitude of roles as a matter of course. With the demise of long-term contracts and the closure of many reps, that schooling ground for young actors has now all but disappeared.

Young actors also learn by imitation. In his time at the Belgrade, McKellen worked with Leonard Rossiter in the pre-London try-out of David Turner's *Semi-Detached*. But a particular early mentor was the company's regular leading man in his first season, Bernard Kilby. He was the one who kept his head above water as Trigorin in the ill-fated *Seagull*, and in *Much Ado* he was compared favourably with recent other Benedicks at Stratford. The Belgrade reverted once more to Agatha Christie in April 1962 – *Ten Little Niggers*, as it was then still called. Kilby was playing Judge Wargrave. One night he fell heavily, performing his stage death. Rushed to hospital in the early hours, he had two operations for an intestinal rupture the following day. The show went on. With no understudy, that night the director, Geoffrey Edwards, put on the costume and got through the part without a prompt. A week later

Kilby was dead. He was 39. Back in November 1961 he had told the local *Sunday Mercury* his only ambition in the theatre was 'just to keep working'. It was a simple, no-nonsense actor's statement, which McKellen would take very much to heart.

Among the sixteen or so roles played by the young McKellen at the Belgrade between September 1961 and June 1962, one is worth noting particularly. *End of Conflict*, written by Barry England, was one of Anthony Richardson's attempts at a new play. Set in the Chinese communist border country on the mainland opposite Hong Kong in 1951, the play involved a rather talky clash between a bunch of regular army types and Simon, a young subaltern straight from Downing College, doing his National Service, played by Ian McKellen. It was the first in a line of military and ex-military roles that would run right through to the Captain in *The Dance of Death* in New York, London and Sydney more than forty years later. For a man with such a strong pacifist background, and who had come within days of signing papers as a conscientious objector, it is ironic that McKellen should have made such an illustrious career out of playing soldiers.

Elspeth Cochrane came up from London, liked what she saw, and would later become McKellen's first agent. She was not the only one to see and be impressed by the young McKellen at the Belgrade. At her encouragement Robert Chetwyn, artistic director of the Arts Theatre, Ipswich, also made the trek up to Coventry to see *Semi-Detached*.

'He was untrained, but he obviously had the talent,' remembers Chetwyn. 'I don't think he quite knew what he'd got, but I sensed that he had something very powerful.' Pressed as to exactly what that 'something' was, Chetwyn finds it hard to explain. 'You can have two actors who are equal in what they're capable of, but one becomes a big star and one has a comfortable career and no one has ever heard of them. The thing which makes a star actor is charisma.' But that simply brings us round to another word which is hard to define. It's a question people often come back to – just what was it that made people sit up and take notice when they saw the young McKellen on stage?

There's one thing Chetwyn is specific about. 'I thought he had incredible range.' Shakespeare, Osborne, O'Neill . . . 'One thing he really didn't have a clue about,' he says at last, searching his memory for what was missing in the young actor's repertoire, 'was the light drawing-room comedy of the period. I remember giving him a part in *The Gazebo* by Alec Coppell. He was rather disdainful of it at first and then he got so pleased with himself when he got laughs that he changed his attitude about comedy and stopped looking down on it.'

Interestingly, Chetwyn felt McKellen at that time was 'not at all sure how well equipped he was as an actor'. He'd gone from school plays to student drama to rep, missing out drama school and picking up technique as he went. McKellen's Cambridge contemporary, Corin Redgrave, says he wishes he had gone to drama school but, publicly, McKellen has tended to be rather dismissive of specialist actor training. Nickolas Grace (*Brideshead Revisited, Robin of Sherwood*), just out of the Central School of Speech and Drama in 1970, remembers McKellen privately taking a similar attitude to Redgrave, however. 'One of the first things he said to me was that he really regretted not having been to drama school. He used to see me do my warm-up on stage every day and he felt he'd missed out on the voice and movement training which as an actor is the most important thing to have inside yourself.'

Like Coventry, Ipswich gave its public as wide a variety of theatre as they could be made to swallow. The difference in Ipswich was that the audience was more loyal. In Coventry they would pack the Agatha Christies and avoid like poison anything that looked risky. In Ipswich they came because they trusted the company. The theatre was much smaller too. In fact it had been a village hall and then a cinema and would transform itself once more into the Elim Pentecostal Church after the rep left for the new Wolsey Theatre in 1979. And most important of all, there wasn't the crushing £17,000 a year that Anthony Richardson had to find in mortgage repayments.

James Cairncross worked with McKellen in Ipswich. He remains quite sure of the reason for the theatre's success at this period: 'The old theatre in Ipswich was very cramped. The dressing rooms were fairly primitive. The place owed its success, I think, almost entirely to Robert Chetwyn. He achieved more in a fortnight's rehearsal than any director I've ever worked with.'

Chetwyn had evolved a rehearsal system in the hard school of weekly rep in Harrogate. Actors with a big part in one play had a small one in the next. Simple thrillers were rehearsed in a matter of days, so that extra time could be 'borrowed' for more complex plays. At Ipswich in fortnightly rep this translated into a week on easy plays and three weeks on harder ones.

'He was determined,' says Cairncross, already a highly experienced actor. 'He wasn't a ruthless man but he knew exactly what he wanted. You trusted him after a bit.'

Chetwyn had his schedule worked out to the minute: read-through Monday morning; give the actors their moves that afternoon and all next day. Then go back to the beginning, and work over the script again in detail, 'discovering' the play with the actors as they went along. 'I'm always quite pleased when an actor doesn't really know what they're going to do with a part,' he says, 'because I'm usually in that state myself. I know where we're going to finish, but not how we're going to get there. I find that out in rehearsal. And that's the point of theatre. You're depending on the actor to do a great deal for you. You can't do that in television or film.' The climax of the rehearsal period came with two dress rehearsals on the Monday, another one on Tuesday and then the opening on Tuesday night.

Eager to learn, willing to accept a note from his director, though increasingly questioning if he didn't agree, McKellen developed fast under Robert Chetwyn's guidance; because the other difference between Coventry and Ipswich was that Chetwyn actually directed the plays. Of the fifteen productions McKellen did at the Belgrade, the Artistic Director, Anthony Richardson only took charge of five. At Ipswich McKellen would appear in 21 plays in the space of thirteen months. Chetwyn directed fifteen of them himself. This is a phenomenal work-rate for both actors and director, and over a period of time can certainly lead to staleness. For the young McKellen it was phase two of his education in the professional theatre.

Chetwyn gave McKellen a series of substantial roles. Before Christmas he played the lead in a dramatisation of *David Copperfield*. Then on 5 February 1963 he opened in his first leading role in Shakespeare – Henry V. 'It was quite a thing to give him Henry V so soon,' remembers the director, 'but he wasn't at all fazed by Shakespeare or the script.' Chetwyn didn't know McKellen had played the part before at Bolton School, but the director still recalls the young actor's eagerness to learn, both in rehearsals and during the two-and-a-half-week run. 'I have this very clear memory,' he says, 'of sitting in my tiny office right at the top of the building with *Henry V* on stage. I was doing some work, and Ian came rushing up the stairs and he was so excited because he'd got something right he'd been struggling with.'

Chetwyn no longer remembers exactly what it was that his young star had 'got right', but this eagerness to continue working and developing a performance through the run of the play would become a feature of McKellen, the mature actor. And that's whether the reviews are good or bad. For *Henry V* at Ipswich he got excellent notices, but he knew there were aspects of the role which weren't working. So, not for him the fixing of a performance on the first night and then two weeks or two months or two years of repetition. What he learned at Ipswich is that a performance in the theatre is never complete. Every night a role has to be recreated for a new audience. No two nights are exactly the same.

And every performance contains within it the possibility of improvement, of discovering something new. That's if the play and the part are
good enough. McKellen would find – and continued to find –
repeating small roles, where there is less to discover, more difficult; and
even leading roles in plays with less complex or interesting characters
than those of Shakespeare could bore him rigid.

'It was at the time when you tried very hard to excuse Shakespeare's
politics,' comments Chetwyn on his 1963 *Henry V*, 'the way in which
he glorified war. And we tried to put in quite a lot to go against that.'
One particular production gimmick Chetwyn introduced was more to
do with the lack of numbers in the cast. Instead of having his Henry
address a band of followers on stage in the famous speech before
Harfleur, Chetwyn placed what soldiers he had in the auditorium and
told McKellen to use them and the audience as his army. In the intimate
surroundings of the Arts Theatre the actor could begin 'Once more unto
the breach . . .' at a whisper rather than the usual bellow. Again, that
connection with the audience, that sense of reaching out to each
individual in the theatre, would become a trademark of McKellen the
stage actor. And the contrast between the intimate style of performance
which was possible in a small space like the Arts Theatre, Ipswich, and
the big scale needed to reach the back row at the 900-seater Belgrade –
or Bolton School Hall for that matter – would become still more obvious
one day in Stratford, when McKellen created one of his most famous
roles – Macbeth – in a theatre that seated just over a hundred.

'*Henry V* was a highlight of Ian's time at Ipswich,' says Robert
Chetwyn, 'but so was *Luther*.'

John Osborne's play about Martin Luther had opened at the Royal
Court in 1961, starring Albert Finney. Born three years before McKellen
and also hailing from Lancashire, Finney is an actor with whom
McKellen would often be compared in the years to come. In September
1963 Finney recreated the role on Broadway. That same year he also
achieved international stardom in the title role of Tony Richardson's film
of *Tom Jones*. That double of appearing in a hit on Broadway at the same
time as opening in a major film would be an ambition that McKellen
would take another forty years to achieve.

Meanwhile in April 1963, five months before Finney took the play to
Broadway, Robert Chetwyn was mounting the first production of *Luther*
outside London. 'To be honest,' he says, 'the reps were not lining up to
do it. It had a big cast, it was tricky stuff and not a crowd pleaser.'

Having seen the original production, Chetwyn felt the play's rapid
shifts of place and time were confusing for an audience. He wrote to

John Osborne, asking if he could put in a character called Footnote who would explain what was going on. The playwright agreed. 'He said he would come and see it but he never did,' adds Chetwyn. The part of Luther played to the strengths of the young McKellen with his extreme emotional intensity. 'I thought he was rather better than Albert as Luther,' Chetwyn goes on. 'Ian was very straightforward. Albert's performance was harder to get into for an audience.'

Ian's closest friend during his time at Ipswich was Gawn Grainger, also on a long-term contract with Robert Chetwyn. Grainger later married the actress Zoë Wanamaker, who would appear alongside McKellen in Trevor Nunn's 1989 Othello at the RSC, as well as the 1997 film Swept from the Sea and another adaptation of David Copperfield, this time for the BBC in 1999. Thirty years on from his young David at Ipswich, McKellen would play Mr Creakle in the television version. It was at this point that McKellen was meeting – or being reunited with – other people who would be important to his future career. A one[?] return to the Belgrade Theatre for The Big Contract, Barry Engl[...] follow-up to End of Conflict, reunited him with his old Cambridge Trevor Nunn. Nunn was in his first job under the ABC TV scheme fc[...] trainee directors. Within a year Peter Hall would summon Nunn to Stratford, and within five years he would be running the Royal Shakespeare Company at the age of 27.

But if Trevor Nunn would ultimately be the most important collaborator in McKellen's stage career, it was an actor in Ipswich who was about to help him take his most important step so far.

James Cairncross came up to join the company at the Arts Theatre, Ipswich in July 1963 for a new play called I, John Brown. Written by John Hall and featuring McKellen as a school teacher named Andrew Acre, according to Cairncross the production was 'victory under fire. It was a shambles of a play.' But shambles or not, Cairncross was impressed by his young co-star. 'He'd got star quality,' he observes. 'As they say, you've either got or you haven't got class. It shines out of your arse.'

Again, what exactly constituted that star quality is not something Cairncross is able to define. But it left him sure that Ian McKellen should be going on to greater things. A veteran of four and a half years in the London production of Salad Days in the early 1950s, Cairncross came back to see the Ipswich company's shot at the Julian Slade/Dorothy Reynolds musical. Already a rep standard and something of a joke in the acting profession, it was McKellen's first excursion into the world of musical theatre. 'Ian played with total integrity,' observes Cairncross with a smile, 'while somehow managing to convey the impression that the whole thing was a lot of rubbish.'

Cairncross had contacts in the theatre well beyond the world of musicals. He'd worked with John Neville at the Bristol Old Vic before Neville and Richard Burton became the twin lions of the British classical stage in the mid-1950s. Neville had been asked to mount the inaugural season at the brand new Nottingham Playhouse alongside Frank Dunlop, artistic director of the old theatre. 'I said to John you ought to have a look at this young chap I've been working with,' Cairncross goes on, 'so he and Frank Dunlop came to see him.'

The production they saw at Ipswich was John Arden's savage anti-war drama *Sergeant Musgrave's Dance*. McKellen was once again donning military uniform – this time nineteenth-century uniform – as Private Sparky. Cairncross had returned to play the old soldier, Attercliffe.

It was September 1963. Rehearsals for *Coriolanus*, the opening production in Nottingham, were due to start in November. Dunlop and Neville had already travelled the country looking for young actors. But this was something different. 'He was remarkable,' says Dunlop of the 24-year-old McKellen. 'Dazzling. Of all the people we saw, he was the one who impressed us most.' Not a man given to overstatement, Dunlop was quite sure of what they were looking at. 'He was obviously going to be a star.'

McKellen completed his contract at Ipswich as the juvenile lead in Bill Naughton's Lancashire comedy *All in Good Time*. He had a couple of weeks off before rehearsals were to begin for Nottingham. He went back to Bolton.

'He came to see us,' remembers Geoffrey Banks, 'and, I blush to remember it now but by way of breezy conversation I said, "Are there many queers in the company?" '

There had been no hint, no rumour, no whisper at school. 'But,' says Banks, 'down at the Little Theatre there were people whose ears were much closer to the ground than mine and they knew.' And the reason that the amateur actors at Bolton's Little Theatre had reason to know of McKellen's homosexuality is that, according to Geoffrey Banks, it was there that McKellen met the first of his two long-term lovers, Brian 'Brodie' Taylor.

Banks tells the story of their meeting like this. 'He was home and he thought, Where shall I go? I'll go down to the Little Theatre. And there was a rehearsal going on and their eyes met across a not very crowded room.'

Brodie was a teacher of PE and history, but not at Bolton School. 'He was below the salt at a kind of comprehensive, I think,' says Banks. Michael Shipley, another pupil at Bolton School and amateur actor at the Little Theatre, uses the same expression – 'below the salt'. It's said with humour, but perhaps there's still something there of the great class divide between the grammar school boy and the non-grammar school boy.

Geoffrey Banks knew Brodie well. They had met when Elizabeth Banks was at the Little Theatre playing opposite the young teacher in *The Way of the World*. Banks's description of the young Brodie makes him sound like something out of a 1930s drawing-room comedy. 'I remember Brian erupting into a ward when my wife was in hospital,' he says, 'and he was wearing tennis shorts with a bottle of Lucozade in one hand and a tennis racket in the other, and he strode down the ward commandingly and everybody stopped talking and thought, Who is this God-like figure? Because he really was a golden boy – golden hair and very tanned and so forth. Very long lashes.'

Michael Shipley, on the other hand, places a first meeting between McKellen and Brodie much earlier – in 1958 when McKellen was playing Sebastian in the Little Theatre's *Twelfth Night* before Cambridge. 'Brian was extremely lively and personable,' remembers Shipley, 'and got very closely involved with the high church people at St Augustine.'

Whichever is right, what is certain is that by the end of 1963, despite having met many gay men in the world of the professional theatre, McKellen was embarking on the first of only two long-term relationships, with a boy from his old home town. There is a search for security there. And there is the perennial McKellen search for family, because what one friend remembers most clearly is how close McKellen was to Brian Taylor's mother, Doris.

Rehearsals for *Coriolanus* began in November 1963. McKellen was staying in regional theatre. He was even taking a modest pay cut. But this was no ordinary rep. It was to be run by a triumvirate which included not only John Neville, arguably the pre-eminent classical actor of his generation, but also Peter Ustinov who, though he didn't actually do much for the new theatre, did lend considerable prestige to its first season as well as a new play – *The Life in my Hands*. Frank Dunlop, who had operated the old playhouse in a converted cinema in Nottingham's Goldsmith Street, had also run the Bristol Old Vic and would go on to create the Young Vic in London.

The Belgrade, Coventry, may have blazed the way for the post-war development of regional theatre, but in many ways the Nottingham Playhouse was the jewel in the crown of the repertory movement. The old theatre had epitomised the make-do spirit of rep, with a stage just twelve feet deep and dressing rooms under the stage with ceilings so low

play began. More importantly for McKellen, Guthrie wanted to bring out what he saw as the homoerotic nature of the relationship between Coriolanus and Aufidius. This was no arbitrary director's concept. The language Aufidius uses in Act 4, when Coriolanus comes to join him against the Romans who have banished him, is full of sexual charge. What McKellen found much more difficult was the moment Guthrie wanted right at the end of the play after Aufidius has killed Coriolanus for betraying the Volsces. Aufidius's final speech shows a complete change of mood. After the violence of the killing, he says, 'My rage is gone, and I am struck with sorrow.' Before the speech Guthrie wanted McKellen to let out a great cry of pain as he held the dead body of his enemy/friend in his arms. McKellen couldn't do it.

'If you're not prepared to commit yourself to something bigger than you are, you have no right to be playing this part,' Guthrie told him. He was asking the young actor to raise his style of playing to a heightened level, to measure up to the scale of these superhuman creatures of war Shakespeare had created.

Rehearsals moved to Nottingham. Facing the same difficulties which had led Robert Chetwyn to cast the audience as the English army in *Henry V*, Guthrie was using a large number of amateurs to swell the size of his Roman crowds. Equity rules didn't limit the length of rehearsal time as they do today. So, as Richard Digby Day remembers, 'He sat there with Judith Guthrie, who was a chronic alcoholic at the time, of course, and they used to bring their sandwiches and a Thermos and sit there all day. And we had to rehearse into the evening because that was mostly only when the amateurs could be there.'

It was the freezing winter of 1963–4. Michael Crawford and John Collins found their digs so cold, they slept in the new theatre at night, until they nearly set fire to the place and were thrown out. First night was approaching, and still Guthrie was unhappy about that crucial final moment. He was pushing McKellen beyond his comfort zone – always the place where actors do their best work, and sometimes the place where they fall flat on their faces. The point is to take the risk. That is what McKellen was learning to do. Blessed with a beautiful speaking voice and a decent physique, Ian McKellen could perfectly well have been that actor Robert Chetwyn talked about, the one who 'has a comfortable career and no one has ever heard of'.

Chetwyn called the difference charisma. Watching the work on *Coriolanus*, Richard Digby Day remembers 'the enormous energy and attack and the daring of it all'. Marielaine Douglas, another company member, agrees: 'Such energy and physicality!'

But McKellen did not find the moment which crowned it all until the dress rehearsal, the day before opening night. Despite those extra rehearsals he was still frightened of the climactic moment Guthrie wanted. Finally the director strode down to the footlights. He knew what the problem was – the young actor was afraid to draw on real feeling for such an extreme moment. 'We're not going to think you're silly,' he told McKellen. 'You're looking more silly not doing it.' And there at the dress rehearsal he finally got it. A great, wailing cry, full of pain and anguish filled the auditorium.

Packed to the rafters with civic dignitaries, theatre folk and national critics, the opening night was an unqualified triumph. And McKellen caught his share of the superlatives. Predictably perhaps, it was that extraordinary last moment that got much of the attention. *The Times* hailed, 'Ian McKellen, a new actor with a prodigious range of hysterical passion which here rises to its climax in a long wailing threnody over the hero's body.'

That cry over the dead hero's body was a crucial breakthrough for McKellen. Robert Chetwyn had noted his lack of confidence when he came to Ipswich, his own continuing uncertainty about whether he had what it took to be a professional actor. McKellen never thought of himself as a born actor. In fact, he once called himself a slogger, who learned his trade in three years' apprenticeship in rep, developing a confidence he didn't have naturally. It took many years for him really to learn Guthrie's deeper lesson that the job of the actor was to reveal himself to the audience and make them empathise with the character he was playing. But he grasped straight away the simpler truth that audiences are excited by danger. From the opening night of *Coriolanus*, and the cry over John Neville's prostrate form, Ian McKellen developed into an actor whose trademark was an absolute fearlessness. It was to bring him plenty of brickbats from critics who criticised him for overacting, as well as more of the extravagant praise which greeted his Aufidius and indeed everything he touched during that golden season at Nottingham. But much more importantly it enabled him to create radically original, hugely theatrical characterisations which thrilled theatre audiences as far afield as a National Theatre tour can take you.

And what a season it was. 'Everything he did was wonderful and completely different and yet him, which is a mark I think of great acting,' offers Frank Dunlop. Peter Ustinov's play about capital punishment got mixed reviews, but Ustinov himself was hugely impressed. Watching McKellen in rehearsal, he was amazed to see the young actor putting inflections into speeches which he had never thought of.

Frank Dunlop directed a hugely successful production of *Saturday Night and Sunday Morning* with McKellen in the leading role of Arthur Seaton, already made famous in the film by – that name again – Albert Finney. Arthur's cheerfully anarchic message – 'All I'm out for is a good time. All the rest is propaganda' – appealed directly to the young audience which theatre is so often searching for in vain.

Director and star enjoyed their researches for the production. 'We were in Nottingham where *Saturday Night and Sunday Morning* was supposed to happen,' remembers Dunlop. 'It was the first adaptation of the book done on stage and Sillitoe worked with us and we used to go everywhere the squaddies went. Joan Heal and Ian and I would go to these awful sleazy pubs with a concert on and they'd be full of soldiers looking for a bit of crumpet and they used to hate us because they thought we were posh. At that point Ian was just a lad – he liked a drink and getting mixed up in trouble. They heard our voices and we didn't realise that maybe one or two of us spoke louder than usual because we were actors. It was very exciting.'

On their tour of the drinking dives of Nottingham, Dunlop and his actors also discovered a local pop group, led by a young guitarist named Alvin Lee. The group was immediately recruited for the production. They would go on to become Ten Years After and play at Woodstock in 1969.

At the beginning of February Frank Greene, the man behind all the main school plays at Bolton School, came with a party of old boys to watch his star pupil on the professional stage in Nottingham. After the performance he hurried backstage with a characteristically firm hand-shake for his young protégé. For a school teacher to see such success in someone he has helped is enormously satisfying. A week later, on Friday 14 February, Frank 'Charley' Greene had a heart attack and died during the Masters v. Boys Badminton match. His last words were an apology to a colleague. He was 63. McKellen contributed a brief eulogy to the March edition of the school magazine. Contributions also arrived from Irving Wardle, drama critic at *The Times*, and Leslie Halliwell, who would produce the first edition of his *Filmgoer's Companion* the following year. Working quietly in Bolton all those years, Greene had had quite an impact on the world of British drama.

McKellen's extraordinary season at Nottingham climaxed with the title role in the rarely performed *Sir Thomas More*, written in collaboration by a string of journeyman seventeenth-century playwrights with at least one scene by Shakespeare. According to Frank Dunlop, who directed the play, he had always planned to offer McKellen the part. Richard

Digby Day, who assisted Dunlop, remembers things differently, suggesting there had been disagreements between the two artistic directors. 'The atmosphere by now had begun to be quite bad, and I [felt like I] had become a go-between for John [Neville] and Frank. They were in offices in separate parts of the building and didn't speak.' According to Day, the original plan had been for John Neville to play Sir Thomas More. This was clearly no longer possible. 'Frank tried to think of others to do Sir Thomas More, but then decided it was ridiculous that Ian shouldn't do it.'

One young actor, Steven Berkoff, two years older than McKellen and newly arrived in the company, remembers the first day of rehearsals for *Sir Thomas More* in his autobiography, *Free Association*: 'We had just sat down to begin our first reading when in walked this very young man with bushy hair wearing blue jeans and a jeans top. He was playing Sir Thomas More. You've got to be kidding: he looks far too young. But when Ian started to read he had an authority which belied his years.'

Just turned 25, McKellen was indeed far too young for the part. Edith Macarthur, playing Lady More, was 38, and says, 'He made me feel very old.' But, with the aid of a thick layer of stage make-up, McKellen succeeded in transforming himself into the very image of More, and though reviewers did not think much of the play, once again they admired its leading man. Emrys Bryson in the *Nottingham Evening Post* wrote: 'After a season in which he has done anything from Calderon to Sillitoe, twenty-five-year-old Ian McKellen proves that as Sir Thomas More he is indeed a man for all seasons. Gravely spry, courteously dignified, he gives the role and production an authority remarkable for such a young man.' Of course, Bryson hadn't seen McKellen's Justice Shallow or his Pope in *Doctor Faustus*, or he would have known that a mask of ageing make-up had often produced the young McKellen's best performances.

It was a difficult time at the Nottingham Playhouse. With Dunlop already planning to leave, inevitably people started taking sides between the two directors. McKellen avoided it all adroitly, according to assistant director Richard Digby Day. 'At a time when the company was very divided he managed to keep out of that. He was a very good company member and good at leading from the front in *Sir Thomas More*.' It's the first of many such statements; the ex-head boy of Bolton School would step easily into the role of company leader.

The other thing colleagues testify to constantly is McKellen's sense of fun, his mischievousness. 'We saw a ludicrous production of *Dracula* in Derby – Ian, Michael Cadman [another actor in the company] and I,'

Day goes on. 'We went into a photo booth and Ian put in paper teeth and we took a photograph of him biting Michael and me.' Day was living in a house on Standard Hill, the kind of place that gave actors' digs a bad name – no hot running water, stinking of damp. 'It was run by an elderly spinster named Flora Burnham,' Day remembers. 'One night some stones were thrown at my window and it was Ian: "I've locked myself out. Can I spend the night with you?" So I let him in and we'd just got into bed when there was a knocking on the door – "Mr Digby Day, Mr Digby Day, you've got somebody there, they'll have to leave at once." So,' he concludes with a twinkle, 'that was my night with Ian McKellen!'

But Day goes on to say something else too: 'I never felt that I really knew him. I think it was very difficult to get to know him.' One of the gang throughout the week, at the weekend, McKellen was not to be seen. 'He was terrifically in love with Brodie then,' comments Day. 'Always looking forward to him coming for the weekend. At the weekend they would disappear into a sort of home milieu.'

Day offers one other story about the young McKellen, which shows a different side of the rising star – his impatience with anything he considered second rate. During rehearsals for *The Mayor of Zalamea*, a heavily cut and doctored version of Pedro Calderon de la Barca's play of the same name, in which he was playing the lascivious Captain Don Alvaro, McKellen was less than happy with one of the other actors. 'When he came on, the temperature on stage distinctly dropped,' admits Richard Digby Day.

The plays ran in repertoire at the Nottingham Playhouse with three or four different shows in a week until July, when McKellen left the company. He had been hailed by the national critics and seen by everyone who was important in the London theatre. The season was his passport to success. Phyllis Calvert, about to go into rehearsals for *A Scent of Flowers*, James Saunders's follow-up to *Next Time I'll Sing To You*, was among those who saw him. Producer Michael Codron was still looking for a young actor to play the key supporting role of Godfrey, and Calvert sent him up to Nottingham to see McKellen. 'I remember Phyllis Calvert telling me that she insisted on him being given the part,' says Richard Digby Day.

So, without even having to audition, McKellen was catapulted onto the West End stage. From £8 12s at the Belgrade in August 1961, he opened at the Duke of York's on St Martin's Lane on 30 September 1964 at £40 a week, rising to £45 after production costs were met. In an attempt perhaps to prevent the young actor's head from becoming too big, the press flyer spelled his name wrongly – McKellan.

A Scent of Flowers is a poetic meditation on what drove a young girl named Zoë to suicide. The play begins with her dead on stage in a coffin and allows her to interact after death with the other characters, including her stepbrother Godfrey, McKellen's part. The coffin stays on stage throughout. It was too much for the citizens of Golders Green on the production's pre-West End try-out. Unable to figure out what was going on, the audience started walking out during the first act. Nor were the London critics by any means united in their praise. But the play was a hit, winning James Saunders an *Evening Standard* Award as Most Promising Playwright, and bringing McKellen the first of several shelves full of statuettes in the shape of the Clarence Derwent Award for Best Supporting Actor.

Denis and Gladys McKellen made the journey down from Barrow Bridge for the opening night – proud parents sharing their boy's success. Only, of course, Ian's real mother, Margery, wasn't there and hadn't been for thirteen years. Within a week his father would be dead as well.

It was Saturday 3 October. Denis and Gladys had been out for the day, up to Kendal to the Lakes. On the way back they hit traffic just south of Preston on the old A6. Denis turned off to take a short cut through Brindle on a narrow country lane and home to Barrow Bridge the back way. John Walker, a local farmer, was coming the other way in his Land Rover. He saw a car coming towards him and stopped. The other car kept coming.

'I was sitting there waiting for him to stop, but he didn't,' Walker told the inquest later.

The two cars collided head on. There were no seat belts in those days, of course. Gladys was injured but survived; Denis had severe chest injuries. He lived for four days in hospital without regaining consciousness. McKellen did not go to the hospital. Of course, there's the old theatrical adage that the show must go on, but under such circumstances he would certainly have been allowed time off from *A Scent of Flowers*. But, just as at twelve he had not wanted to attend his mother's funeral, so at 25 he did not see his father before he died.

He did go up for the funeral, held at the Congregational Church on Chorley Old Road the following week. There were representatives there from Bolton School, from the local Rotary Club and any number of civic dignitaries. After the service they all went back to 34 Barrow Bridge Road. It was a fine autumn day and Gladys McKellen laid out food and drink in the front garden. Purely by chance Geoffrey Banks, McKellen's old teacher and mentor from Bolton School, who by this time had left and was working at another school, happened to be passing.

'His home was on one of my favourite walks,' remembers Banks. 'We lived on opposite sides of Moss Bank Park. I had a double free period and I'd gone out to clear my head. I walked past Ian's place and the funeral was taking place that day. I tiptoed past and I hadn't gone more than twenty yards when I heard my name being shouted and he's running down the pavement after me.'

With a class to teach back at school, Banks declined McKellen's offer to join them. But teacher and ex-pupil talked for a few moments on the pavement.

'It must have been pretty horrid for you, sitting on stage with a coffin every night,' suggested Banks.

'O God, yes!' came the reply. But horrid or not, McKellen was back at the Duke of York's for the Monday night show.

McKellen had consciously followed his father's example in the way he built his career. Denis had started at the bottom and worked his way up to Borough Engineer. His son had decided to spend three or four years in rep learning his craft, not aim for television or a quick entry to the West End. Denis's early death left many regrets. As McKellen put it in a *Daily Mail* interview in February 1998, 'Just when I was feeling confident, and perhaps we'd have been able to have an adult relationship, my father died. So there was a lot of unfinished business.'

Neither of his parents lived to see him called the leading classical actor of his day (as he was within five years) but McKellen's 'unfinished business' is much more personal. They had brought him up to be truthful in all things. And he hadn't been – he'd never told them he was gay. 'To my dying day,' he told Michael Parkinson on his show in February 2004, 'I shall regret that I never completed my relationship with my parents by telling them such a central thing about myself.'

One of the luminaries to come and see *A Scent of Flowers* was Maggie Smith who was about to play Beatrice to Robert Stephens's Benedick in *Much Ado About Nothing* for Sir Laurence Olivier's recently formed National Theatre. Impressed by the young McKellen, she persuaded Olivier to come too. As ill luck would have it McKellen was 'off' with flu the night Olivier came, but he was asked to join the company anyway. It seemed like the next rung on a steady ascent of the theatrical ladder, and McKellen accepted with alacrity. In the event it turned out to be one of his least happy acting experiences.

Cast in the same thankless role he had struggled with at Coventry – Claudio – McKellen never found his feet at the National Theatre. 'There were a number of actors of my age and range in the company, and there was a sense of competition which I as a socialist did not find helpful,' he told *The Times* in 1971. Maybe he was joking with the political interpolation, but the competitive side of a theatre company was one McKellen had not met before.

For a young actor, theatre companies can go two ways: they can be co-operative, mutually supportive families, or they can be competitive and every-man-for-himself families. And the actors at the time included Albert Finney, Derek Jacobi and Edward Petherbridge, with Ronald Pickup and Michael York walking on in the Dogberry and Verges scenes, and a very young Christopher Timothy listed in the programme among four 'Inanimates'. But this was a Franco Zeffirelli production, so almost anything was possible! Add to this array of talent, all vying for the audience's (and director's) attention, an appalling blonde wig, several layers of make-up applied by Zeffirelli himself while sitting on the actor's knee, and a ludicrous stick-on moustache, and it is little wonder that McKellen failed to improve on his earlier attempt at the part.

Deeply unhappy, hating working with Zeffirelli, according to Elspeth Cochrane McKellen was soon wanting out of his eight-month contract. It was just as well he hadn't signed for the three years Olivier had offered. *Much Ado* was his only appearance on the stage of the Old Vic. He went on to the Chichester Festival Theatre for the National's summer season to do bits in John Arden's *Armstrong's Last Goodnight*, in which his name was missed off the programme, and *Trelawney of the Wells*. He never appeared with his schoolboy hero Olivier. When the great man offered to extend his stay, McKellen declined. Joining such a starry company had been a mistake. After his triumphs in Nottingham and a prestigious West End debut, McKellen had been in danger of disappearing back into the ranks. It was not a situation he would ever put himself in again. 'Ian isn't an ensemble player,' observes Geoffrey Banks. 'He's a star.'

3. WE ARE AMAZED . . .

There was a story doing the rounds early in 1966 about a recent dinner party at which Ingrid Bergman had been guest of honour. Arriving late after a performance of *A Lily in Little India*, a new play by Donald Howarth he was doing at the St Martin's Theatre, Ian McKellen walked in on a discussion about what was wrong with the British theatre. Without hesitation, the newcomer announced, 'It's the star system.'

'But we have to live,' said Ingrid Bergman. 'Won't you give us a chance?'

'No.'

Considering that he currently had third billing in the West End behind Jill Bennett and Jesse Watson and was already on the way to becoming a star himself, there is some irony in the story, which may very well be apocryphal anyway. But having turned his back on Olivier's National Theatre, McKellen aligned himself for the next ten years and – arguably, despite lengthy sojourns later with both the RSC and National Theatre – permanently against the major subsidised companies. With his knighthood and his status as 'great classical actor', it is easy to see McKellen as a creature of the theatrical establishment. But uniquely among his famous contemporaries McKellen made his name away from London and the big companies. He made his name in the provinces on tour. The colossal success and extravagant acclaim that was his by the end of the 1960s was won with the kind of relentless touring schedule that is many actors' idea of hell, but which for McKellen, the child who back in Wigan wanted to run away and join the fairground, is what theatre is all about.

But before the touring began his first stop was the smaller London theatres. In rapid succession he did *A Lily in Little India* at the Hampstead Theatre Club, transferring to the West End for a short run. Then he was at the Royal Court in a new Arnold Wesker play. Then a Shaw double bill at the Mermaid. No old-fashioned long runs. Always a new opening night. Always in front of the critics and the public. And picking up the *Plays and Players* Award for Most Promising Actor of 1966 along the way.

In April he did his first photographic feature for the *Sunday Times*. In open-necked shirt and denim jacket, with an improbable hat hooked over one foot, he still looks like a Cambridge student, posed with cigarettes and coffee cup. The face is soft, unformed. But the prominent, thuggish nose and the contradictingly sensitive mouth are there, along with the bags under the eyes and big ears, inherited from his father. The image is languid, relaxed, poised.

New plays and Shakespeare – those are the ways you get taken seriously as a theatre actor in Britain. Zeffirelli's *Much Ado* had put McKellen off Shakespeare for the time being, so he stuck with new plays. By November 1966 he was in Oxford rehearsing a new translation of Alexei Arbuzov's *The Promise*, which had already been a hit in Russia but was new to the west. Three characters, three acts and one set, the play is set in Leningrad, spanning the period from the siege of 1942 up to 1960. It's a love triangle with three unusually good parts for young actors, giving them the chance to change through the course of the evening from optimistic youth to wounded and disillusioned middle age. But the main reason McKellen was there was the actress who was to play Lika, the girl that both men love, Judi Dench.

McKellen had been watching Dench's career carefully. Five years his senior, she seemed to have been choosing jobs less on where they were happening, than on who was involved – much as he had done going up to Nottingham to work with John Neville. He would always remain perfectly happy to work away from London and the major companies, provided that he worked with people he thought were good and, increasingly as he went on, ideally with people who were his friends. It is the attitude which says that theatre is not buildings and places, theatre is people.

The third member of the cast was Ian McShane, then a rising young film actor and another Lancashire lad, hailing from Blackburn. He was the would-be engineer, Marat, to whom McKellen's Leonidik finally surrenders the girl in the great romantic gesture which is the climax of Act 3. Dench for one was sure the play was uncommercial. She was proved wrong.

The first night in Oxford was full of London critics, there to check on these three young lions of the British stage. The show seemed to go well, and cast and director went out to celebrate. They found themselves in the same restaurant as a group of theatre critics. Now there is an unwritten law that cast and critics do not mix after the show. Up at the Dirty Duck, the theatre pub in Stratford, critics and actors drink in the same bar after press nights but always at scrupulously separate tables. But this night was different. The critics were unanimous in their enthusiasm for the play and the performances of its three stars. They invited the actors and director Frank Hauser to join them, and bought drinks all round.

Transferring to the tiny Fortune Theatre in London, *The Promise* settled into a long run. Again, reviews for the play were excellent. Dench rather stole the personal notices, though Harold Hobson in the *Sunday Times* went overboard about McKellen: 'There are moments in [his] performance . . . which must rank with the highest achievements of acting I have seen.' But a warning note was struck in Dennis Whitman's review in *London Look* with the first appearance in a McKellen notice of the dread word 'mannered', which has dogged his career ever since and which has a ring of that review of his schoolboy Henry V in the *Boltonian* in 1957 – 'the pointing of some lines appeared rather odd'.

What critics have principally been referring to when they call some of McKellen's performances mannered is his voice. And it is at moments of high emotional intensity that the mannerisms usually surface: the jaw goes slack, words emerge in a slur from the corner of the mouth; the last words in the line are swallowed by emotion. Soliloquies find him hurrying from one thought to another, but this can turn into rushing and become monotonous; lines are sometimes stressed in ways that seem to make no sense; vowels become elongated and distorted beyond recognition; extreme changes of pace mean the sense is lost. At his worst he speaks as if choking on passion, and a generalised wash of emotion totally obscures the text.

Trevor Nunn put it delicately in an interview in the *Sunday Telegraph* magazine: 'With a heightened text and Ian's concentration on its musical and rhetorical qualities, he can become not entirely credible.' Not surprisingly, what Nunn believes McKellen needs is a good director. And McKellen himself agrees. 'I like a director who bullies,' he told Joy Leslie Gibson in 1979, then qualified the statement quickly. 'No, I don't mean that literally. I like a director who refuses to let me be satisfied until he has got the best I can do out of me.' At that time he cited Tyrone Guthrie, Nunn and John Barton as examples. He also included Robert Chetwyn. In fact, McKellen would remain fiercely loyal to his director at Ipswich rep, at least up until 1989, when so much was changing in his life.

Seen by Princess Margaret and Lord Snowdon at the end of March, *The Promise* was one of the hits of the year. Noel Coward was in the theatre the same month, and came away describing the acting as perfect.

McKellen and Judi Dench were forging a working relationship and personal friendship which would take them on to other, greater heights at the RSC and survive as a close personal alliance. Yet their approach to rehearsal is quite different. Dench is well known for doing a lot of work at home, and coming to rehearsals with what sometimes looks like a finished performance. McKellen's approach is the opposite, preferring extended discussion and trial and error in rehearsal. Sometimes he analyses aloud as he works through a speech, as if in soliloquy. It makes him slower at developing a character than Dench. Working with McKellen in 1989 on Trevor Nunn's *Othello*, Zoë Wanamaker found it a relief how uncertain he remained of his lines even up to the previews. 'I'm quite a slow worker,' she admits, 'and I think he is too.'

But Judi Dench and Ian McKellen would find other things in common. They shared a taste for complicated games, especially word games, and she eventually invited him to join a group of games players in London. At the Fortune McKellen also discovered her liking for playing games on stage. One night Richard Chamberlain, then at the height of his fame as Doctor Kildare, was in the audience. 'Judi and I were terribly excited,' McKellen told John Miller while he was writing the biography *Judi Dench: with a crack in her voice.* 'I suppose we both fancied him. We could see where he was sitting in the small theatre and wondered if he'd come round. During that show there was a lot of singing the Dr Kildare signature tune under our breath.' Of course, it wasn't only the London audience who flocked to see McKellen in his first really major hit in the West End. Geoffrey Banks made the journey down the A6 from Bolton. Before the show he called at the ground floor flat at 25 Earls Terrace, where his old pupil was now living.

Number 25 was the one on the end of the terrace at the unfashionable, westernmost end of Kensington High Street. In the 1990s the whole row was done up. In 2000 Harry Potter author J K Rowling reportedly paid £4.25 m for one of the newly refurbished houses. But back in the 60s the houses on Earls Terrace were all divided into flats. McKellen liked to regale visitors with the story of how Gerald du Maurier's parents had lived there briefly before moving to Hampstead, and that the star actor had almost certainly been conceived in the house. But really 25 Earls Terrace, which still looks a bit like the side entrance, was on the cusp of the less than salubrious Earls Court.

McKellen was sharing the flat with his lover Brian Taylor. Brodie had quit his job in Bolton and moved south. McKellen's observation that if he had become a teacher rather than an actor his homosexuality would have had to be hidden at work is backed up by the fact that, in London, Brodie had not taken another job as a teacher, a profession in which it remains virtually impossible to be 'out'. Michael Shipley stayed in contact with his old friend from Bolton Little Theatre. 'I remember calling at his antique shop once down the King's Road,' he says. 'Then later he worked for television or a film company.' Eventually Brodie would become a theatrical agent, going into partnership with Nina Quick.

Geoffrey Banks recalls that afternoon in 1967 before the performance of *The Promise*. 'Liz and I had tea with them. And this was the first time that their relationship was explicit and he was throwing it open to his old teacher.'

Although it would be more than another twenty years before McKellen finally came out to the public and to his family, this was another stage on the journey. His homosexuality was no secret in the acting world. Now he was making the conscious decision to come out to his old schoolteacher. Perhaps not surprisingly, McKellen seemed nervous. 'We arrived,' Banks goes on, 'and he was the one who was going, "Oh, there aren't enough forks" and so forth and was worried about domestic things. Brian just stood with his back to the fire and held forth. But once we were on our way to the theatre, Ian was back to his old self, chattering away.'

Judi Dench found the six-month run a trial of strength. *The Promise* is a long play and with only three characters, inevitably the three actors have little time off stage. Intervals were occupied with costume and make-up changes, as the characters age eighteen years. 'By Saturday night,' she told Sheridan Morley in 1978, 'I was so tired I used to have to chalk up the number of scenes left on my dressing-room wall and then cross them off one by one.' By the time a transfer to Broadway was being discussed, she had had enough. In August Prunella Scales (*Fawlty Towers, After Henry*) took over at the Fortune with Derek Fowlds (*Yes Minister, Heartbeat*) in McKellen's part and Colin Campbell in McShane's as Marat. Rehearsals for New York began in mid-September 1967. Eileen Atkins, who had had a hit already on Broadway that year in *The Killing of Sister George*, was playing Lika.

For the two Ians it was their first time on Broadway, and the transfer looked like the continuation of a triumphal progress for McKellen. But, as he was to find out again, success in London's West End by no means guarantees success on the Great White Way. On opening night, 14 November 1967, there were pickets outside the Henry Miller's Theatre. Led by Roy Scheider, New York actors were protesting, with the kind of paranoid protectionism which has marred relations between British and American Equity for years, at the presence of British actors on Broadway. More seriously, the all-powerful New York critics didn't like the play, audiences stayed away, and the show was closed inside three weeks.

It was no more than a hiccup. Back in London McKellen wasn't short of offers, and within weeks he was into rehearsal for Peter Shaffer's *Black*

Comedy which had opened originally in Chichester, before enjoying a successful run at the Old Vic. *Black Comedy* is a one-act play which depends for its comedy on the simple device of beginning with stage and auditorium lights off and then switching them on when the plot calls for a black-out. Shaffer had written another one-acter, *White Liars*, to make a double bill for the West End transfer.

McKellen had a gift in the two roles he played as part of the double bill: Tom, the bogus pop singer in *White Liars*, and Harold Gorringe, 'an outrageous antique-fancying pouf', as Peter Lewis put it in the *Daily Mail*. Most thought *White Liars*, with its web of deceit and surprise, a bit too intricate and clever for its own good, but McKellen was, without doubt, the hit of the double-bill. At the time he himself dismissed his performances as full of disguises and physical tricks, but on the other hand was delighted when a visitor to his dressing room didn't realise he'd played both parts. Disguise and revelation – there are still the mixed feelings of a man hiding his true self and an actor trying to absorb Tyrone Guthrie's lesson about revealing himself on stage, while still delighting in theatrical sleight of hand.

After the Peter Shaffer double bill Ian McKellen went off to Ireland to make his first major feature film, *Alfred the Great*. However, the shooting schedule allowed him enough days off to plan his next move in the theatre. It was the move which would establish him as the foremost classical actor of his generation.

While McKellen had been learning his trade at the Belgrade Theatre, Coventry, Richard Cottrell, one of the Cambridge theatre mafia who would be so crucial to McKellen's career from now on, was founding Prospect Theatre Productions with Iain Mackintosh and Elizabeth Sweeting. Successful summer seasons in Oxford and a commitment to touring, the magic word that opens the coffers of the Arts Council, propelled the company onto a wider stage. By 1968 Toby Robertson, another Cambridge man, was artistic director, Richard Cottrell was Associate Director, and Prospect had established a reputation for solid productions of the classics, some well known, some less often performed. It was at this point that they asked Ian McKellen to play Richard II for a five-week tour of the provinces in November and December of 1968.

It was not necessarily the kind of offer to thrill a 29-year-old actor who had behind him a series of West End successes, a first film and a visit to Broadway. McKellen applied his criteria for choosing jobs. Did he want to play the part? Did he want to work with these people? The answer to the first question was a definite yes. What about the second?

With a part like Richard II, one of Shakespeare's star vehicles, the director was arguably more important than the other members of the cast. Toby Robertson had directed Prospect's Shakespeares so far; now it was Cottrell's turn. Over a week in Ireland, Cottrell and McKellen discussed the play. It was soon clear that they were on the same wavelength, and the actor committed to the job.

The twin keys to the play, as they saw it, were firstly to understand and establish clearly for an audience the family relationships, and secondly to get a handle on Richard's own concept of kingship. The medieval belief in the divine right of kings is at the heart of *Richard II*. According to this precept, a king was anointed by God himself, and was effectively his representative on earth. No human hand therefore, including his own, could remove him from the throne. The result in more personal terms is obvious – kings tended to think they were God. This was McKellen's way into the character. Adopting an approach to Shakespearian characters which would become an important part of his method throughout his career as a classical actor, McKellen next looked for modern parallels.

'I based Richard on a film star I'd been working with – one who kept his own little court around him like a monarch,' he told *Illustrated London News* in January 1970. The stars on *Alfred the Great* were David Hemmings and Michael York, McKellen's own contemporaries, who had set themselves up in rival Irish castles during the shoot near Loughrea in County Galway. That level of star behaviour looks like a possible model for McKellen's Richard. But he may also have been drawing on his experiences on location in the summer of 1966 for *The Bells of Hell Go Ting-a-Ling-a-Ling*, starring Gregory Peck.

It was not that he copied mannerisms he had observed; it was simply a way into the character's psychology, a way of connecting Shakespeare to his own experience. Another contemporary figure he drew on was the Dalai Lama, a modern incarnation of the god-head who, still more appropriately for Richard II, had been driven from his position by an invading army, in his case the Chinese occupying Tibet.

Expanding on his approach to Shakespeare to Joy Leslie Gibson in June 1979, McKellen said, 'Classic drama can only be worthwhile, if closely tied to the world today.' It is a point of view which pervades all of modern Shakespearian production, certainly from the time Peter Hall took over the RSC in 1960. It derives from a work of Shakespearian criticism by the Polish-born critic, scholar and philosopher of theatre, Jan Kott, entitled *Shakespeare our Contemporary*, published in Britain in 1964.

'No one who met him,' wrote Michael Kustow in Kott's *Guardian* obituary in 2002, 'as I first did at the Royal Shakespeare Company in the 1960s, will forget his impishness, his ceaseless vitality, his voice rising to excited falsetto at some choice paradox.'

The effect of Kott's book was to lift Shakespeare out of the museum, to blow away the library dust and to allow the plays a distinctive meaning for those living in the long post-war shadow of Hitler and Stalin and the atomic bomb. A fighter in the Polish resistance to Nazism, an *apparatchik* and later a dissident in communist Poland, Kott's own life gave his discoveries in Shakespeare an unprecedented authenticity and authority.

'What I have in mind,' Kott writes, 'is not a forced topicality . . . Shakespeare does not have to be modernised or brought up to date . . . What matters is that through Shakespeare's text we ought to get at our own modern experiences, anxiety and sensibility.'

It is a crucial distinction. The *Richard II* that McKellen and Cottrell were planning was to be located recognisably in the medieval world, most obviously through costuming, but also in the use of formal patterning in the blocking. But what came alive, at least for the young audience of 1968 and 1969, who flocked to see the production, was what the play had to say about the clash between the generations. Here was a Richard who might be a medieval monarch, but who, in his gorgeous clothes and his irreverence for his elders and with his student-like mates was recognisably young. Not a distant, incomprehensible sun-king, battling it out with a bunch of helmeted heavies, but a young, intensely attractive leader, ranged against the crabbed old age of John of Gaunt and his cronies and his prematurely middle-aged son, Bolingbroke. That was what made the young king's fall, with all his faults on full view, so moving. The audience saw its own concerns – the generation gap, as it was then called – explored and illuminated in the play.

'One magical day in rehearsal,' remembered McKellen in an interview in *Woman and Home* in 1984, 'we discovered a gesture, a regal, priestly upraising of the arms, symbolic but deeply felt . . . On it I quickly built the rest of the character.'

This is deeply revealing both of the process of rehearsal and the way in which McKellen created his performance as Richard: it's 'we' who found the gesture – and it's not the royal 'we'. A rehearsal is a place where discoveries are made in collaboration between director and actors. Critics often praise a director's insight or a particularly telling moment from an individual actor, but to distinguish exactly whose idea something was in rehearsal is often more or less impossible. Many directors will confine themselves almost entirely to selecting from what the actors offer, rather than making positive suggestions themselves. McKellen in his description of the discovery of that all-important gesture, a gesture etched clearly in the minds of all who saw the performance, acknowledges that collaborative nature of rehearsal. And on that gesture, he goes on, he 'quickly built the rest of the character'. It's what the great Russian actor, director and teacher Michael Chekhov called 'psychological gesture' – a single physical gesture that encapsulates for the actor the whole of a character. That upraising of the hands, with which McKellen's Richard announced his connection to God, expressed both for him and for the audience his entire conception of the part. It was the gesture with which he made his first grand entry. It was the gesture with which he stilled the wrangling lords in the first scene. And when in the scene before Flint Castle the gesture failed to bring Bolingbroke and his supporters to their knees, Richard's loss of power was embodied in a moment.

At the same time, McKellen found a complete contrast to the stately pace and hieratic gestures of Richard the sun-king in the informal body language and colloquial speech rhythms of his early scenes with Bushy, Bagot, Green and Aumerle. This was the young man off duty among his friends – playful, irreverent, arrogant, likeable and extremely human. And it was his discovery, when those friends are put to death, that 'I live with bread like you, feel want,/Taste grief, *need friends*,' which began Richard II's growth as a human being and made his tragedy so moving. Never frightened since Bolton School of a little 'odd pointing of lines', McKellen came down on that '*need friends*' with a burning intensity which allowed the audience to see suddenly into the heart of Richard the man. Director Richard Cottrell remembers the thrilling moment in rehearsal when McKellen found that emphasis. As important as the sun-king gesture and like the howl over the dead Coriolanus's body, it was a defining moment for the character. And this sudden focus on a particular instant in performance would become one of McKellen's distinctive ways of illuminating his Shakespearian heroes.

Of course, there were those who said it had all been done before. Audrey Williamson went so far as to write to McKellen pointing out how he had stolen different bits from John Gielgud, John Neville, Paul Scofield, Alec Guinness and Maurice Evans, including Gielgud's ceremonial entrance and Guinness's rhythmic pacing in prison in Act V, which McKellen had actually borrowed from a polar bear in London Zoo. McKellen made his response in *Shakespeare Quarterly* in 1982: 'When

I'm doing Shakespeare or any play I assume that the audience watching it has never seen the play before. I try to play *Hamlet* or *Richard II* or *Macbeth* with the same commitment and freshness as if those plays had been written only months before and the audience has no idea of what is going to happen. I don't play to the critics who are coming to see their tenth *Hamlet* this season and who are likely to be interested in what I do that's different, something that may illuminate a corner of the play they haven't noticed before. No, my commitment is to the audience who don't know anything about *Hamlet* at all.' This is the reason why for so long he preferred to stay away from Stratford, where the rustle of audience members turning the pages of the script is often audible from the stage.

Richard II did a week in Cambridge, a week in Brighton, a week in Newcastle, a week in Leeds and a week in Guildford. A whole coach party from Barrow Bridge turned up at the Leeds Grand, crowding into the star's dressing room after the show. Five theatres, forty performances and that was it, but such was the acclaim and such the ballyhoo in the national press that no one was surprised when Prospect announced that the production would be revived the following year. This time it would play at the Edinburgh Festival, followed by a tour, including brief stopovers in Vienna and Bratislava and then on to London to the Mermaid Theatre. What did surprise and what made this tour the remarkable theatrical occasion that it became was that McKellen was not only going to reprise his Richard II, but he was going to alternate it with the title role in Christopher Marlowe's *Edward II*. Derek Jacobi had dropped out; so had Gary Bond. Originally slated to play Gaveston in the Marlowe play, McKellen had finally agreed to take on both kings.

Probably written no more than a couple of years before *Richard II*, Marlowe's play makes a fascinating companion piece. With its story of a weak monarch deposed by his over-mighty subjects, its scene in which the king surrenders the crown and the final murder in prison, *Edward II* was clearly an influence on the young Shakespeare. For most of the audience in 1969, though, *Edward II* was chiefly interesting – indeed shocking – for its graphic portrayal of the homosexual love of Edward and Gaveston. And where earlier modern productions of the play, including director Toby Robertson's own student production at Cambridge with Derek Jacobi in the title role, had tended to play down this aspect of the play, McKellen would bring it to the forefront of the drama in a passionate kiss with James Laurenson's Gaveston within minutes of the play's opening.

Paul Hardwick was retained as John of Gaunt from the previous year's company, but for the most part it was a new group of actors who assembled around McKellen for rehearsals at the end of July 1969. Among the newcomers, Prospect stalwarts Timothy West and Robert Eddison were taking over as Bolingbroke and York respectively, with West also playing the chief antagonist, Mortimer, in *Edward II*, and Eddison taking on the small but telling role of Edward's murderer, Lightborn.

Also among the cast was Nigel Havers (later to star in films such as *Farewell to the King*, *A Passage to India* and *Chariots of Fire*) in his first professional job as acting assistant stage manager (ASM). 'I was the most junior member of the gang. I was seventeen. I remember rehearsing at the Donmar Warehouse, which was then just a space, and being terribly impressed just watching Ian. He was absolutely mesmeric in rehearsal.'

Having already played Richard, McKellen was focusing mainly on developing the character of Edward. 'I remember one very hot afternoon when I was making the tea,' says Havers, 'watching him suddenly grasp the scene when he hears about Gaveston's death. He let out this sort of primal scream – amazing. He didn't use it in performance. I think it was just him getting something into his psyche.' What McKellen was following was Tyrone Guthrie's principle that at some point in rehearsal the actor must experience the full, real feeling behind each moment, so that he can reproduce it in performance. It was what he had been searching for at that dress rehearsal of *Coriolanus*.

Lucy Fleming, niece of the writer Ian Fleming and daughter of British screen actress Celia Johnson, took over as Richard's Queen Anne, a part originally offered to Felicity Kendal. Fleming also played Edward's niece. Lucy Fleming remembers those rehearsals too: 'There were times when he was just marking it, but once he turned it on, it was stunning to listen to and to act with – the intensity of his acting. It was fascinating, awe-inspiring.'

After the 1968 tour the newspapers were already full of the 'Olivier from Wigan' tag that would follow McKellen for years. In truth nothing more than lazy journalistic shorthand, coupled with the sly metropolitan condescension that considers the juxtaposition of the name of the great Sir Laurence with a Lancashire coal town as the height of wit, it was nevertheless the kind of press to go to an actor's head. Nigel Havers for one found McKellen had not begun believing his publicity, however. 'He wasn't grand at all. Being the lowest of the low you can be treated quite badly, and the other ASMs started off by thinking I was some kind of toffee-nosed bastard because of the way I spoke and my dad [Lord Havers QC, later the Attorney General]. But Ian was very nice. Richard Cottrell was tough. He had this stutter, and he used to get really furious at us and shout because he couldn't get the words out. I never understand why directors have to shout – as if any actor gets it wrong on purpose – no point. But anyway, Ian used to be very defensive of us. I felt he never treated me as anything other than an equal.'

Lucy Fleming remembers the director quite differently. She thinks the relationship between McKellen and 'Cotty', dating back to Cambridge days, was important to the success of the production. 'Cotty was very sensitive, very gentle, very good, very intelligent,' she remembers. 'He kind of drew one out. Quite a shy man actually. I think he was very good with Ian because he didn't over-direct him.'

It's a comment others make about Trevor Nunn's working relationship with McKellen. When a director knows and trusts his leading actor, he doesn't push. He lets him take his own time in developing a part, intervening as and when the actor seems to want or need it. It is similar to a comment on Tyrone Guthrie's approach: 'He assumed that the majority of the actors knew what they were going to be doing anyhow,' or Robert Chetwyn's: 'You're depending on the actor to do a great deal for you.' Mutual trust is the key to a successful actor–director relationship.

McKellen had taken on a tremendous challenge. Apart from the sheer stamina required to play these two enormous parts in repertoire, he had to differentiate between two roles which are in some ways similar. What McKellen needed was as great a contrast as he had found between Tom and Harold Gorringe in the Shaffer double bill. In the rehearsal rooms in Covent Garden he began to develop two radically different performances. For instance, where Richard's early scenes were all poise and grandeur with slow and stately movement, as if he had castors beneath those golden robes, as Edward, McKellen prowled, skipped and paced the stage, an adolescent in love, a man younger in spirit if not in fact than Richard – simpler, less intelligent.

Both plays cover an extended period of history. For Edward, McKellen and his director decided on make-up changes through the evening to suggest the passage of the years. Despite a modest budget, designer Tim Goodchild's costumes for *Richard II* had already been a crucial part of the success of the show. 'When I first came on,' recalls Lucy Fleming, 'I had a train about twelve foot long. At Edinburgh Ian and I had to start down in the basement and come up different ways because of the length of the train.' In fact, King Richard's costume was a triumph of theatrical effect over production costs, looking highly authentic, but actually made of modern furnishing fabric and a lot of gold paint, dressed up with rhinestones, raffia, coins and even some metal beer-bottle tops. And that enormous train was covered underneath with polythene to stop it getting ripped and filthy. Trying to look as different as possible, Kenneth Rowell produced for *Edward II* a set hung with lengths of chain, which were echoed in the costumes, giving the whole play a much more primitive look than *Richard*. The rainbow-hued costumes for *Edward II* were rather 1960s, but at least added to the contrast. Even the programme chipped in, showing on its cover the gilded Richard of Act 1 alongside the haunted old Edward of Act 5. They are barely recognisable as the same actor.

They did a warm-up week of *Richard II* at the Forum Theatre in Billingham in the north-east of England – 'ghastly place: we all stayed in that awful tower block next to it and the whole place smelled,' offers Lucy Fleming – and then they moved up to the official opening at the Edinburgh Festival. But this was no fringe affair. Prospect Theatre Productions was at the Festival for the first time, and Ian McKellen as Richard and Edward at the Assembly Rooms was the theatrical event of the year. Walking into the gloom of Edinburgh's historic Assembly Rooms for the first time on a rainy Sunday afternoon, the cast felt nervous and unwelcome. Timothy West, whose two tough-minded antagonists to McKellen were a crucial part of the success of the 1969 tour, could scarcely believe they were about to perform in this gothic vault – let alone in a play which began with two men kissing each other on the mouth.

Interestingly, when he was drawing up plans with architect Bill Howell for the Young Vic, which opened in 1970, Frank Dunlop cited the Assembly Rooms in Edinburgh as exactly the kind of performance space he wanted – a square room, with a single gallery and seats on three sides, leaving a long tongue of acting area sticking out into the audience. Both Dunlop and Joan Littlewood, legendary head of Theatre Workshop, despite dismissing the place initially as 'impossible', finished by considering the Edinburgh Assembly Rooms one of the most exciting theatrical spaces they had ever directed in.

Some who saw the productions that year thought McKellen's Edward II markedly inferior to his Richard. Typically for McKellen he looked for a psychological sub-structure to Edward. He wanted to create a portrait of a man, very young at the beginning, full of potential, who turns into a tyrant because his love for Piers Gaveston is thwarted by those around him.

The advantage of this for the actor is that it gives him what is called a through-line for the part: the character has a journey to go on from youth to maturity, from innocence to bitter experience, from love to tyranny. For McKellen in particular it had the added advantage of bringing the character close to his own experience – Edward is a homosexual in a society which will not allow him to love as he wishes. But Marlowe's is not a play of psychology; indeed his plays are basically pre-psychological. Whereas in Richard you have at times the prototype for Hamlet, the first modern man, with his introspection and his painful journey towards self-knowledge, Edward, despite occasional gestures at development, ends more or less where he begins – lamenting for his Gaveston. What you need to play Marlowe is perfect technical command of the actor's instrument – his body and his voice – and perfect control of the iambic pentameter: Marlowe's mighty line. And this McKellen did not have. Where psychology had illuminated Richard, taken him on a credible journey from medieval sun-king to human being, psychology cast a wash of emotion across Edward which frequently obscured the text.

But any fear that *Edward II* might not find an audience was soon quashed when Councillor John Kidd, having attended the opening night, insisted the Chief Constable investigate 'this shocking and filthy production'. From then on wherever the show went there was not a seat to be had.

From Edinburgh the productions moved to Bernard Miles's Mermaid Theatre in London and the chorus of critical approval reached a crescendo. 'The ineffable presence of God himself enters into Mr McKellen's Richard,' boomed Harold Hobson in the *Sunday Times*. And while Hobson was actually making a comment on the success of the actor's researches into the divine right of kings, rather than saying McKellen was a god, the distinction hardly seemed to matter at a time when young fans of the blues guitar were daubing the walls of Britain with the legend 'Clapton is God'.

Such was the demand for tickets at the Mermaid, that London's Piccadilly Theatre was rapidly reserved for the end of the tour. It was the show that everyone wanted to see. One night in his dressing room McKellen introduced Noel Coward to Rudolf Nureyev. An unnamed member of the royal family even told him after one performance that the production had taught her something new about being a monarch.

More revealing perhaps than the general level of press interest was the feeling of McKellen's fellow actors. In the opening scenes of *Richard II* Nigel Havers and the rest of the spear carriers had the kind of job which can drive an actor to distraction. 'All eight of us were carrying banners,' he remembers, 'and we stood there for the first twenty-five minutes of the play not allowed to move a muscle, which is quite a long time. But

I was absolutely exhilarated watching him. Right through that tour I used to look forward to it.' Twenty odd years later on the National Theatre tour of *Richard III*, McKellen would face virtual mutiny from actors forced to stand at attention in exactly the same way through his long scene with Queen Elizabeth. Yet Havers says he enjoyed it – every night. Just watching.

Havers also offers this testament to the continuing work that went into keeping the two shows sharp. As Edward, McKellen wielded a huge sword – 'phallic', says Havers – in a dramatic gesture at the end of the first half. 'He would just put his hand out,' recalls Nigel Havers, 'and I would launch this sword and he would just catch it without turning. It was a very dramatic moment. And we rehearsed it every single night before the performance – just to make sure we were on tune. And he never dropped it.' This emphasis on precise, physical stage business, designed to define character – in this case showing Edward as warrior – would become another of McKellen's trademarks as a classical actor.

On the other hand Lucy Fleming offers some insights into the inevitable unevenness that can creep into a long tour. 'I remember him on first nights in places being magical,' she says, 'and then he got a bit bored perhaps and I didn't feel he was fully connected to me. It's very difficult to maintain the kind of passion and emotion that he went through playing those parts. I remember once at a matinee he had all his soldiers with him and he made them giggle and then turned around and did this farewell scene with me. I got quite cross about it actually because they were all corpsing behind me. He was so electric when we opened, and then sometimes you'd think, Come off it, you're not doing it properly.'

After the Mermaid the tour took them to Vienna as part of British week. 'There was a London bus driving around all the time,' recalls Lucy Fleming, 'and there were embassy receptions and things like that.'

'I got pissed and left the passports in a restaurant,' puts in Nigel Havers, '– all fifty-five of them. Had to go back at four in the morning and wake everyone up.'

Then in October 1969 they all got on a bus and made the trip across the frontier to Bratislava in Czechoslovakia, behind the Iron Curtain. Just over a year earlier Soviet tanks had rolled across the border to put an end to Alexander Dubcek's 'Prague spring', an attempt to create 'communism with a human face'. The Czechoslovakian people had stood in the streets with placards, unable to resist the might of the Red Army. Any visit from a western theatre company would have been important at the time but *Richard II* was electrifying. The audience interpreted this story of a leader deposed by an invading army as their own. Writing in the *Sunday Telegraph Magazine* thirteen years later, McKellen could still remember the scene in Act 3, when Richard weeps for joy to be back in England once more, and calls upon the plants, insects and animals of his kingdom to resist the invader, strange sounds began to come from the auditorium: 'the plash, the gasp, the snuffles, the mewing. I have never heard it since, an audience crying. They were grieving.'

At the end of the show they stood and cheered. They wept. They chanted. They threw flowers. The new powers-that-be were appalled. They cancelled the next day's press conference, moved the cast to a new hotel, and told them they weren't allowed out except to go to the theatre. No clearer endorsement of Jan Kott's thesis could possibly be imagined: 'What matters is that through Shakespeare's text we ought to get at our own modern experiences, anxiety and sensibility.' In a play nearly 400 years old the Czechoslovak people had seen enacted their own recent history.

It was that tour which established McKellen at a stroke as the leading young classical actor of his generation. James Cairncross and Robert Chetwyn couldn't explain it. Lucy Fleming tries to define just exactly what was so good about the young McKellen: 'You couldn't take your eyes off him. You were just fascinated by what this man was doing.' But why? 'He drew you with him. You just wanted to go with him.' And then she starts to put her finger on it. 'I think it's to do with a sort of ease, a relaxation – that you know as an audience you're totally comfortable and you'll go anywhere with him. He's got that complete confidence on stage.'

Nigel Havers puts it like this: 'He's not frightened of anything and those actors are very powerful. They have no stage fear at all. They're totally at home on stage. And they say, "F*** off, I don't give a shit!" No nerves.'

McKellen's performances were packed with moments of extreme daring: the exaggeratedly studied movement of Richard; the tremendous pace and clarity; the thrilling upward inflections; the sudden, surprising emphases; the abrupt explosions of fury; the sudden psychological insights. Moments of risk. A reminder of that dress rehearsal in Nottingham in December 1963 with Tyrone Guthrie urging his young Tullus Aufidius to have one more go at the cry of pain and sorrow over John Neville's dead Coriolanus. McKellen had overcome his fear of that moment, mastered it, and found that it was the greatest point of danger in a performance which made the greatest impact. Fearlessness. F*** off, I don't give a shit! No nerves.

Richard II and *Edward II* closed at the Piccadilly Theatre on 21 March 1970. According to Nigel Havers, 'The run at the Piccadilly was cut short because Ian was going to do a movie which got canned at the last minute. He was going to do the *Flashman* film, and he just cut it. We were full, doing fantastic business.'

The abortive *Royal Flash*, which didn't get made until 1975 with Malcolm McDowell in the lead, was just one of many false starts in movies. As far as theatre was concerned, the logical next step for McKellen, just coming up to his 31st birthday, was Hamlet. And the obvious place to play it was the RSC, now under the control of his old Cambridge chum Trevor Nunn. It didn't happen. The exact sequence of events is not certain, but what seems to have happened is that Nunn did ask him to come to Stratford to play Hamlet, but he was insisting on a longer contract than McKellen wanted to sign and the two couldn't agree on who should direct. Had an agreement been reached in 1970, the history of McKellen's Hamlet might have been very different.

As it was, he went back to Prospect – only McKellen didn't want Toby Robertson directing. Lucy Fleming had noted in rehearsals for *Edward II* that there wasn't the rapport between Robertson and McKellen that the actor had with Richard Cottrell. 'Toby used to change things at the last moment,' believes Nigel Havers. 'He would be backstage during the show and you'd be just about to go on and he'd say, "No, no, go on the other side." He'd be directing you while the play was going on.' Instead, McKellen brought in his old friend from Ipswich days, Robert Chetwyn.

Over the coming months they met regularly in Chetwyn's London flat in Ecclestone Square to plan the production. They went through the text of *Hamlet*, discussing every detail, leaving nothing to chance. 'Tell the story' has been every director's watchword since Bertolt Brecht began to influence British theatre in the 1950s. Chetwyn was no exception. 'I wanted to find a very simple way through all the complexity,' he says. What should they do with the soliloquies? And particularly with the most famous of them all – 'To be or not to be . . .' – which didn't seem to advance the plot at all. McKellen talked to his old mentor in Cambridge, Dadie Rylands. 'Cut it,' was his terse advice. And for a while McKellen and Chetwyn considered following it. But how can you cut the most famous 35 lines in world drama?

While the *Hamlet* tour was being set up for 1971, McKellen was back under the directorship of his friend Richard Cottrell, who had parted company with Toby Robertson and Prospect, and was running a company out of their old student stamping ground, the Arts Theatre in Cambridge. It was another wonderfully contrasting double – Captain

Plume in *The Recruiting Officer*, George Farquhar's eighteenth-century comedy, a chance for high style and plenty of gags, and Corporal Hill in a revival of Arnold Wesker's first hit, *Chips With Everything*, a brutal comedy drawing on Wesker's experiences during National Service.

A year out of the Central School of Speech and Drama, Nickolas Grace was among the cast. 'Cotty's always been really good at finding people,' he comments. 'We had Stuart Wilson, Julian Curry and Susan Fleetwood. And Jonathan Kent was just walking on and understudying.' Grace remembers rehearsals for *Chips* particularly. What Cottrell and McKellen knew was that to make the play work the recruits and their Corporal had to be welded together into an ensemble. It was no good if they interacted as a star and a bunch of young actors. 'We did a lot of those things we'd learned at drama school but had never actually put into practice,' says Nickolas Grace. 'Like improvising – all the young RAF trainees together. What was great about Ian was that he absolutely threw himself into it and was one of us. We all had to do square-bashing – squaddie stuff – right up until the day we opened, and he took that terribly seriously.'

It was one more in McKellen's line of military men, dating back to *End of Conflict* in Coventry, another National Service play. Only this time McKellen could use his native Lancashire accent for Corporal Hill. Wesker came up to Cambridge to see it, and declared the production at least as good if not better than the original at the Royal Court in 1962.

This was a first time on tour for Nickolas Grace. 'Ian showed me something which I hadn't always seen in rep with big names coming in that you could do this work and you could have fun at the same time. There were lots of young guys around and he was the commanding officer. And what he's really good at is being the leader of the company, getting in there and saying, "Come on, let's all go and have a cream tea in the cake shop down the road." Or in Southampton we all went riding in the New Forest. He took us under his wing, me and Jonathan Kent and Stuart Wilson.'

McKellen as company leader. This is a role that is crucially important on the road, and at least part of what it involves are very ordinary things like remembering people's birthdays. They'd reached Swansea, when Nickolas Grace's birthday arrived. When he got to the theatre that night, McKellen was already there.

'Oh by the way,' said McKellen casually, 'we're having a party for you later tonight.'

After the show they all went back to the cottage he was sharing with Julian Curry in Port Einon. 'There were jellies and cake and all those silly things,' remembers Grace. 'He liked all that. His nickname was "Troupe". Cotty called him that. "Come on, Troupe," Cotty would say.'

Julian Curry was already a friend from Coventry days. McKellen also struck up a rapport with Susan Fleetwood, playing Sylvia to his Captain Plume in *The Recruiting Officer*. She was soon calling him 'Troupe' as well. And both actors were there on the opening day of rehearsals in February 1971 when McKellen's *Hamlet* got under way in the dark and rather forbidding interior of the London Welsh Club on Gray's Inn Road. McKellen had a friend directing (Robert Chetwyn); for the key roles of Horatio and Ophelia he had two more mates in Curry and Fleetwood; his old friend James Cairncross was First Gravedigger; Nick Grace was there too, playing Second Gravedigger and Player Queen. It was exactly the recipe McKellen would always want for creating his best work. And star and director were in agreement: 'Ian and I knew what we were doing with it,' says Chetwyn. 'If Hamlet and the director are in tune then the rest falls into place around that.'

Only it didn't.

They had decided to play Hamlet as a very young man, not someone who can't make up his mind, but a youth totally bewildered by the rush of events in the first three and a half acts. Chetwyn had also made some important decisions about design. Michael Annals had devised an extraordinary set, made up largely of huge mirrors at the back of the stage. 'I didn't want a specific period,' says Chetwyn. 'But I wanted to make it accessible to an audience. I wanted a timeless production.' So Hamlet's costume, for instance, while nodding to the renaissance in a drawstring shirt, had more than a hint of the early 1970s with a fringe jacket which wouldn't have looked out of place on a rock 'n' roll singer. 'The production was all about youth culture against middle age.' That was how McKellen remembered it in an interview for the *Independent* in 1989.

'I hate making speeches at the beginning,' says Robert Chetwyn. 'It gives this awful feeling that this is how it's all going to be, and theatre isn't like that. There are so many myriad ways of getting to the end point. And every actor has to find his own way or be helped.' The problem would be that at least some of the actors would soon feel they were having to find their own way largely in the dark. 'We used to talk about it in the pub,' remembers Nickolas Grace. 'What's he trying to do with the play? Because [we didn't feel] it had ever been explained to us. We'd come every day and just hope for the best.'

Faith Brook, who played Gertrude as an alcoholic, remembers one rehearsal in particular. She and McKellen were working on the closet scene in which Hamlet confronts his mother for marrying her dead husband's brother. Since Olivier's interpretation, so heavily influenced by Freudian psychology, the scene has often been played with strong incestuous overtones. The rehearsal had rather run out of steam.

'I've tried everything to suggest things to you – you think of something,' said Chetwyn. 'What do you want to do?'

'I want to cry,' said Faith Brook.

'Then for God's sake cry,' said the director.

They ran it again with Gertrude crying from about halfway through the scene, when McKellen's Hamlet started to shake her physically. McKellen stopped.

'I can't cope with the tears,' he said, meaning his Hamlet had to respond to his mother's crying. The rehearsal continued with McKellen changing the way he played the latter part of the scene in the light of Gertrude's tears.

It sounds like a rehearsal process working well, with director and actors co-operating, interchanging ideas, adapting and developing a scene in the light of new discoveries. But many in the cast, certainly among those playing the smaller parts, felt adrift. Nickolas Grace was most worried by what he saw as a change in McKellen himself. 'Ian was wonderful at first to all of us. But then he seemed to cut himself off. And I thought, Oh God, Ian's changed. But now I understand.' Grace felt Chetwyn didn't seem to have a strict line on what he wanted Hamlet's approach to be. 'So Ian appeared to go off and do his own thing, which was at times very renaissance and beautiful and full of wonderful poses, and at other times during the run he'd turn back upstage to us and go, "Agh!" ' (And Nick pulls a face, as if to imitate McKellen saying, 'What the hell are we doing here?')

Meanwhile Chetwyn was having his own difficulties with Prospect. He says now that although Toby Robertson had claimed to be happy about not directing McKellen's Hamlet, Chetwyn felt that, 'He didn't like it at all really. And he kept wanting to know what was going on. And later he . . . invited the press to a schools matinee in Edinburgh.'

Nickolas Grace takes up the story at the point at which the production opened at the Nottingham Playhouse, scene of McKellen's early triumphs. 'All the mates from Prospect like Richard Cottrell came, and the vibes on that first night were pretty awful, because they were all trying to say, "Well done", but couldn't. And Ian was frustrated and saying, "Well, what's wrong with it? What can we do?" It was very sad.'

The critics hated it. 'McKellen gives a sudden, shuddering emphasis to lines which seem to bear little or no relationship to his or any other interpretation of the play,' wrote Peter Ansorge in *Plays and Players*. It was the same method which had thrown that 'need friends' into such sharp relief in *Richard II*. Only this time no one was buying.

Some felt the critical response was predictable. 'He'd had an enormous success as Richard and Edward,' comments James Cairncross who was playing First Gravedigger and had the wisdom of two other Hamlets behind him, 'and it was quite logical that the very same critics who praised him to the skies in Edward and Richard tore him down a bit.'

Certainly there were successes – on the European leg of the tour in particular. 'In Rome,' remembers Faith Brook, 'pretty well everybody in the audience was on drugs and we had this mirror set. In the court, for instance, it looked as if we had hundreds of people on the stage. And they thought, Wow! Twenty Hamlets! I remember Ian standing on the first night in Rome and we'd taken about fifteen curtain calls, and he was hanging onto the curtain and he said, "I feel like Donald Wolfit," ' – something of a joke in the acting profession by the 1960s for his old-fashioned style.

Nick Grace remembers Rome too. 'They'd got the posters wrong, and they all said "Jan McKellen". And they were all screaming, "Jan! Jan! Jan!" in the theatre. And there were people screaming and shouting at the stage door.' The social scene was good too, led by young scions of the Italian royal families of the movies, Rossellini and Antonioni. 'It was real decadence. I remember there were parties when I thought, My God, this is what Rome's all about. Ian loved that. We both went back there for a holiday after the tour was over.'

Bruised by the critical reception in the British press, by the time the production was getting ready for the Cambridge Theatre in London in the summer, McKellen himself was sounding distinctly paranoid. 'I suspect a lot of people hate me as an actor,' he told Michael Owen of the *Evening Standard*. 'I fully expect to get the worst notices of my life.' He put part of the blame on the fact that there had been too many other productions of *Hamlet* that year, and audiences and critics in particular were simply sick of the play. Certainly, Alan Howard had just done it up at Stratford, Jonathan Miller had directed a production, and the Cambridge Theatre itself had already played host to Alan Bates's Prince at the beginning of the year. Playing Hamlet that year, McKellen told the *Observer* a couple of years later, with a delightful image from his favourite walking country in the Lake District, was 'like climbing Great Gable on Bank Holiday Monday'.

The atmosphere in the company was not good and quite a number of the actors playing smaller parts had already decided to jump ship before

London. More seriously it was soon clear that a major recasting of the larger parts would be necessary. Ronald Lewis, who was playing Claudius, announced that he wanted equal billing with McKellen at the Cambridge. The management wouldn't have it. 'Ronnie had been something of a film star,' comments Robert Chetwyn, 'and was a good actor, but he was a very delicate kind of guy. I think he felt he should have been in Ian McKellen's position. He had that kind of start. He was a Richard Burton type and he kept doing wonderful work but not quite top league.' John Woodvine, who would later feature in McKellen's *Macbeth*, took over.

Then at the last minute Geoffrey Chater left, and James Cairncross, already doubling First Gravedigger and the voice of the Ghost who appeared only as a series of reflections in Michael Annals's mirrors, became Polonius as well.

'The show lost some of its guts when it came into London,' comments Faith Brook. 'Too much doubling up to save money.' She herself was indignant when cost-savings at the Cambridge finally led to Eddie Kulukundis walking into her dressing room and asking her to take a pay cut.

Into the middle of all this walked David Ashton, a young actor in his first West End job. 'I was just playing nothing – a couple of lines and then running about with a spear and then running about with another spear,' he says. But Ashton soon had pretty clear views on what was wrong. 'There wasn't a core to the production. It was almost like a boulevard Hamlet . . . Ian played it like a kind of Wilfred Lawson juvenile – fluting voice. He played him as someone very far out on a limb somewhere – quite disturbed – but I thought he could have found a lot more depth if he'd been pushed.'

Faith Brook offers, 'I think when he was doing Edward and Richard there were some things he got rather fond of doing and he was still doing them in *Hamlet*. Mainly vocal things – odd inflections. I think he was vocally very mannered. I remember thinking, You like the sound of your own voice.'

Sure enough, reviews at the Cambridge were little better than they had been on tour. Nicholas de Jongh in the *Guardian* thought the play had got worse. Irving Wardle in *The Times* thought it had got a bit better. One critic left the theatre so sick of watching *Hamlet* he thought there should be a ten-year moratorium on productions of the play.

McKellen himself ended with mixed feelings. He knew the production had succeeded in his basic aim of reaching an audience less familiar with *Hamlet* than the national critics. In Aberdeen a fourteen-year-old girl came up to him at the stage door shaking with excitement. 'I thought you were going to be killed,' she stammered out. 'I thought Laertes was going to kill you.' That was the audience he was playing for. But looking back on the part nearly twenty years after he played it, he decided he had rushed at it, going too much for angst and bewilderment and pain, and not finding Hamlet's humanity. Summing the experience up for the *Independent* in March 1989, he sounded impatient with the play itself as well as his own performance: 'Peter O'Toole was right when he said it was just one long wank from beginning to end – pure self-indulgence. So much of the play encourages you to be self-obsessed and neurotic . . . any actor more than thirty is dreary – Hamlet should be eighteen – a kid – otherwise his behaviour is inexcusable.'

McKellen had conceived the part as a very young man. Perhaps the problem was simply that at the age of 32, he thought he was too old for the part, so he pressed for youthful effects and lost truthfulness. It would be a problem he would face again in *Romeo and Juliet* five years later. The difficulty for McKellen's conception of Hamlet, is the practical one that an actor young enough to make a convincing university student, which is, after all, what Hamlet is supposed to be, is almost always going to lack the technical expertise to play the part.

Nickolas Grace had been worried about McKellen during rehearsals for *Hamlet*, as he appeared to cut himself off from the company and stopped interacting with the other characters on stage. Was he really turning into the nineteenth-century star actor which some of the critics accused him of being? David Ashton thinks not. 'I thought he was a very generous man to work with. He had a kind of knack, although he was a star, of being very easily with you and you didn't feel there was any condescension. He was an actor in a company of actors. Whenever we were on the stage rehearsing together you felt that he treated you as an equal. He was like that with everyone.'

It's almost identical to what Nigel Havers had to say about rehearsals for *Richard* and *Edward*.

4. TAKING CONTROL

Actors are like strawberries. They lie there looking cute, saying, 'Pick me! Pick me!' But sooner or later every strawberry might think he'd like a turn at picking. In the 1970s Ian McKellen would make the attempt to move away from the essentially passive position of the actor waiting for a director to employ him, and take control of his own career.

He had already directed a couple of plays at the Liverpool Playhouse in 1969 between the two Prospect tours of *Richard II*. At that time he was quite clear that he didn't want it to take over his career. But in the aftermath of his not altogether successful Hamlet in the early months of 1972, directing looked as if it might be the way to go. First he did *The Real Inspector Hound* at the Phoenix, Leicester with Edward Hardwicke and Derek Jacobi; then he went to Watford to put on Joe Orton's *Erpingham Camp*. These shows were quality regional productions, but McKellen had bigger plans.

Shipping magnate and impresario Eddie Kulukundis had brought McKellen's *Hamlet* into London when Prospect refused. Now Kulukundis was eager to mount a production of a musical which had been one of the hits of the 1971 Edinburgh Festival. Based on Shakespeare's *Henry V*, the show rejoiced in the title of *Hank Cinq*. McKellen couldn't be in it because his singing wasn't good enough. Instead, Kulukundis asked him to direct. Michael Annals, creator of those *Hamlet* mirrors, agreed to design, and began building models, which were consciously reminiscent of Olivier's film of *Henry V* with cut-out groups of soldiers and cardboard banners. Then, with McKellen speaking the lyrics to the songs, the pair did the rounds of potential backers.

No joy. *Hank* sank without trace. And though he went on to direct *A Private Matter* at the Vaudeville in 1973 and *The Clandestine Marriage* at the Savoy in 1975, both Alastair Sim vehicles produced by Binkie Beaumont, directing would not prove the way forward for McKellen. Indeed he seems to have found actors waiting passively for him to feed their imaginations and tell them what to do a somewhat alarming experience.

'I am more confident on stage than I am at home,' McKellen told Michael Owen in an *Evening Standard* interview in July 1971 – a very rare excursion into his personal life. 'In my private life I'm ineffectual. I can't make decisions. I used to be sure of myself and saw a distinct pattern for the future but now I'm confused.'

It wasn't only the question of whether he should move more into directing that was preoccupying him. His relationship with Brian Taylor was breaking up. All that McKellen has said is that the relationship 'changed' in 1972, and Brodie doesn't talk willingly about his time with Ian McKellen, observing simply that, 'There isn't really anything I want to get off my chest.' But at any rate 1972 saw Ian McKellen moving out of the flat at 25 Earls Terrace, and buying his first house, a knocked through Victorian terrace at 17 Camberwell Grove. He'd gone from the unfashionable end of Kensington High Street to an even less fashionable corner of south London, though Albert Finney did have a place in Camberwell at the time too.

South London's besetting problem of not being well served by the underground train system was not such a difficulty for McKellen. He was well-known at the time for going everywhere on a moped. Visiting 17 Camberwell Grove in 1978, journalist Michael Owen noted the figurines of Shakespeare on shelves and the copies of the *New Statesman* and the *Guardian*, announcing the owner's leftward leaning politics.

In among the directing jobs at the beginning of 1971, McKellen had gone up to Sheffield to be part of the opening of the brand new Crucible Theatre in Chekhov's one-act skit on the Russian theatre, *Swan Song*. The play is about a 68-year-old ham actor named Svetlovidov who falls asleep drunk and gets locked into the theatre after a performance. He proceeds to regale the prompter, who sleeps in the theatre at night because he has nowhere else to go (shades of Michael Crawford and John Collins in Nottingham), with over-the-top extracts from his greatest roles. David William was directing. But who should they get to play the small but crucial part of the Prompter?

McKellen and Edward Petherbridge had been friends since Olivier's National Theatre company in 1965. McKellen had left and become a star. Petherbridge had stayed, had a huge success in 1967 in Tom Stoppard's first play, *Rosencrantz and Guildenstern Are Dead*, but then somehow failed to get the kind of leading Shakespearian roles for which he seemed so well suited. Finally, after a total of six years with the National, he quit the company in 1970. McKellen mentioned to his old friend that he was doing the Chekhov two-hander in Sheffield. Petherbridge agreed to play the tiny role of the Prompter. That job and the two men's friendship would give birth to a revolutionary idea.

Edward Petherbridge looks and sounds like a well-bred English gentleman, but actually his background is very different. Like McKellen he hails from the north of England – the soot-blackened back streets of 1930s and 40s Bradford in fact. He was born in 1936 into a family a clear social class down from the McKellens – his father was a mill worker and the Petherbridges lived in a back-to-back. There are other intriguing similarities with Ian McKellen. McKellen lost his mother as a boy; Petherbridge's mother had a stroke while pregnant with him, from which she never fully recovered. At sixteen Petherbridge was taken on at a stage school in Bradford, where they proceeded to iron out his Yorkshire accent, rather as Bolton School and Cambridge did for McKellen, just in time for both men to miss the wave of northern actors like Finney and Tom Courtenay who had kept theirs. A conscientious objector, Petherbridge refused to do his National Service, but unlike McKellen whose place at Cambridge saved him, at the age of nineteen Petherbridge served three months in Wormwood Scrubs prison.

Eight years in weekly rep followed by six years at the National had left Petherbridge in much more acute need of a greater degree of control over his working life than McKellen. Between them, and with the encouragement of David William, during rehearsals for *Swan Song* the two men hatched plans to create their own theatre company. Potential recruits were approached. Robert Eddison was one of the first. There were no auditions – everyone had to be by personal recommendation. 'Ian rang me up out of the blue,' remembers Frank Middlemass, another early recruit, who had worked with Edward Petherbridge in weekly rep in Penzance. 'I was living in Nevern Square in Earl's Court at the time. He came over, but he didn't have to talk me into it because I thought it was a very interesting thing to do.'

Margery Mason was a slightly later addition. A friend of hers had already been recruited. 'Tenniel Evans rang me up at my home and asked me to join the company. It had to be friends, or friends of friends.' Only Eileen Atkins turned them down. She was already committed elsewhere.

They called it the Actors' Company, and they had their first meeting in McKellen's sitting room in Camberwell in November 1971. Item one on the agenda: finance. The touring arm of the Arts Council would fund them, but not directly, because they had no track record. So McKellen turned to his old friend Richard Cottrell, who agreed to take the whole enterprise under the wing of the Cambridge Theatre Company. Cottrell also agreed to direct and to help choose plays for the first season. McKellen went to see Bill Thomley, drama director of the Edinburgh Festival. After Richard and Edward, Thomley was only too happy to have any company with McKellen in charge. That was one date sorted out. Except that McKellen wasn't supposed to be in charge. At their early meetings – and anyone who was involved with the Actors' Company remembers those interminable meetings – the key, basic ground rules had been thrashed out: 'Equal pay and billing for all, a sharing of leading as well as smaller parts – a company of equals.' *No one* was meant to be in charge.

Equal pay meant just £50 a week on that first tour. Equal billing meant alphabetical order on all the posters. Now a commonplace at the subsidised companies, this would be an area that would cause endless trouble with funding bodies who wanted the star names – and specifically McKellen's – more prominent.

The 'company of equals' that was finally assembled was a mix of youth and experience, character actors and leading players: Caroline Blakiston, Marian Diamond, Robert Eddison, Robin Ellis, Tenniel Evans, Felicity Kendal, Matthew Long, Margery Mason, Ian McKellen, Frank Middle-mass, Juan Moreno, Edward Petherbridge, Moira Redmond, Sheila Reid, Jack Shepherd, Ronnie Stevens and John Tordoff.

The statement of intent they included in the programme went further than discussion of billing and sharing good parts. There was what sounded like a broader political agenda as well:

'There is an increasing dissatisfaction in the British Theatre (and, indeed, in society generally) for that kind of dominating head of a large enterprise who accumulates authority to himself and merely employs his staff rather than co-operates with them. Small groups of young British actors have set up democratic ensembles; but the Actors' Company seems to be the first group of established actors who draw collectively on decades of experience and take control of those basic decisions which affect their work. Decisions about what plays to do, where to perform them, for how long, how they should be budgeted and cast and directed. The actors thereby become their own artistic director. Put simply, the workers are in control.' Everyone was in charge.

They could have gone further and abandoned directors altogether. But the fact that it was the actors hiring the director, rather than the other way around, did produce a shift in the relationship. Edward Pether-bridge, for one, thought they drew the teeth of their directors.

Some were more into 'workers control' than others. Margery Mason, who had been a member of the Communist Party, took to the weekly meetings and the rejection of the theatre's traditional hierarchy with enthusiasm. 'Ian was very intent on not being the star,' she remembers. 'He bent over backwards to make sure everyone contributed. Ted used to talk a lot, but Ian would never monopolise meetings. He battled to keep it democratic. At the start particularly we were very nice to each other and we greeted each other not with a lot of actor luvvy stuff but with real affection. It had a very good feeling.'

On the other hand there were others among the group, particularly the older actors, who were committed to the work, but less keen on those meetings. 'Robert Eddison never said much in meetings,' Margery Mason recalls. 'I don't think he liked that side of it much.'

'The business discussions and all that sort of thing bored me absolutely blue,' admits Frank Middlemass. 'All I wanted to be really was an actor. I don't think it was Ronnie Stevens's cup of tea either.'

'Meetings were more or less mandatory,' says Margery Mason. 'And at least weekly. At the end of one meeting I said, "I've been counting: Ian's spoken three times; Jack [Shepherd]'s spoken once; and Ted's spoken seventy-three times." ' Not everyone got on and Margery recalls that she personally clashed with Jack Shepherd; Frank Middlemass also remembers discussions being blocked at times by a small minority.

As for McKellen, he was in his element. While some members of the Actors' Company struggled with the demands of rehearsal, performance and forward planning, McKellen, notorious for unrelenting energy, took it in his stride. 'The only one who really knew what he was doing was Ian himself,' thinks Frank Middlemass. 'He's got the sort of brain that can cope. I think most actors are too volatile. They're creatures of emotion. And you needed a business brain as well for the Actors' Company.' And all those meetings with open-ended agendas must have reminded McKellen of the Quaker meetings of his youth.

Margery Mason is quite clear too about who was at the helm: 'It was Ian's company, and that was recognised by officialdom and press alike.' So was McKellen in charge after all?

The programme statement makes clear that in principle the company was making collective decisions about which plays to do, who would direct them, where they would be put on and who would play which role. Then there were decisions on design and budgeting to be made. But in fact the plays for the first season had been decided and the casting done by the time most members of the ensemble joined. Richard Cottrell was going to direct his own translation of the Feydeau farce *Le Dindon*, which he'd called *Ruling the Roost*. David Giles, best known for his TV work, including the small screen version of McKellen's *Hamlet*, had been asked to direct John Ford's Jacobean tale of incest and murder, *'Tis Pity She's a Whore*. And a new play by the novelist Iris Murdoch, set in medieval Japan and called *The Three Arrows*, would be directed by Noel Willman, the Irish character actor who had won a Tony award for Best Director for *A Man for All Seasons*.

With the plays chosen, it wasn't long before one of those key, basic ground rules – 'a sharing of leading as well as smaller parts' – ran into trouble too. Ian McKellen was to play the lead in *'Tis Pity*. In *Ruling the Roost* he would play what looked like the virtually non-existent part of a hotel pageboy. But he was also cast as Yoremitsu, the lead in *The Three Arrows*.

It would be easy to be cynical about the casting at the Actors' Company. Yes, McKellen played more leading roles than anyone else, and yes, when he did play minor parts like the Pageboy, according to Frank Middlemass, 'He came on and pinched every scene.' But Margery Mason avoids cynicism and is at once more indulgent and more realistic. 'He's an idealist,' is her comment on McKellen. 'And he's also a star. And the two things battle a bit. I don't think he pushed himself, but it wasn't as equal as all that, because people wouldn't let it be. The Arts Council wouldn't let it be for one. They wouldn't have funded it, if Ian hadn't been playing big leads.'

The tour was set to follow roughly Prospect's *Richard/Edward* itinerary, opening in Billingham on 22 August 1972, before going up to the Edinburgh Festival. After that the Actors' Company fulfilled their obligations to Richard Cottrell by providing him with an autumn season at the Cambridge Arts, then off on the road to Brighton, Oxford, Leeds and Newcastle.

Edward Petherbridge may have thought the company drew the teeth of its directors, but Frank Middlemass remembers rehearsals of *The Three Arrows* with Noel Willman rather differently. After one or two bruising encounters with the irascible Irishman, he and Margery Mason decided to do a private rehearsal of one big scene. The following day they brought their work to The Howff, the arts centre in Hampstead they were using. 'We did it to perfection,' remembers Middlemass. 'Noel said something slightly dismissive to Margery. Then he turned to me and said, "Yes, Frank, I can see what you're trying to do but you're merely coming across as terribly unpleasant." '

Much better known as a novelist than a playwright, Iris Murdoch herself came to The Howff, a Scots word for a meeting place, but offered little to the actors. 'We were all in awe of her,' remembers Frank Middlemass, 'and the curious thing was I think she was in awe of us, because we were from a foreign world. I had a charming letter from her soon afterwards and she said, "Thank you for being so kind because I was so frightened." '

Critics and audiences liked *The Three Arrows* least of the three plays, and it was dropped after the first season. But the other two were a success, and the press interest in the unusual set-up of the company was intense. After his experience with the Actors' Company McKellen would always do all the interviews and profiles and press junkets he was asked to. He learned the vital importance of publicity, whether you're selling John Ford in Leeds or J R R Tolkien in LA.

'*Tis Pity* was very very effective,' remembers Margery Mason who was cast as Putana, maid to the incestuous Annabella, played by Felicity Kendal. 'Felicity was pregnant at the time so there was a lot of difficulty about her being dragged about. And she was corseted in like mad.' McKellen, she recalls, was already developing his liking for trying out new ideas in performance, sometimes without telling his fellow performers: 'He would do unexpected things like you'd suddenly find him throwing himself down on the floor.'

The production was updated to the Edwardian period, with McKellen's tortured Giovanni making his first entrance in bicycle clips. The aim was to clarify the social relationships between the characters and make Ford's blood-curdling tale more real and therefore much more shocking – precisely what Tyrone Guthrie had been doing when he set his *Coriolanus* in the Napoleonic era.

As for *Ruling the Roost*, though Edward Petherbridge and Robert Eddison were ostensibly the male leads, McKellen as the Pageboy developed an extended gag which got him noticed by all the reviewers. *Punch* commented, 'In one superbly managed piece of business Ian McKellen's pimply Buttons, "suffering from puberty", and Robert Eddison's crabby old army doctor furiously exchange coats back and forth until both are left coatless and quivering.'

As the Actors' Company opened to packed houses at the Royal Lyceum Theatre in Edinburgh in September, the *Evening Standard* back in London was reporting the National Theatre as 'wooing' McKellen for *The Misanthrope* and *The Bacchae*. They would woo in vain. With the Actors' Company an obvious success, plans were already being developed for the following year.

'We were all heady with our unwonted sense of being in control,' remembers Margery Mason, 'so we decided to cut ourselves free from Cambridge and set up as a permanent company, hopefully with an eventual London home. The Arts Council then took us under their wing and practically every minute not spent on stage was devoted to meetings in which we thrashed out our constitution, policy and future programme.'

The break with Richard Cottrell and the Cambridge Theatre Company was amicable but necessary. That first season's arrangement had left them looking as if they were still beholden to an old-style management.

Soon the British Council was talking about financing an extension of the following year's tour to take in New York. McKellen and Petherbridge's idea was on the up and up.

'The Actors' Company is a way of life,' Petherbridge told the *Guardian*'s Janet Watts. 'The involvement is absolutely total. It's a tribal situation: but without the big chief or a witch doctor. We don't think the sun shines out of everybody's performance, but there's no paranoid huddling in corners.'

But not everyone was prepared to make it a way of life. When the company re-assembled in the summer of 1973, Felicity Kendal had left to look after her newborn baby. Jack Shepherd, Moira Redmond and Ronnie Stevens were all gone, and so was Frank Middlemass. 'I do remember,' he says, 'a terrible feeling of guilt when I decided not to do the next season, but I'd realised that I was all right at the acting, but the rest used to keep me awake, worrying about the responsibility of making decisions that would affect the whole future and success of the thing. I was intimidated by what I was trying to do and felt I was incompetent.'

Among the newcomers were Paola Dionisotti, who took over as Annabella when the company revived *'Tis Pity She's a Whore*, and John Woodvine, who had stepped into the breach before as Claudius when *Hamlet* came into the Cambridge Theatre. As well as *'Tis Pity*, they decided to retain *Ruling the Roost* in the repertoire, and to add Chekhov's *The Wood Demon*, an early draft of *Uncle Vanya*. Chekhov, with his absolute requirement for strong ensemble acting, was an obvious choice for the Actors' Company, and *The Wood Demon* had the advantage of being less frequently performed than his best-known plays. David Giles returned to direct. McKellen would play Kruschov, the Wood Demon himself, a highly emotional, heart-on-sleeve character who seemed tailor-made for the actor.

David William, who had been there in Sheffield when McKellen and Petherbridge were first hatching plans for the Actors' Company, came in to direct Congreve's *The Way of the World* which, according to Margery Mason, 'saw our first open competition in the field of casting, since most of our actresses naturally wanted to play Millamant'. In the end Caroline Blakiston got the part with Petherbridge as Mirabell. McKellen agreed to play a Footman. Robert Eddison recalled him being less than gracious about playing such a tiny part.

With a twinkle in his eye Nigel Havers recalls Timothy West telling him a dream he had around this time: 'In the dream he's asked to go to Centre Point with Ian, right to the top. And there's this theatre company, and they say, "Mr West, we'd like to invite you to join this company of actors. It's all democratic. Everyone plays all different sized parts. For instance this week Ian McKellen's playing Hamlet. And next week he's playing the footman. Of course, the play is called *The Footman* . . ."'

The Brooklyn Academy of Music was planning a British season for the turn of the year. The Young Vic and the RSC were already going. Now they wanted the Actors' Company to follow them in. It was a highly prestigious offer, but the Americans wanted Shakespeare. With typical democratic thoroughness, the company proceeded to read and discuss the suitability of every one of the Bard's 37 plays. Eventually, they decided on *King Lear* with Robert Eddison in the title role. McKellen would play Edgar, a good part but not a starring role.

The last link in the five-play repertoire was to be a piece devised and directed by Edward Petherbridge, based on the writings of the controversial psychiatrist R D Laing, a seminal figure of the 1960s. Part of the so-called 'anti-psychiatry' movement, Ronnie Laing believed that behaviours classified by society as 'mad' were really no more than the individual's attempt to overcome the madness of the world in which he or she has to live. He argued for institutions where a natural process of healing could be allowed to take place, and where the use of psychoactive drugs would be strictly limited. The book, *Knots*, which Petherbridge was using, was not a work of psychiatry, but a collection of sketches, showing the way people tie each other in emotional knots. An example, printed in the programme, gives a fair impression:

Jill: You think I'm stupid.
Jack: I don't think you're stupid.
Jill: I must be stupid to think you think I'm
        stupid if you don't: or you must be lying.
        I am stupid every way:
        to think I'm stupid, if I am stupid;
        to think I'm stupid, if I'm not stupid;
        to think you think I'm stupid, if you don't . . .

And so on.

There had been a version on the radio already. What the Actors' Company did was to find the comedy in these tortuous exchanges, and to add brilliantly theatrical, visual counterpoints to Laing's words. So a duologue beginning 'I'm upset you're upset' was performed by two actors juggling with fixed grins on their faces. Or the sequence 'Jack feels guilty that Jill feels guilty' was turned into a pantomime song sheet for the audience to sing along. Petherbridge got a chance to use his mime skills. Juan Moreno showed the audience how good a juggler he was. Caroline Blakiston presided over all at a mini-Wurlitzer organ. It was ensemble performance at its best. Only Margery Mason decided not to take part.

'I'd met Laing at a party,' she remembers, 'where he lay on the floor, replying by shrugs or monosyllables to anyone's attempt at conversation and then, refusing food or drink, took himself off.' Her experience of meeting the man put Mason off Petherbridge's concept. Later she regretted her decision. 'I think it was one of the most interesting things the company did, and perhaps showed what our democratic, participatory set-up could achieve at its best.'

The Wood Demon and *The Way of the World* were a sell-out at the Edinburgh Festival, and then set off on tour until November. *Knots* was originally planned for the Royal Court, but when that fell through, the Shaw Theatre on Euston Road offered the company a slot in December. From there it was on to New York and then back to the Wimbledon Theatre for a month playing all five shows in repertoire, followed by another UK tour, ending up in Norwich in June 1974. But almost at the beginning of the whole enterprise, McKellen dropped a bombshell.

At the beginning of the second season the Actors' Company had taken on Graham Marchant to help with organisation and Clare Fox as company manager. Margery Mason describes her as 'sorely tried'. Some of the reasons why become clear from the minutes of one Actors' Company meeting held at the Central School of Speech and Drama. Clare Fox saw herself as 'the only person with practical production experience' in a theatre company with none of the usual management team and a decision-making process so tortuous that vital decisions were put off until the last minute and then made in a panic. Clare Fox also spoke of a lack of communication and 'numerous occasions when I did not know what was going on'. The scale of the Actors' Company's enterprise had quite clearly become too great for an everyone's-in-charge approach.

A few weeks into the tour Ian McKellen called a full day's meeting of the entire company to discuss the future. The kind of organisational difficulties of which Clare Fox despaired could not go on. McKellen suggested a radical change of policy. He proposed they should appoint an artistic director. 'It seemed like the beginning of the end,' Edward Petherbridge told Janet Watts later. Though it was not overtly stated, there was only one possible choice – McKellen was to be in charge after all.

Or was he? Through a long, tortuous day the company discussed the proposal. Finally they rejected it. It was the moment when Ian McKellen's career could have gone in a radically different direction. If the Actors' Company had voted him in as artistic director in October 1973, then he might very well have gone on to head the RSC and the

National Theatre, as Richard Eyre and others thought he should. With an actor rather than a director at the helm, those companies might have developed in very different ways.

Having rejected the idea of a single artistic director, however, the Actors' Company descended into self-parody, setting up a bewildering array of committees. Before long there was a Future Committee, an Executive Committee, a Publicity Committee. There was even a committee in charge of organising parties. On 17 December 1973 McKellen was still telling the *Evening Standard*, 'I am sure that the future of theatre is in companies like ours.' With him as artistic director those words might just have been true. As it was, McKellen had already decided to leave. After years of playing hard to get, he had accepted an offer from the Royal Shakespeare Company.

In the meantime, *Knots* opened at the Shaw with a fifteen-minute curtain raiser called *Flow*, written by the academic Gabriel Josipovici in a faintly Beckettian manner, and *King Lear* went into rehearsal at the London Welsh Club on Gray's Inn Road, the very same less-than-inspiring rehearsal space where McKellen's *Hamlet* got started.

Robert Chetwyn had begun his rehearsals without a speech, and the actors had finished up complaining they didn't know what the production was about. David William began his rehearsals with a long speech, explaining his concept, showing the designs, and the actors still weren't happy – which, as far as directors are concerned, goes to prove that actors will whinge no matter what. Margery Mason snoozed through the speech. 'I don't remember what the concept was now,' she admits. She woke up for the designs, demanding, 'Where are we going to sit down? There's nothing arranged.' Actors' Company members were not inclined simply to accept what the director said without question. As for McKellen, after seeing Alan Barlow's set design, with its lengths of cord that could be lit to represent masonry, forests, sky or rain, he immediately dubbed the production *String Lear*.

The minutes of another meeting back in November in the Stalls Bar of the Manchester Opera House show the extent to which the actors were allowed input into the visual dimension of the production, with each cast member in turn telling David William and Alan Barlow how they saw their character's appearance in *King Lear*. Again, the relationship is very different from the normal situation where it's like-it-or-lump-it on the first day of rehearsal.

Certainly rehearsals threw up one surprise, as McKellen developed his characterisation for Edgar in the section on the heath when he becomes 'poor Tom'. 'One day he suddenly took off all his clothes,' remembers

Margery Mason who was playing Old Man (sic) in the hovel on the heath. 'And it was freezing cold at the Welsh place. No one was expecting it. Not even the director. And to our great credit we took no notice at all. And when Robert Eddison said the bit about the "poor, bare, forked animal", he got hold of Ian by his ankles and held him upside down. So of course his willy was waving back and forth.' Edgar might not be the leading role, but the performance was sure to be noticeable!

At 10.50 on the morning of Thursday 24 January 1974 the Actors' Company took the coach from Victoria Station to Gatwick Airport. By 2.50 p.m. local time they were in New York, courtesy of British Caledonian. With many company members new to the city they did the tourist sites – Empire State Building and lunch at Sardi's, courtesy of the New York drama critics. Clive Barnes, the much-feared critic of the *New York Times*, able to close a show with a stroke of his pen, was not present.

'I stayed at the Chelsea Hotel,' remembers Margery Mason. 'I shared a room with Marian [Diamond] and she got out the second day because there were cockroaches.' The hotel where Dylan Thomas died and Bob Dylan wrote 'Sad Eyed Lady of the Lowlands' lived up to its Bohemian reputation. 'While I was there,' says Mason, 'someone was carried out, because they'd committed suicide.'

The Brooklyn Academy of Music, or BAM as it is usually called, is a great barn of a place more suited to opera and dance. The main auditorium seats over two thousand. But every spring the management brings in international companies and tries to lure an audience across the Brooklyn Bridge. It doesn't always work. Press coverage was vital. A group of the actors would turn out for interviews, but the journalists always wanted to talk to McKellen. 'He was desperately trying to get reporters to speak to everyone,' recalls Margery Mason, 'saying, "Well, Margery, why don't you take that one?" '

The opening night of *The Wood Demon* was a nervous affair. McKellen had failed before in New York with *The Promise*. But the enormous theatre was packed, and there were laughs in the first scene, which settled the actors down. They were at a news-stand on 72nd Street in the early hours to find out the verdict from Clive Barnes. He liked it.

Then things started to go wrong.

The weather in New York was clement for February, but the Atlantic Ocean wasn't, and the sets and costumes for *King Lear* were still on the high seas as opening night arrived. In an impromptu meeting in the BAM car park they considered the options. Cancel the performance? No one wanted to do that. Borrow from the RSC who were still in town? Wrong period. Finally they agreed to do the show in their own clothes with a speech from the stage explaining the situation and offering money back to anyone who wanted it. Only eight of an audience of nearly two thousand took up the offer. As so often in such situations, the actors raised their own game in an emergency and the audience responded to seeing something out of the ordinary. The performance ended with a standing ovation.

Knots did five nights only in BAM's smaller auditorium, while *The Way of the World* joined the repertoire in the main house. The company was a hit and, as ever in New York, that meant they were in demand. They did a session talking to the students about Shakespeare at the Actors' Studio, home of Lee Strasberg and the Method School of acting, and once again it was, 'Why don't you ask one of the others?', as McKellen tried to stay out of the limelight, tried to maintain that feeling of a company of equals. 'We went to a party,' recalls Margery Mason. '[It was at] this fantastic apartment overlooking the park. And there was one room for pot smokers and one room for drinkers.'

McKellen stayed with a New York friend, and went to see Carol Channing in a revival of *Lorelei* at the Palace Theatre. He discovered the horrors of the Brooklyn subway, getting stuck between stations one day on the way to BAM; he developed a liking for American food – sandwiches, milk, pecan pie and Jell-o. Ten years later in a piece for the *Observer*, a colleague at the BBC suggested McKellen's palate had stayed in American mode: 'He likes nursery food – cakes, sweets, jellies. He likes coming here [the BBC] because of the puddings.' Back in New York McKellen also picked up his first US acting award, the Drama Desk Award, for his performances in *The Wood Demon* and *King Lear*.

After the excitement of New York it was back to the rather less glamorous surroundings of the Wimbledon Theatre in south London. Wimbledon was chiefly famous at the time for the Wombles, small, mole-like puppets with an infuriating song, which were currently all over the television. But for a month starting 26 March 1974 the Actors' Company made Wimbledon famous for theatre. Critics who saw the company's five productions in repertoire thought all the old shows had improved – a sure sign of an ensemble working well together. They had begun to write about the company rather as the Coventry papers had commented on the progress of the young actors at the rep. Robin Ellis has 'developed into a commanding actor' said *The Times*. 'The most dramatic advance has been made by Marian Diamond,' opined the *Observer*.

Only *King Lear* failed to win the same plaudits. Robert Eddison was generally considered under-powered and over-parted, not coming into his own until the elegiac scenes towards the end. Trevor Grove in the *Evening Standard* noted that 'McKellen's *coup de nudité* left the schoolgirls in the audience deeply impressed.' Margery Mason remembers one audience member at a matinee shouting out, 'Nice one, Cyril!' as McKellen revealed all.

There was a palpable air of excitement behind these reviews – a feeling that something really different was being done in the British theatre, that an important new company was in development. The theatre was packed. McKellen took his turn with the rest of the company, manning the phones in the box office. Writing in *The Lady*, J C Trewin wondered, 'Who is going to occupy the Old Vic when the National Theatre moves to the South Bank?'

It was a question that had occurred to the Actors' Company already. In fact the search for a permanent base had preoccupied them throughout 1973. Seasons in Oxford and Bath had been proposed. But what they wanted was a theatre in London. The Royal Court, Greenwich, Richmond, Wimbledon and the old Coronet cinema in Notting Hill were all floated. None came to anything. And, of course, the axe hanging over the whole thing was that McKellen, their 'in' with the Arts Council and biggest box office draw, had already said he was going.

So why did Ian McKellen leave the Actors' Company? His answer has changed over the years. In 1976 he told the *Observer* it was because he 'couldn't persuade [the others] to run their own rep'. But five years later he told *The Times*, 'To be honest I was fed up with playing the small parts.' No doubt the reasons for his defection were mixed, and greatly affected by the RSC's offer to let him sign for just over one year rather than the usual two, and to play only in London and not in Stratford. But part of it must go back to that meeting in October 1973, when McKellen couldn't persuade the company to change direction and appoint an artistic director. 'It would be awful if the next two years were as undefined as the last two years,' McKellen said in a meeting on 2 January 1974. The language betrays a real loss of patience with the way the Actors' Company had been run.

In the event the company did continue without Ian McKellen. Edward Petherbridge did some more directing himself. Then he too left. Robin Ellis went on to TV fame in *Poldark* the following year. 1975 saw Felicity Kendal begin an extended residency in Everyman's cosiest sexual fantasies on *The Good Life*. Margery Mason rejoined a rather less star-studded Actors' Company a few years later to do a British Council tour. 'I was the only founder member,' she remembers, 'and swanned into the first meeting with cries of joy, dispensing hugs and kisses in all directions as had been our wont, to find the rest of the cast a little startled by such over the top behaviour.'

McKellen talked about directing the Actors' Company. He talked about doing *Three Sisters* with them. But he never returned. He also raised the idea of the Actors' Company infiltrating the RSC or the National, changing things from the inside. Fast forward to 1985, ten years after McKellen quit the Actors' Company itself, and he got a chance to do exactly that. It was Ian McKellen's second and last major excursion into management.

Ever since the move to the South Bank in 1975, the National Theatre had been criticised as a monolithic enterprise, lacking a clear artistic identity, where actors frequently felt undervalued and neglected. In 1984 Peter Hall decided to do something about it. On 22 October he announced he was chopping the juggernaut into five separate bits. Each of the five companies would play in all three auditoria, putting on three plays in a year. Hall himself remained, of course, in overall control and ran one group. Peter Wood and Bill Bryden each took on a group. David Hare and Richard Eyre ran one group jointly. All directors so far, except for playwright David Hare. But for the third company, Hall turned to the man who had been his leading actor through the 1984 season, Ian McKellen.

'When I first arrived,' McKellen told Peter Roberts of *Plays and Players*, 'I said to Peter Hall that I was going to be very nosey about the way the National Theatre is run and perhaps be critical of it. I think that it was as a result of this attitude he said that this company . . . was going and was I up to running it?' In other words Hall was calling his bluff. You think you can do it better? Go ahead. McKellen's response was that he would only do it if Edward Petherbridge could work with him. Hall agreed.

'Edward and I were doing *Love's Labours Lost* up at Stratford,' remembers Emily Richard, Petherbridge's wife, 'with Ken Branagh playing the King of France and Roger Rees as Berowne. Ian would come up and sit in our funny little cramped cottage and then Edward would go down to the National Theatre and they'd have these endless meetings.'

Yes, it was back to those meetings: Which plays? Which actors? Which directors? Only this time it was just the two of them making the decisions. McKellen wasn't going to repeat the long drawn out nightmare of the Actors' Company's decision-making process. Other treasured shibboleths were also abandoned. Equal pay and billing? 'Very difficult in the context of the National Theatre,' McKellen told Peter Roberts in June 1985. Equal responsibility for policy and decision-making? Petherbridge talking in the same interview: 'Very difficult.' Essentially they were operating in the conventional manner of joint artistic directors, just as McKellen had wanted at the Actors' Company.

Of course, there's plenty of scope for friction in two-person meetings too. Emily Richard says there was none. 'They work very well together. They're completely different,' she observes. 'Edward is possibly more mercurial.'

McKellen seems to think the reverse. 'I'm a silly old optimist. He's the practical one,' he told Heather Neil in May 1985.

In the same year Petherbridge said of his long-time friend in an interview for *Plays and Players*: 'I think that among the very many things that Ian can do and I can't is inspire people. It's something to do with natural leadership. If he wants to start something, there's a queue following, whereas when I try to be a leader and turn around, there's no one behind me.'

McKellen will have none of it. 'I've never been good at being a leader,' he told the *Independent*.

So what's the truth? Just how does the relationship work? Petherbridge again, talking to John Higgins of *The Times*, said, 'Well, we make each other laugh a lot. We are aware of the eccentricities in each other's make-up. I suppose we are a lesson to each other. Ian always looks on the bright side. I look on – perhaps – the Laing side.' As the McKellen/Petherbridge company was formed, *The South Bank Show* was in the middle of preparing a documentary called 'A Year in the Life of Ian McKellen' for LWT. They certainly seem to have wanted to dramatise the importance of the friendship between the two artistic directors. Emily Richard recalls, 'When Edward came back from New York by Concorde after doing *Strange Interlude*, I wanted to go to Heathrow and meet him, and LWT said, "No, no. Ian McKellen is going to meet him." ' Mrs Petherbridge was understandably less than delighted.

Neither McKellen nor Petherbridge wanted to direct themselves at the National, but what they did want to do was to bring in directors they admired, who hadn't worked there before. They approached Philip Prowse, *eminence noir* of the Glasgow Citizens' Theatre, and a real outsider as far as the National was concerned. Then they had an even more radical idea. What about a woman?

Sheila Hancock had just been directing the small scale tour at the RSC. She had been part of early plans for the Actors' Company, but dropped out when her mother fell ill. On the afternoon of 12 January 1985 she got a phone call from Edward Petherbridge's dressing room in Stratford. It was Ian McKellen. Would she like to direct *The Critic* in the Olivier Theatre at the National?

By this time Prowse had come back to them, saying that yes he was interested, and he would like to do *The Duchess of Malfi* in the Lyttleton. The play for the Cottesloe was left undecided. For one thing the National's studio theatre was currently closed due to funding cuts, and McKellen and Petherbridge also wanted company input on choosing at least one of the productions. But they did have an idea about who they wanted to direct – Mike Alfreds. Best known for radical dramatisations of big novels in which the actors moved in and out of character, telling the story, swapping parts, even playing the scenery, Alfreds had founded Shared Experience in 1975. But he had never worked on the South Bank.

Finally McKellen approached Tom Stoppard with the idea of the playwright directing his own *The Real Inspector Hound* as the other half of a double bill with *The Critic*. Two comedies about the problems of putting on theatre written some 300 years apart – the pairing looked inspired. But it did invite dangerous comparison with Olivier's famously contrasting pairing of *The Critic* with *Oedipus Rex* at the Old Vic in 1945, especially when it was announced that McKellen would be playing Olivier's old role of Mr Puff – critics could be heard dusting off the old 'Olivier from Wigan' material.

Only then did they start to think about the rest of the casting. The original plan was for 25 actors. Cut-backs reduced this to a maximum of seventeen. The plan was for all the actors to be in all the productions, playing large parts in one show, smaller parts in the others and understudying each other. Shades of the Actors' Company again. But this time there was no nonsense about Pageboys and Footmen. McKellen would play big parts in all of them.

In some ways though, McKellen and Petherbridge were clearly trying to revive the feeling of the early days at the Actors' Company, when the success on stage had been founded on a real spirit of comradeship off stage. 'I hope [that spirit] will be evidenced in our productions here too,' McKellen told *Plays and Players* in June 1985.

Roy Kinnear, a senior recruit to the company and veteran of actors' participation with Joan Littlewood, took a more sceptical line. He remembered Littlewood's method at Theatre Workshop, when the actors got to participate in the choice of how many loo rolls were bought and she got to choose the plays. Kinnear accepted the theatre as a dictatorship. 'In the end,' he said in an interview for the *Observer*, 'an actor's always doing what the director wants, and you've got to have someone to blame. But it's nice to have the semblance of democracy.'

As with the Actors' Company there was a manifesto for the programme. But this one was signed by the twin artistic directors only. It read like this:

'In the decade since Laurence Olivier retired from the National Theatre at the Old Vic theatre, British theatres have been ruled not by actors but by directors. Coincidentally over the same period, there has been a total decline in the numbers of acting companies working together for long periods. Those regional theatres, where actors of our generation learned our business, cannot nowadays afford to retain such companies. Even in this theatre, there is no pattern of prolonged contracts such as are available to actors working in the national theatres of Europe. British actors are in danger of becoming mere casual employees.

'We are delighted to accept Peter Hall's invitation to organise a company of seventeen actors – Eleanor Bron, Selina Cadell, Simon Dutton, Sheila Hancock, Greg Hicks, Jonathan Hyde, Roy Kinnear, Julie Legrand, Hugh Lloyd, Stephen MacDonald, Ian McKellen, Claire Moore, Edward Petherbridge, Laurence Rudic, Dikran Tulaine and Tristram Wymark. Neither of us will direct the plays. Every member of the group will be understudying – signed Ian McKellen & Edward Petherbridge.'

Inflicting a nice little nip on the hand that fed them, there was an actor's critique of director's theatre there as well as a swift dart at the National itself. What was much more astounding was the group of actors they had chosen. Petherbridge was still in New York with *Strange Interlude* when the final casting was decided amidst complex negotiations between the directors, chaired by McKellen. He listened to the list of actors over the transatlantic telephone line. There was a brief pause. Then he suggested they should scrap *The Duchess of Malfi* and do a panto instead.

Jonathan Hyde, a stalwart of the Glasgow Citz, was Philip Prowse's choice. Claire Moore had only ever done musicals. Stephen Macdonald was making a return to acting after several years as a director at Dundee rep and the Lyceum in Edinburgh. Eleanor Bron admits she was 'thunderstruck' when the offer arrived. She, Sheila Hancock and Roy Kinnear were all known as comic actors and looked pretty strange casting for *The Duchess of Malfi*. Hugh Lloyd was best known for sit com and light entertainment on the TV. And so on. It took time for this disparate group of actors to grow into the ensemble McKellen and Petherbridge had in mind. And *The Duchess of Malfi* didn't help.

McKellen had encountered the two poles of the director's method early on in George Sawtell and Frank Greene back at Bolton School. In Philip Prowse and Mike Alfreds that contrast would be taken to extremes. And there was no doubt about which kind of director McKellen liked better.

According to one member of the company, Philip Prowse, habitually dressed in black, and avowedly more interested in the visual dimension than the actors, tended to describe what he wanted the end product to look like, rather than guide his performers in achieving it. Actors schooled in the RSC tradition of detailed analysis and discussion of a text had trouble adjusting. The rigidly stylised nature of the production was set from the opening sequence which was a parade of all the actors across the stage – two steps – stop – two steps – stop. Tempers grew frayed.

'Edward sent off some rather hot memos to Philip Prowse,' recalls Emily Richard. When it came time for press interviews as opening night approached, Prowse refused to appear. Immediately before opening night on 4 July 1985 there was a huge company row. And opening night itself was chaotic with a series of technical blunders – wrong lighting cues, furniture not appearing, stage flats not locked down properly. Generally the reviews admired Prowse's design, lamented much of the verse speaking and thought Eleanor Bron out of her depth as the Duchess.

The double bill of *The Real Inspector Hound* and *The Critic* opened next in the Olivier Theatre. McKellen had always maintained that the wide open spaces of the Olivier could only be filled by larger-than-life shows like Richard Eyre's 1982 production of *Guys and Dolls*. So why he thought *The Real Inspector Hound*, a chamber piece if ever there was one, was going to work on the notoriously difficult Olivier stage is hard to say. Critics again complained of not being able to hear. *The Critic*, with its spectacularly collapsing set and a high camp performance from McKellen, was better received, though reviewers seemed unable to decide whether he was doing an Irish or a north country accent. However, McKellen came in for some of his harshest criticism from one of his fellow actors. Bill Moody had played one of the citizens in an award-winning version of *Coriolanus*, starring McKellen, and which had just closed in Athens. Moody thinks it was as much the director as the actor who was to blame, but he didn't mince words with McKellen. 'I told him it was crap,' he confesses. 'I said, "What you're doing is totally wrong. It's just not real. And Jonathan Hyde is acting you off stage." '

Moody explains his objections: 'He was acting acting. Here's this character who's trying to get into society; he should have been trying hard to be a gentleman, not behaving like a buffoon.' McKellen had encouraged his fellow actors to offer their opinions during the troubled genesis of *Coriolanus*, but after the conversation Bill Moody wondered if he hadn't gone too far. 'I thought, F***, who am I to tell Ian McKellen what to do? And probably he took no notice, but I hope he had a think about it.'

None of it mattered anyway, because the public were delighted with a double-bill of comedy at the usually serious National Theatre, and the show did capacity business throughout its run. But by far the most interesting production the McKellen/Petherbridge company put on was the one directed by Mike Alfreds. A success in its own right, the show would mark an important development in Ian McKellen's way of working on stage.

Mike Alfreds read over a hundred plays before finally deciding to do *The Cherry Orchard* in the Cottesloe. McKellen was cast as Lopakhin, the man of peasant stock, who ends up owning the cherry orchard itself. The small space was ideal for creating the detailed, naturalistic performances which are crucial to making Chekhov work, but it was Alfreds's rehearsal method which really made the difference.

An Alfreds rehearsal puts the emphasis on process not product. He is aiming to create a world on stage in which the actors will feel free to play in a sort of controlled improvisation. It's precisely the opposite approach to that of Philip Prowse. And Alfreds himself seems to have little time for some of his fellow directors, likening them to traffic cops, telling everyone where and when to move. The Alfreds method also makes a good contrast to the tight schedule described by Robert Chetwyn. But then there's a world of difference between fortnightly rep in Ipswich and the National Theatre, where there's the luxury of seven weeks of rehearsal.

In the National rehearsal room Alfreds began with the basic approach of Konstantin Stanislavski, who was after all the original director of *The Cherry Orchard* in 1904 and the creator of the Stanislavski system of acting. No early blocking. First the actors researched their characters in depth through a careful study of the script, making lists of what the other characters said about them, what they said about themselves and what they said about others. Then, without using the words, Alfreds would get the actors to play the actions of a scene – what they were physically doing from moment to moment. But nothing was set.

Many directors like to leave the blocking open and fluid for as long as possible, not closing off options until shortly before opening night. But Alfreds goes one further. In *The Cherry Orchard* there were no set moves at all. His aim was to keep every performance alive and immediate – no repetition from night to night; no stale, mechanical shows. The result is that from night to night performances will vary enormously, and some will be much better than others. But this kind of unpredictability is, taken to its logical extreme, what theatre is all about. Sit in the cinema and you'll see exactly the same as last night's audience and the night before's. In the theatre every performance is a one-off. In a Mike Alfreds production, it's a one-off extraordinaire.

For McKellen the method was a revelation. Ever since *Richard II* or even *The Promise* he had tried to find ways to keep a performance alive – sometimes by playing what seem like silly games in performance with his fellow actors. Margery Mason had been thrown during *'Tis Pity She's a Whore* by McKellen's habit of doing unexpected things in performance. It's a way of keeping the excitement level up on stage, which should have a corresponding effect in the auditorium. So a desire to experiment and improvise was already there. Now he was being given licence to be as different as possible every night. Lopakhin has a big scene in Act 3, when he returns drunk and elated after the auction, having bought the estate in which his grandfather was a serf. Sheila Hancock played Madame Ranevskaya, the old owner. One night he would crush her to him in a bear-hug, kissing away her tears. The next night he might be on the other side of the stage, hurling the same lines at her, full of hatred and disgust.

McKellen explained what Alfreds taught him to Robert Cheshyre in 1992: 'The instruction is never to do anything unless you believe it. You are not pretending; you are feeling. With that goes the freedom to move wherever you want. If you are genuinely sensitive to each other, that will produce wild variations.' He admits *The Cherry Orchard*'s good reviews were because the critics happened to see a good night. Other nights were disastrous. 'If people want to see how I've developed,' he went on, 'they have to look as much to my working with Mike Alfreds as to my having come out. The two are related, since they are both about not being artificial, not lying, but living in the moment.' It's a big statement, because McKellen usually credits coming out as having transformed him both as an actor and a man. And 'living in the moment'? It means looking as if you're making it up on stage as you go along, as if it hasn't been rehearsed at all – just like life.

The McKellen/Petherbridge company did a week in Paris with *The Critic* and *Le Véritable Inspecteur Hound*. They did a week in Aberdeen with *The Cherry Orchard* and three weeks in Chicago with all four plays. And that was the end. McKellen seems to have been pleased it was over. The responsibility of decision-making had weighed more heavily than at the Actors' Company. The burden had fallen more directly on him. No actor has ever been asked to run a company at the National again.

McKellen and Petherbridge at the National Theatre in 1985/6 were likened to Olivier and Richardson at the Old Vic in the 1940s. But notoriously, of course, the twentieth century was the century when university-educated directors took over the theatre from the actors. Did it have to be that way? After all, when the National Theatre came into being after 115 years of trying, it was Laurence Olivier at the helm, not Tyrone Guthrie. After the Actors' Company and the McKellen/Petherbridge double act, there would be those who were sure McKellen would sooner or later go down the same road as Olivier. With rumours of Terry Hands's retirement from the RSC in 1989, the *Independent* tipped McKellen as successor. Richard Eyre, by then director of the National, put his money on the same man.

Five years later, as Eyre himself was thinking of quitting the National, he took McKellen out to dinner to ask if he would take over the job. McKellen seems to have been tempted. But could he face what he'd seen Eyre go through – being trapped in the job, no chance of freelance work, getting slated in the press when things went wrong?

As late as 2003, on the announcement of the appointment of the star of *American Beauty* and *The Usual Suspects*, Kevin Spacey, to run the Old Vic, McKellen was wondering whether he should not be doing the job himself. 'Frankie [Frances de la Tour] said I should do it,' he told Bryan Appleyard, another Old Boltonian. 'Why leave it to Kevin Spacey? I felt young again. I said, "Are you on?" She said, "I'll be there, dear." '

It was certainly not that McKellen lacked the organisational capacity or the artistic vision to lead one of the major companies. He had proved that already. Ultimately the instinct of the freelance, which had kept him away from the RSC and the National for so many years, seems to have proved too strong, however. And, after all, as Emily Richard puts it, 'If he'd done that, he wouldn't have been able to do the films.'

5. THE CAMBRIDGE CONNECTION

On 12 August 1974, a week short of the thirteenth anniversary of his first professional job as an actor, Ian McKellen finally made his debut with the Royal Shakespeare Company in the title role of John Barton's production of *Doctor Faustus*. He was 35. For a man who has come to be thought of as the leading classical actor of his generation, it is easy to forget that McKellen took so long to join the country's leading classical company. And even then he only sort of joined, because *Doctor Faustus* opened not in Stratford, or indeed London, but at the Nottingham Playhouse. In fact, McKellen's first year and a half with the RSC looked much more like a continuation of his freelance career – touring and appearing in a series of plays in London – than a major change of direction. In his first nineteen months with the company he would play a total of just five nights in Stratford.

Set entirely in Faustus's book-lined study in a set created by Michael Annals, the designer behind the *Hamlet* mirrors and the abortive *Hank Cinq*, this *Doctor Faustus* was, in many ways, a typical Barton production. The programme described the play as 'adapted by John Barton with the cast', which actually meant that chunks of Marlowe had been cut, and bits of the English Faust-book interpolated, along with some 550 lines of Barton's own blank verse. The Seven Deadly Sins were human-sized puppets; the Good and Bad Angels were glove puppets, worked by Faustus himself; Helen of Troy was a mask; there was even a plan to cast Mephistopheles as a ventriloquist's dummy, before wiser counsels prevailed and Emrys James was cast instead. Critics who saw the production either at the Edinburgh Festival or when it reached the RSC's London base at the Aldwych in September, were not generally enthusiastic about McKellen's performance. Caryl Brahms, writing in the *Guardian*, called his Faustus 'a dotty young don in a Carol Channing *Hello Dolly* wig'.

At the Aldwych McKellen added to the repertoire two more typically high-energy, barn-storming performances as the eponymous con-man of Franz Wedekind's *The Marquis of Keith* and Philip, the Bastard in Shakespeare's *King John*. The latter was his only excursion into Shakespeare during this first stint with the RSC, and just as he had only sort of joined the Stratford company, so this was only sort of Shakespeare. Barton had again cut the young Shakespeare's text, slipping in bits from two other Elizabethan plays about King John along with more original Barton. The production had not been well received the previous year. Nor was it now, as McKellen took over from Richard Pasco, though the role, one of Shakespeare's outsiders in a line with Richard III and Iago, was in some ways an interesting warm-up for those later triumphs. When the show closed, McKellen kept the Bastard's boots to wear on his moped.

In the summer McKellen took time out from the RSC to appear in a new play by David Rudkin (whose plays have included *Afore Night Come* and *Artemis*) called *Ashes*. Directed by a young Ron Daniels and produced by Michael Codron, the production opened at the Young Vic and went no further. No one liked the play, a grim account of a couple's struggle with infertility. McKellen played the bisexual husband. Previous attempts at accents had not been wholly succesful and nor was his attempt to do an Ulster accent. This one generated a similar puzzlement to his Mister Puff at the National – was it north country? Was it Irish?

In October he was back at the Aldwych once more in George Bernard Shaw's *Too True To Be Good*. More importantly, he was reunited for the first time since 1967 with the actress who would go on to partner him in what remains arguably his greatest stage performance, Judi Dench.

Shaw called *Too True to Be Good*, which he wrote in 1932 at the age of 76, 'a political extravaganza'. The play was not a success at its premiere in spite of a powerful performance by Ralph Richardson. But under Clifford Williams's direction, the RSC cast, led by Judi Dench as a bogus nurse and Ian McKellen as her boyfriend, the burglar, focused on the comic potential of the script, playing down the politics. At the climax of the play, McKellen's burglar turns into a hellfire preacher, and lets go with both barrels: 'We have outgrown our religion, outgrown our political system, outgrown our strength of mind and character . . .' Grandfather William Henry McKellen would have been proud. Ian McKellen felt he and Dench brought something else to the play – passion. It would be a crucial ingredient up at Stratford the following year.

A surprise hit at the Aldwych – *Woman's Journal* declared somewhat improbably that McKellen 'had the ladies in the audience swooning at his burglar in a one-piece bathing costume' – the play transferred to the Globe in time for Christmas. While there, McKellen, who Nigel Havers declares is without nerves, had his only recorded experience of stage fright.

He was in a restaurant in Soho after the show one night, when he overheard two actors, Douglas Campbell and Bill Squire, who had just seen his performance. 'They criticised my diction, damned my physique and agreed on my total failure as an actor,' McKellen remembered in *The*

Times in February 1996. More than that, the two actors particularly referred to Tyrone Guthrie who had also been a big influence in Campbell's career, directing him in *Oedipus Rex* in Stratford, Ontario in 1955. The suggestion was that the great director would be turning in his grave if he could see the ham his protégé, Ian McKellen, had become.

Actors love slating each other's performances, and it was just bad luck that McKellen should happen to overhear this particular discussion, and at the time he laughed it off. But the following night on stage, the whole experience suddenly came flooding back. It was during Act 2, which is set on a beach, and which featured McKellen in the one-piece swimsuit *Woman's Journal* had liked so much. He was facing out front, and Bill Squire and Douglas Campbell's words floated back into his head. Did the entire audience think the same thing? The scene ground to a halt. McKellen turned his back on the audience. Judi Dench managed to help him through the rest of the scene, but it was four months before he fully recovered his nerve. By then he was in Stratford.

In November 1975 Ian McKellen agreed to a season with the RSC in Stratford and London. Negotiations had been tough. And he was not the only one horse-trading with Trevor Nunn that year – Donald Sinden was joining the company too, although he'd said he would only play Benedick if he could also play Lear. McKellen in his turn had agreed to Romeo and Leontes in *The Winter's Tale* on the condition that Nunn would also direct him in *Macbeth* with Judi Dench as Lady M.

After his bad early experiences with the National in 1965, it's not surprising McKellen should have been wary of the RSC. He feared a scenario in which he would get lost as one of a large number of actors in a big company away from his London home. As a freelance actor and even more as the founder of the Actors' Company, he was accustomed to a measure of control over his destiny as a performer. The RSC was the epitome of director's theatre. But the RSC in 1976 turned out to be something quite different from what McKellen had expected.

'I found it broke down into various groups of fairly intimately working people,' he explained to Tom Suttcliffe in the *Guardian*. 'From the inside it was very much smaller than it appeared from the outside.'

Actually, the RSC really was smaller than it had been. Nunn had cut actor numbers down from a height of around 50 to 25. The two huge tubs in the wings labelled 'Mud' and 'Blood', which had characterised the epic-scale productions of the 1960s, had gone. Finally convinced that Peter Hall was not suddenly going to reappear and say he was taking over again, Nunn was creating his own production style with fellow directors John Barton and Terry Hands.

'Trevor worked in a very intimate way,' explains RSC Director of Voice, Cicely Berry, 'working out relationships between characters, looking for the truth. Terry was interested in the epic scale of the plays. John Barton was into the form of the language.'

Crucially, as Artistic Director, Nunn was also learning to work at relationships with his company. Nickolas Grace was another actor rejoining the RSC that year. He remembers looking around the rehearsal room on the first day of rehearsals and being amazed at the company Nunn had succeeded in assembling. As well as leading stage actors like McKellen, Dench and Sinden, there was Francesca Annis who had starred in Roman Polanski's blood-soaked film of *Macbeth* in 1971 and had just had a huge success on British TV as Emma Bovary. There were stars of the future like Roger Rees, Greg Hicks, Ian McDiarmid, Richard Griffiths, Robin Ellis and John Nettles. There were RSC stalwarts like John Woodvine, Michael Pennington, Bob Peck and Michael Williams. A very young Peter Woodward was in his first job. And Cherie Lunghi, just three years out of drama school, was playing Perdita in *The Winter's Tale*.

But to Nick Grace, just as amazing as the company he was in were the words coming out of the director's mouth. 'I want you to know,' said Nunn, 'that I've learned from my experience at the RSC as director, and I'm going to be here for you. If ever you need me, I'm contactable in my office and I'm going to be a leader to this company.'

'I thought, I don't believe that,' admits Nickolas Grace. 'Because I'd been in the company before from '72 to '74 and you could never find Trevor – that was the joke, to be Trevved was he'd hug you and then disappear.'

Nunn continued his speech: 'I'm the ring master and you're the performers. But, if you think I'm wrong, I want you to tell me, and, if I think you're wrong, I'll tell you.'

I don't believe that either, thought Grace.

There were other sceptics there that day in January 1976 in the RSC's dusty rehearsal room in Covent Garden. Michael Williams muttered, 'Yeah, yeah, well put your money where your mouth is,' as Nunn talked on about the quality of the cast. As ever, the RSC was not exactly paying the actors a fortune.

But Nunn really was determined to create a new atmosphere. He was certain that at its best the RSC in Stratford could be a place where the actors could develop between them a level of trust and understanding, which was impossible in companies brought together for a single play. And that feeling could permeate all their work on stage together. Cicely

Berry is certain where that feeling of trust originated. 'Trevor created an atmosphere where everyone felt they could contribute,' she explains. 'When they all moved up to Stratford, Trevor was always in the green room, talking to people. Ian really responded to the family atmosphere of the place. He liked that.'

McKellen himself uses exactly the same kind of language – the language which suggests what it always is that he is looking for in a theatre company or a film unit. Joining the RSC, he told Michael Billington in 1982, was 'like coming home'.

For McKellen the first play into rehearsal was *Romeo and Juliet*. It was fifteen years since he'd worked with Trevor Nunn. The director found being back with his old Cambridge sparring partner rejuvenating. Here was an actor who liked to be extended in rehearsal, but who also knew how to extend the director. Simple answers wouldn't do. He wanted to explore complexities, subtleties, shades of thought in the language. Some directors would have found it intimidating. Nunn was delighted. That shared Cambridge background of Leavis and Rylands put them instantly on the same wavelength. 'Ian is restless, curious, daring,' Nunn told Michael Billington, trying to describe McKellen's method of constant experiment, constant search for new approaches in rehearsal. 'He loves living dangerously.' It's that fearlessness again. But for McKellen, as stimulating as rehearsals with Nunn, were the classes in voice, movement and text which were (and remain) part and parcel of the way the RSC operates in Stratford. Very much a tenor in *Richard II* and *Edward II*, McKellen began to widen the range of his voice in sessions with Cicely Berry.

'Mainly my work with him was freeing the voice,' explains Berry. 'Ian was an actor who worked from nervous tension, so there was quite a lot of tightness in the neck, which narrowed his voice.'

McKellen's version of how sessions with Cicely Berry worked, from the *Telegraph* in March 2003, was, 'Cis is small and shy, yet she radiates the energy of a healer as she lays her hands on your back, your ribs, your neck, your forehead, soothing the body so that it can breathe freely and confidently.'

'Ian was very eager to work with me,' Berry goes on, 'and he worked really hard – pretty well every day if we could. His voice became stronger, more confident. He learned to sit down in the voice and find his own response to the language.'

Sit down? Find his own voice? The language becomes obscure. 'The process of finding your voice,' McKellen explained to Janet Watts in March 1976, 'is knitted to the process of becoming more aware of yourself. The more you're willing to find out about yourself, the more whole your voice will be. It's a matter of rooting poetic words in your own needs as a person, and sharing that experience with an audience.'

Cicely Berry's method only really becomes clear when you start to try some of her exercises. Everyone is frightened of Shakespeare's language: school kids who fear they will fail their exams; audiences who fear they will not understand; actors who fear they cannot speak verse. Cicely Berry aims to take that fear away. She aims to make actors stop worrying about whether they or anyone else will understand, and let the language do the work itself. So she makes her actors do silly things like run round the room chasing each other while acting a scene. Or sit on the floor rocking like a toddler as they speak a speech. Or stack chairs in the corner of the room while they utter some immortal line or other. Anything to take the mind off the words – to let them come out freely.

Nickolas Grace gives another perspective: 'You'd go to Cis's room upstairs at Stratford and you'd lie on the floor and say, "Cis, help me with this text." Then you'd go through the speeches or you'd just lie on the floor and gossip for an hour. She was there as a therapist – that was what she was brilliant at, apart from being a brilliant voice teacher.'

Coupled with movement classes from Gillian Lynn and text classes with John Barton, it was the drama training McKellen had never had. In 1982 Barton made a series of TV programmes with members of the company, including Ian McKellen, which went a long way to explaining his and Trevor Nunn's approach to Shakespearian text. Those programmes, shown on London Weekend Television, and the book based on them, *Playing Shakespeare*, come as close as anything to spelling out the house style at the Royal Shakespeare Company.

Barton saw director and actors as 'explorers or detectives', collaborating in a minute examination of the text for meaning, character, verse-form and, most elusively, poetry. He wanted a way of speaking Shakespeare which got away from the dreaded 'poetry voice', a way of speaking which sounded as if the actors were 'inventing a phrase at the very moment it is uttered' – no old-fashioned singing of the text, but an attempt to 'find and fresh-mint the language'.

Barton offered ways into the language for those actors who found Shakespeare intimidating. Some of his approach would be familiar to those who struggled at school to comprehend the iambic pentameter, Shakespeare's five-beat verse line. The point though is that it is scholarship in the practical service of theatre. That is what created the modern RSC, married to a Stanislavskian belief in the reality of the characters in the play – a certainty that there is a truthful motivation for every line uttered by every Shakespearian character. And there's one other ingredient. Nickolas Grace defines Trevor Nunn the director as 'a mixture of Stanislavski and Cambridge verse-speaking and pure show-biz. That's what makes him the greatest there is.'

But for all the power in the acting company and the work that was going on behind the scenes, it still had to be put into practice on stage. And it didn't happen all at once.

As ever McKellen had a clear line on the part. 'Romeo's mad,' he told Robert Cushman of the *Observer* in January 1978. 'He's a suicide case. He can't reconcile the enormity of love with the business of having breakfast and being nice to people.' The problem was that, at 36, McKellen felt he was too old. As far back as January 1970 McKellen had told an interviewer he thought he was too old to play Romeo. Six years later his performance in the part was dominated by anxiety about his age. As in *Hamlet*, when he wanted to play younger than himself, McKellen overcompensated. Above the mirror in his dressing room he had a postcard of Guy the Gorilla from London Zoo. It was there as an object lesson in how to sit still, do nothing and yet rivet an audience's attention. But by opening night for *Romeo*, McKellen had not learned Guy's lesson, injecting a manic energy into his performance in an attempt to suggest adolescence.

The Winter's Tale ran into different problems.

By this time the extraordinary group of actors who had met on that first day in Covent Garden were beginning to weld themselves into an ensemble, and the reason why many of that company still think of this as the golden age at the RSC began to become clear. Nickolas Grace was playing Florizel in *The Winter's Tale*. He describes the level of trust that developed between the actors during rehearsals – exactly the trust that Trevor Nunn had been hoping for: 'You could say to people, "I don't quite understand why you're doing that," without them going, "Hey, hold on, this is my territory and don't you dare step on what I'm doing." We'd got into this environment where you could really challenge each other in the right way without knocking each other, so that if you came to me with some wonderful idea, I'd take that idea and go one level higher, and you'd take what I'd give you and you'd go higher. And you felt all the time you were actually getting better together as a company.'

It was the atmosphere of mutual support – the family atmosphere – that makes a theatre company a good place to work. The opposite of the atmosphere McKellen had found at the National in 1965.

The problem on *The Winter's Tale* was the director – there were three of them.

'It was a nightmare,' is Nickolas Grace's opinion. 'And I felt really sorry for Ian. Trevor was doing the opening section, John Barton was doing Bohemia and Barry Kyle was trying to dovetail and wasn't. We didn't know what the f*** we were doing. We were mostly concentrating on the Bohemian side, but . . . the rehearsals were so ad hoc.'

McKellen remembers it the other way around – Barton was directing him at the court of Sicilia and Nunn was doing Bohemia – so it must have been chaos! Though *Romeo* improved after some pretty shocking notices, and eventually moved to London for the Aldwych season, *The Winter's Tale* was dropped from the repertoire.

For the 1976 season the stage and auditorium at Stratford had been transformed into something resembling Shakespeare's Globe with an audience gallery on stage and the front stalls angled inwards. The whole thing was an attempt to overcome the feeling of dislocation between stage and auditorium, which so many actors have felt at the main Royal Shakespeare Theatre. But just across the car park was a building where no such problem existed. It was a corrugated iron hut, which the RSC had christened The Other Place in 1974 to make it sound better. But it was still a corrugated iron hut. In that hut McKellen was about to create theatre history.

Trevor Nunn wasn't actually that keen on doing *Macbeth* that year. He'd directed Nicol Williamson and Helen Mirren in the play only two years earlier. There was neither the money nor room in the repertoire to fit it into the main house, so with a budget of just £200 Nunn finally agreed to do the play at The Other Place, basing the production on the Williamson/Mirren version. Anticipating later attempts to cut seat prices, like the National Theatre's Travelex season, tickets would be just a pound each – top price in the main house was five pounds.

The confined and brutally simple environment of The Other Place, so perfectly suited to his search for the domestic element in Shakespeare, would transform Nunn's earlier work on *Macbeth*. As for McKellen, it made him into a different actor.

By 1976 Ian McKellen was clearly established in the minds of public and critics alike as an actor unafraid of the grand gesture, if you liked his acting, or as a mannered throw-back to the bad old days of legendary ham actor Donald Wolfit if you didn't. He had learned his trade belting out *Henry V* in the cavernous hall at Bolton School. He had barnstormed his way around Britain and Europe in highly theatrical tours of *Richard*

II, Edward II and *Hamlet*. The Other Place allowed him to transform his way of playing Shakespeare.

The difference between acting in a studio and a big theatre is that in a small space there is nowhere to hide. The audience are close, very close, and you can see them. You can see their faces. In a big theatre you play soliloquy out front and you can look over the tops of the audience's heads or you can pretend to look them in the eye, but you can't really see because you're blinded by the lights and they are in the dark. In the Other Place you could really look them in the eye. If you dared. Questions like 'Is this a dagger that I see before me?' become direct and immediate. In the pause after the short line, 'She should have died hereafter,' McKellen could catch the eye of individual audience members, before sharing the despair of 'Tomorrow and tomorrow and tomorrow . . .'

With virtually no money to spend and a tiny space in which to design, all the grandeur of John Napier's 1974 black and white church interior disappeared. In its place was a dark ceremonial circle painted on the bare floorboards and a set of upturned wooden beer crates ranged around the perimeter. The cast of twelve sat there when they weren't in the scene. Costumes were courtesy of local charity shops – for McKellen and John Woodvine as Banquo a couple of long leather coats which didn't fit, a tea-towel dyed black for Judi Dench to wear on her head as Lady Macbeth. Most of the costumes were black. Griffith Jones wore a white robe for Duncan, and Roger Rees as Malcolm had a white polo-neck sweater. The simple props were laid out on a table in full view of the audience. A thunder sheet, operated by the actors, hung stage right.

For the first two to three weeks of rehearsal, McKellen asked Nunn not to impose any ideas on him. He knew the director might have Nicol Williamson's performance still in his theatrical memory. Nunn agreed. McKellen's aim was to find his own way into the part, and then connect that to what Nunn wanted. He looked, as ever, for modern parallels. It was only two years since Richard Nixon had resigned from the American presidency in disgrace. Was Macbeth Nixon? No, the director came back at once. Macbeth wasn't Nixon. He was his opposite. He was Jack Kennedy. The Macbeths at the beginning of the play were Jackie and Jack, the golden couple. That gave them a high place to fall from.

It's not that McKellen was going to go on stage and impersonate Kennedy, any more than he'd tried to look like the Dalai Lama as Richard II. It was a way into the part, a way of relating it to the world he knew, a way 'to get at our own modern experiences, anxiety and sensibility' as Jan Kott put it. And McKellen had plenty of difficulties in connecting to the world Macbeth inhabits.

'I don't believe in witches and I don't believe in God,' he explained in *Playing Shakespeare*, 'and Macbeth clearly believes in both those concepts. I've never killed a man and he is a professional soldier. I've never murdered a man and he does. I've never been married, and so I have to imagine my way into all those aspects of his life by thinking of people I know, or it may be thinking of a modern man, a contemporary whom I don't know personally but who's vaguely in Macbeth's position.' Again it is a Stanislavskian approach – the search for an analogy which, when fed by the actor's imagination, will help him find his character. As well as Kennedy, McKellen thought of Muhammad Ali. What if the greatest sportsman in the world wanted to become the President of the United States? What if he wanted it badly enough to do anything to get there . . .?

McKellen and Dench had proved twice already that they worked well together. This was to be their greatest partnership. Bob Peck, playing Macduff, thinks McKellen needs someone as strong as him at rehearsal or he tends to take over. And though their ways of rehearsing might be different, at a deeper level Cicely Berry thinks they had a similar way of working: 'They were both very serious about the technicalities of the language, but also they both had a great passion.' Passion. It was what McKellen said they had brought to Shaw. But *Macbeth* saw a new level of sexual chemistry between them on stage, which McKellen has rarely achieved with his female co-stars. Ronald Eyre, director of *The Marquis of Keith*, ascribed this entirely to Judi Dench, but it must also have had at least something to do with the close personal friendship between the two actors.

Certainly the *Macbeth* they created was based around a married couple's relationship. Judi Dench's Lady Macbeth wanted the crown not for herself but for her husband, and McKellen's Macbeth was guided less by ambition than by his passion for her. Thus the play became the spectacle of the disintegration of a golden couple, both descending into despair and madness as the terrible logic of their crimes drives them apart.

Watching from the outside – *Macbeth* was his 'play off' – Nickolas Grace says neither Dench nor McKellen was at all certain that what they were creating in the tin hut would work at all. They were particularly anxious about the bareness of the set. 'They were both petrified about it,' he says.

The Saturday before the press night of *Macbeth*, McKellen finished a matinee of *Romeo and Juliet*, hopped in the car, travelled 300-odd miles north to Edinburgh, performed a newly devised one-man show in St Cecilia's Hall on the Sunday evening and was back in Stratford for *Romeo* on Monday night. Which defines the man at this time – a workaholic who could not get enough of performing.

McKellen called the one-man show *Words, Words, Words*. Casually dressed and with cribs scattered around the stage in case he forgot his lines, McKellen interspersed extracts from his own performances – Shakespeare, Shaw, Marlowe – with bits of poetry and entertaining oddities, including an extract from *Roget's Thesaurus* and a passage of government obfuscation from 'VAT News No. 10'. For an encore he read part of the S–Z section of the London telephone directory – Smellie to Smith. In November he nipped over to the Belfast Festival and did one night there as well.

In the years that followed, *Words, Words, Words* would metamorphose into the altogether more professional *Acting Shakespeare*, which McKellen would pull out of the bag whenever work threatened to give him a couple of weeks off. There would be British Council tours to Scandinavia, Spain, France, Cyprus, Israel, Poland and Romania, a month on Broadway in 1983 which earned him another Drama Desk Award, and in 1987 a climactic marathon eight-month trek across the length and breadth of the USA. In fact, the only place he said he would never do the show was London – a pledge that was not finally broken until 1987/8, the year of coming out.

9 September 1976. The Other Place. Stratford. Waiting to go on, Bob Peck zipped up Judi Dench's plain black dress for her. Actors are superstitious, especially in *Macbeth*, traditionally an unlucky play. Peck had to zip that dress every night for the rest of the run. The doors to The Other Place clanged shut, as the lights went down. The actors took their places on their wooden boxes. There was an immediate sense of ceremony. It could have been Quakers at a meeting or witches in a coven. Then, in full view of the audience, the actors created sound effects for the first scene. McKellen rattled a thunder sheet, as the three witches began: 'When shall we three meet again . . .'

Nunn, who had been through a religious phase in his youth, had emphasised the religious dimension of the play, setting up Duncan and his sons as profoundly Christian, to provide a contrast to the witches and a spiritual battleground on which the Macbeths could lose their souls. They played without an interval. In the tiny, claustrophobic theatre, which never sat more than 160, the atmosphere of evil was palpable. 'It was electric that first night,' offers Nickolas Grace who was in the audience. As critic Michael Billington put it, 'It is one of the few occasions in the theatre when I have felt the combination of pity and terror one is supposed to feel in tragedy.' Neville Boundy, a local priest, came night after night and held up a crucifix to protect the actors.

With the audience so close they could have touched the actors, the size of the place was part of the effect, but it was Ian McKellen and Judi Dench's common approach and the strength of the relationship they created on stage which really generated the atmosphere. Neither saw their character as a monster. The key was to understand them as people. Dench found motivation for the 'fiend-like queen' in her love for her husband. While McKellen learned from playing Macbeth that evil as a concept was something he didn't believe in. Macbeth is not an evil man, but a man who does evil things. But because he is always open and honest with the audience, because he is so deeply troubled by the terrible things he does, the audience and the actor who plays him understand Macbeth. They empathise with him. Call someone evil and you've stopped trying to understand why they behave the way they do, and that understanding is crucial for McKellen, an actor who views Shakespeare through the double-lensed microscope of Freud and Stanislavski.

John Woodvine, a veteran of six *Macbeths*, including two as the Thane himself, thought McKellen and Dench found things in the play he'd never seen before. Peter Hall thought it was the only *Macbeth* he'd ever seen which really worked. Richard Eyre thought the same. Fifteen years later, talking to the *Sunday Times*, Trevor Nunn tried to sum up what made the production such a landmark, drawing a telling comparison with Laurence Olivier: 'Ian's version of it is referred to as the great Macbeth of the century. It's a Waterloo of a play, which Olivier never pulled off. A text that most people think of as rhetorical, even overblown, was suddenly conversational, immediate, domestic. Because it was completely recognisable, it was harrowing and therefore unforgettable.'

Conversational. Immediate. Domestic. Recognisable. Working in the 160-seat Other Place had transformed McKellen as an actor. The rhetorical flourishes, the poses, the vocal and physical mannerisms disappeared. With some understatement, he called the experience 'a corrective to my work'. 'It's so rare in the theatre,' he said in *Playing Shakespeare*, 'to get that intimacy in which the audience can catch the breath being inhaled before it is exhaled on a line, and feel the excitement and certainty that what is happening is for real.' Up on the main stage at the Royal Shakespeare Theatre it may be live and it may be real, but it's nothing like as real as in a 160-seat tin hut. The performance won him the *Plays and Players'* London Theatre Critics Award for Best Actor of 1976.

In November, with the company's year-long contracts coming to an end and box-office receipts still at an all time high, Trevor Nunn spoke to the actors. The plan was to extend the runs at Stratford, and then move the whole circus north for a fortnight to Newcastle. Then back to Stratford before a season in London, adding a whole new clutch of plays to the repertoire. McKellen was being offered leading parts in plays by Ben Jonson, Henrik Ibsen and Bertolt Brecht.

'Usually people leave after one year,' comments Nickolas Grace, 'but everyone stayed.' Grace attributes this in part at least to McKellen. 'Ian took it upon himself to be the leader of the company. I don't mean in a grand way. But he said, "If you have any problems then come and talk to me." Judi would be the same, but Judi is different because she has a private life and goes back home and shuts the door. But Ian was always there, saying, "Well, shall we go to Warwick and see a show?" or "Shall we go to the cinema?" and "See you in the pub later." ' Like going riding in the New Forest on the Cambridge Theatre tour, it may not sound important, but for a group of actors away from home, friends and, in some cases, families for a long period of time, this kind of company bonding is vital.

As late as 9 October 1976, McKellen was writing in *The Times* that he 'felt cut off' from home in his 'comfortable RSC flat'. The M40 stopped at Oxford in those days; London was quite a trek. But the quality of the work was too good to walk away from. Like the rest of the company McKellen agreed to stay with the RSC. In March 1977 they moved north. The pilgrimage to Newcastle would become an annual RSC event, but this was the first time. They used the Gulbenkian Theatre, a small, intimate theatre space on the university campus for The Other Place productions and the big Theatre Royal in the city centre for the main house shows, and Newcastle welcomed them with a passion. The season was sold out virtually from the word go – as well as McKellen's Macbeth and Romeo, the company were offering their immensely successful musical version of *The Comedy of Errors*.

Nickolas Grace was playing Dromio of Ephesus, his first taste of major success as an actor. He was already wondering whether he should continue in the part after Newcastle. McKellen was certain with his advice. 'This show is going to transfer to the West End and then Broadway,' Grace remembers him saying. 'And I know you'll think, Oh,

I can't do the same part for two years. But I'm telling you that you should do it, because it makes your mark. If you're really good in something, and people acknowledge you for that, then keep doing it for as long as you can.' It was a lesson he'd learned with *Richard II*, and would apply again.

While they were in Newcastle, rehearsals began at the Gulbenkian for what would be McKellen's other major triumph during this period at the RSC. Significantly it was another show for The Other Place. The complete comic counterpoint to Macbeth, Face in Ben Jonson's *The Alchemist*, is a virtuoso con man. Jonson didn't write characters like his contemporary, Shakespeare; he wrote types, driven by insatiable needs – for money, sex, power. It's what the academics call the Comedy of Humours but as far as acting style is concerned it's basically farce. The problem is that so many of the jokes are impenetrable to a modern audience, not to mention a modern actor.

John Woodvine, as Subtle, was McKellen's partner in crime. Nickolas Grace, who played Abel Drugger, one of the con men's marks, describes the way McKellen approached the part, a description later echoed in a very different context by Antony Sher. 'Ian has such a fine intellect,' says Grace, 'but he tries to approach everything instinctively rather than intellectually. I think he throws himself into things and sees what happens, and then the intellect steps in and fine tunes.' Jump in feet first in rehearsal, then check if you're out of your depth.

Playwright Peter Barnes, best known for *The Ruling Class*, which had been filmed in 1972 with Peter O'Toole in the lead role, was brought in to adapt the script, cutting where Nunn and his actors thought it overwritten and clarifying where necessary. 'Ian and he didn't get on,' remembers Nickolas Grace, and he goes into a routine:

Barnes: [pinched, nasal voice] Oh, there's a gag there. There's a very good gag. Let's just go with that.
McKellen: [mellifluous, actorly tones] I'm not here to do gags.
Barnes: Well, you're missing a gag here.
McKellen: Well, I don't care. I want to understand what this f***ing line *means*!

The upshot was that Barnes and Nunn went away and concocted their script but the playwright kept away from his leading actor. 'But of course Ian loves gags,' Grace finishes, 'and in the end we did the whole thing as a farce – very, very fast with lots of tumbling around and cupboards and doors. It was phenomenal how they did that text at such speed.'

Meanwhile, such was the continuing demand for tickets for *Macbeth* that Trevor Nunn decided to move it to the main house. Refusing the usual dressing rooms, the actors used a single chorus dressing room with a partition down the middle to try to maintain the 'rough magic' they had created in The Other Place. It didn't work. Simple theatrical effects like the single light bulb in the ceiling, which McKellen had set swinging on the despairing 'I 'gin to be aweary of the sun/And wish the estate of the world were now undone . . .' were impossible on the big stage. The all-important contact with the audience was lost. Then Bob Peck got half his ear cut off in the fight at the end, due to the reblocking. Roger Rees had already broken his foot and had to do several performances in a wheelchair. The play's proverbial bad luck seemed to be surfacing.

The experiment in the main house lasted only three weeks, but the actors were all deeply unhappy with the experience and it was a lesson they remembered when plans were set in train for the London transfer. McKellen agreed to *The Alchemist* transferring to the Aldwych, but for *Macbeth* they decided to turn the RSC's old rehearsal room in Covent Garden, where McKellen's *Richard II* had rehearsed in 1969, into a theatre. They called it the Warehouse (now the Donmar Warehouse). It had 180 seats, and the top price was £1.50.

Macbeth played at the Warehouse from July 1977 until January 1978, finally coming back again for a short run at the Young Vic, where Bob Peck thought they were actually at their best. For the audience it remained an intense and totally absorbing experience, though McKellen had looked for and found intentional laughs in the play. The actors, of course, found ways of keeping themselves amused through the long run. There are always more laughs in rehearsals for a tragedy than for a comedy. It's a way of defusing tension. But during the run, the atmosphere on *Macbeth* could become virtually hysterical. At the Warehouse pants and bras were tossed back and forth over the partition in the dressing room. Whenever the cast felt the pace of the show dropping they would do a 'speed run' to re-inject energy into the performance. At the Young Vic one night they all stuck pink, luminous spots on themselves. McKellen had his on the pommel of his sword; Judi Dench put hers on her earring and so on. A prize of a huge pink spot went to the person who could show his or her sticker to the most cast members without the audience noticing.

It all sounds childish but, as with the pranks on *The Promise* or *Richard II*, the effect was to keep the production alive, to keep that edge of danger which made the performances fresh for each audience. Later, after his learning experience with Mike Alfreds on *The Cherry Orchard*, McKellen would achieve a similar effect by making dramatic changes to his performance from night to night.

Back at the Aldwych, *Romeo and Juliet* hit snags when the people at the back of the stalls couldn't see what was happening on Juliet's balcony. Trevor Nunn had TV monitors installed. But *The Alchemist* was a hit, and won McKellen the Society of West End Theatres (SWET) Award for Best Comedy Performance of 1977, though the cast never felt the show worked as well as in Stratford.

McKellen added an interesting one-off to his summer in a single performance of Tom Stoppard's *Every Good Boy Deserves Favour* at the Barbican Concert Hall with John Wood, Patrick Stewart and the London Symphony Orchestra, conducted by André Previn. Early rehearsals took place in McKellen's sitting room in Camberwell with its busts of Shakespeare on the mantelpiece and the incongruous dentist's chair which, for some reason, he insisted on sitting in. But once the whole orchestra arrived, they had to move to the Royal Festival Hall.

The play is a witty and savage attack on the Soviet practice of incarcerating sane dissidents in mental hospitals. Vladimir Bukovsky, the hero of the play who never actually appears and is referred to as 'my friend C', had been released in December 1976 and exiled from the USSR. When he actually turned up to a rehearsal in Covent Garden in June 1977, McKellen, playing Alexander, had to stop in mid-speech. To have the character you are talking about walk into the room as you are rehearsing is an unnerving experience for any actor!

To complete a triumphant two years with the RSC, McKellen also picked up the SWET Award for Best Actor of 1978 for his performance in John Barton's production of Ibsen's *Pillars of the Community*. Judi Dench was there again, this time playing McKellen's lover, and so was a young Ruby Wax, making her West End debut as a fisherman's wife. Some thought McKellen's performance as Karsten Bernick, an apparently upright businessman with a dubious past, his finest to date.

In February he made a rare excursion into new writing, doing a Sunday night benefit for the South African Defence and Aid Fund of *A Miserable and Lonely Death*, a play about Steve Biko. The South African Black Consciousness leader had died of head wounds in police custody in September of the previous year. Alongside McKellen, the cast list included Patrick Stewart, Richard Griffiths, John Woodvine, Ian McDiarmid, Alfred Molina, Nigel Hawthorne, Bob Peck, Peter Woodward and John Nettles. Quite a line-up. Then, just to counterbalance things a little, Brecht's *The Days of the Commune* bombed at the Aldwych – one member of the cast remembers the play as 'like Les Misérables but without the music – just plain miserable'.

The London season was coming to an end, but there was no let up for McKellen. He was working twelve- to fifteen-hour days, and the pressure was higher than ever. And the reason for the hours and the pressure was that for 1978 he had agreed to take on a new role at the RSC. In fact, it had been his idea.

McKellen had noted the absence of actors from the central group running the RSC, and found informal ways to get his ideas across instead. As one of the leading actors in the company and an old friend of the artistic director, he had the ear of the general. What he had whispered in the ear of the general was that instead of returning to Stratford in 1978 he wanted to take a company out on the road. Since the demise of Theatre-go-round, less an RSC tour than a flying visit to some provincial centre, the company had scarcely been outside its strongholds in Stratford and London. There was the season in Newcastle now, but the powers that be at the Arts Council were indicating that grants in the future might depend on a commitment to touring. A meeting between McKellen, Nunn and Jack Phipps at the Arts Council suggested that funding for an RSC tour could certainly be forthcoming.

But McKellen didn't want to do the normal sort of tour.

What he had enjoyed most, what he felt had improved his acting so much with the RSC was the work in studio theatres. So his plan was a small company with a stripped-down set, visiting communities which did not usually see top-quality theatre, and playing in small venues. McKellen would be both actor and producer. That was the reason for those fifteen-hour days

'Ian has a pioneering instinct,' Trevor Nunn told Michael Billington in an interview for the Sunday Telegraph, 'and a capacity for enthusing people, and enjoys the workaholic nature of admin. I think he likes organising and being on the telephone.' What he finished up organising was a fifteen-week tour of 23 towns and villages across the length and breadth of England and Scotland – Poole, Portsmouth, Canterbury, Sheffield, Yarmouth, Dewsbury, Paisley, Dunfermline, Blandford, Exmouth, Glastonbury and so on. With the zeal of a missionary, McKellen was booking the RSC into spaces not normally used for performance at all in parts of East Anglia and the south west with no local theatre of their own. In amongst the sports halls Jack Phipps slipped in a couple of real theatres in Peterborough and Bury St Edmunds.

They would do Chekhov's Three Sisters, with Nunn directing, and Twelfth Night, to be directed by Jon Amiel, another Cambridge graduate whom Nunn had brought in from the Hampstead Theatre Club. McKellen was to play Andrei, older brother to the Prozorov sisters, and Sir Toby Belch. And who should he want with him on a trip like that? Edward Petherbridge, of course. For Petherbridge it was too good an offer to miss. Deciding it was time for him too to jump ship, he quit the Actors' Company.

By this time Petherbridge was living with actress Emily Richard who had joined the Actors' Company in 1976 and whom he married in 1981. Not surprisingly, she immediately wondered if there was something for her in the RSC tour. 'I already knew Ian, and I knew he liked my voice,' she remembers. Some of the company was to be made up from the ranks of the RSC – Roger Rees, Bob Peck and Griffith Jones among them. But they still needed a young actress to play Viola and Irina, youngest of the three sisters. 'Can I audition?' asked Emily Richard.

The audition took place at the RSC's Floral Street offices. Both Trevor Nunn and Ian McKellen were there. 'I have to say I was sick in the kitchen before I went on,' recalls the actress. 'But later that afternoon Ian rang.' She was in. 'I thought it was the most exciting thing that had ever been offered to me.'

Although she had met him before and was living with his old friend Edward Petherbridge, Emily Richard found working with Ian McKellen quite daunting. 'Because he was so incredibly confident as an actor, I felt I had to be a little bit careful with him. In the end I realised no, I don't have to be careful: I can be as mischievous as a sister would be to a brother. But it was quite difficult to begin with.'

Rehearsals for *Three Sisters* began with two weeks of research. Nunn asked each member of his cast to look into an aspect of Russian provincial life in 1900 – the railways, women's status, the weather, the army, education, the Civil Service. It was the director's first shot at Chekhov, but he was convinced that without a detailed understanding of the social background, the actors would never make the play work.

They looked at five different translations before eventually deciding on one by McKellen's old friend and director, Richard Cottrell. Recent high-profile productions of Chekhov, reacting against the solemnity and slowness which bedevils British versions, had tended to go for the comedy. Played against a gold and grey backcloth, without the usual Chekhovian panoply of naturalistic detail, Nunn was going for something different. He wanted to bring out the sense of entrapment felt by the three sisters, Olga, Masha and Irina, in the provincial Russian town from which they long to escape. 'It was a pretty raw *Three Sisters*,' is

Emily Richard's judgement, 'in the sense that emotions were very close to the surface.'

Two years earlier, during his first season with the RSC, McKellen had fitted in a poetry reading with the Russian poet Yevgeny Yevteschenko at the Royal Festival Hall. Preparing for the evening, which as it turned out was interrupted by David Markham, Corin Redgrave's father-in-law, delivering an impromptu denunciation of Soviet Russia from the stage, Yevteschenko had stayed with McKellen in his RSC flat. Some of what he learned from watching and talking to the Russian poet informed *Three Sisters*. 'Ian told us Yevgeny had said there was nothing extraordinary for a Russian to be laughing one minute and the next to burst into tears, and that was how we did our *Three Sisters*. It's something that English actors can find difficult,' observes Emily Richard.

Rehearsals for the Chekhov were going well. Emily Richard brings out one technique of the director's art. 'I've only ever worked with two directors who have the ability to make you think that every good idea is the one you had, not the one they gave you. Trevor's one.' And the other? 'Steven Spielberg.' She played Christian Bale's mother in *Empire of the Sun* in 1987.

But *Twelfth Night* was in trouble. With a week left of rehearsals the company did a run-through in front of Trevor Nunn and Cicely Berry. It was clear to everyone that the production was not working. At the end of the disastrous run-through, a hasty meeting was convened in the car park outside. McKellen was producer of the tour, but the other actors backed what he had to say. The group went back into the rehearsal room to tell Jon Amiel he was being replaced as director.

'There was this pause,' remembers Emily Richard, 'and Jon Amiel had to walk out of the room.'

In the space of a week, abandoning all the usual RSC discussions about nuance of meaning, Nunn redirected *Twelfth Night*, and it was ready – just – for the opening on 13 July at the Christ's Hospital Arts Centre in Horsham. Jon Amiel, who would later find success on TV with *The Singing Detective*, a move to Hollywood and films such as *Entrapment*, turned up for the opening. No one quite knew what to say. It was not his production they were playing.

Sick with nerves in the wings, Emily Richard remembers Edward Petherbridge whispering to her, 'Laurence Olivier told me: "Nerves? Waste of time. It's an indulgence. Just get on and do it." ' And she did. Some venues wanted more Shakespeare than Chekhov, but both productions were a success, and the company added an evening of readings, compiled by Roger Rees, about English obsessions, entitled *Is*

There Honey Still for Tea? after Rupert Brooke's famous line from 'The Old Vicarage, Grantchester'.

McKellen would look back on that tour as the most enjoyable job he had ever done. Jack Tinker, drama critic with the *Daily Mail*, watched the company setting up for one performance, and seemed amazed to report that, 'Ian McKellen pitches in with the building of the stage, hanging and bolting segments of their cleverly constructed portable performing platform with a motley gang of helpers.' Bridget Turner, McKellen's old friend from Coventry, playing Olga in *Three Sisters*, recalls arriving at venues to find McKellen, who had travelled earlier, already putting out chairs for the audience. It was a company of equals again.

The small-scale tour, founded in 1978 by Ian McKellen, would go on to become an integral part of the RSC's year. Twenty years on it would involve five 45-foot articulated trucks, 47 tonnes of equipment and a 400-seat mobile theatre. But back in 1978 there was one yellow van with driver Ted at the wheel, and it was a matter of rearranging chairs or setting up the portable bleachers and then adapting to what was there. No wonder McKellen loved it. It was the nearest thing to running away and joining the fairground you could imagine – putting up the tent, barking for business via the *Peterborough Evening Telegraph* or the *Surrey Daily Advertiser*, doing the show and then on to the next town.

'I remember lying on top of a costume skip in a shower with a pillow,' says Emily Richard, smiling at the memory, 'and I remember Ian lying in the same shower room trying to get some rest before the show. And I used to do these picnics, so that I knew we'd get something to eat – a piece of bread and some fruit and a cup of tea – and Ian used to share it with me and Edward. And we used to laugh because we're in this squash court and we've now got to go on and do Shakespeare and Chekhov.'

There were complaints sometimes about the conditions they were working under, but no one remembers any personality conflicts on that tour. On days off there were 'works outings' to local sites. Once a week the whole company met for Sunday lunch in a pub. According to one company member McKellen and Suzanne Bertish found they were 'kindred spirits' and became particularly close. But it was when the tour reached the Edinburgh Festival in August that McKellen met another kindred spirit who would become what another friend calls the love of his life.

The RSC company were in Henderson's in Hanover Street, then a late-night hangout for Festival goers. Also there after a first night was a young actor named Sean Mathias. 'You knew at once they were going to be together,' says a friend. Mathias was 22, dark and attractive. Born in the posh end of Swansea (Sketty), he had gone from the National Youth Theatre to professional acting. He'd just done a small part in Richard Attenborough's film *A Bridge Too Far*, but otherwise his acting work had been confined to fringe theatre. McKellen was 39, a major star of the British theatre with some status in New York too following the Actors' Company tour.

The adjective sometimes applied to Sean Mathias is 'outrageous'. He was quite a contrast to McKellen, who had had a tendency since boyhood to keep his emotions in check. There are those who think McKellen saw in Sean the person he might have been when he was younger, if only he'd been more confident. The difference in their respective statuses as actors was even more obvious than any personality differences and, perhaps inevitably, this led to conflict in time. Sean would become convinced people in the business saw him as Ian's pretty boyfriend, and wouldn't take him seriously as an actor. Over the eight years their relationship lasted, though, McKellen would do a good deal to help Mathias in the career he turned to as playwright and director. But it would be Sean Mathias's advice which would be crucial to McKellen's next move as an actor. And that move would not be with the RSC.

The small-scale tour ended in October 1978. There were already plans for *Three Sisters* to be revived as part of the new season. But McKellen had had enough. If joining the RSC had been like coming home, then McKellen had certainly become part of the family. He was even godfather to Trevor Nunn and Janet Suzman's son. But he was leaving home again. 'I was getting too comfortable,' he told an interviewer from *Woman* magazine in 1982. 'I wanted to do something different.' When McKellen walks away abruptly from a theatre job, as at the end of *Richard II* and *Edward II*, it's usually because of a movie. This time there was no film. Maybe he did just want a change. But maybe the decision to move back to London had more to do with Sean Mathias. Travelling up and down to the Midlands is no way to start a new love affair – gay or straight.

6. CROSSING THE POND

Ian McKellen was in bed one morning in Edinburgh in September 1978, reading the script of a new play. He was at that time offered a lot of scripts, but this one was something different. It told the story, sometimes humorously, sometimes melodramatically and sometimes with harrowing strength of what it was like to be a homosexual in Germany when the Nazis were coming to power, and of the eventual fate of half a million gay men and women in the death camps. McKellen chucked it across the bed to Sean Mathias and said, 'Should I do this?'

Sean took a look through and came back with an enthusiastic, 'Yes!' And that was how Ian McKellen came to play Max in the original production of Martin Sherman's controversial *Bent*.

That was McKellen's version anyway in an *Observer* interview in March 1998. Sean Mathias told Marianne Macdonald it never happened. 'It was two months before we went to bed. He's wrong. The whole point was that he wouldn't go to bed with me.' But he didn't deny his advice was instrumental in persuading McKellen to take on the role. The director, Robert Chetwyn, tells a different story again of the extended agonising that McKellen, still not 'out' to the public in 1978, went through over *Bent*.

The play had already had a try-out production in Waterford, Connecticut in 1978. The question was what was going to happen next. Sherman had had an earlier play put on by Gay Sweatshop in London. But he wanted his story of the Nazi treatment of homosexuals, based on Bruno Bettelheim's book *The Informed Heart*, to reach a wider audience. Sherman was even considering television. Chetwyn was passed the script by a TV producer friend who was certain the material was too rich for British TV. 'As soon as I read it, I thought of Ian,' says Chetwyn. Sherman, it turned out, had been thinking of McKellen when he wrote it.

So it was Chetwyn who sent the script to McKellen on tour with the RSC in Edinburgh, and whether he and Sean Mathias were in bed together when it arrived or not, McKellen did indeed say, 'Yes.' Then he started having second thoughts.

The leading character of *Bent*, the part McKellen was being asked to play, is a survivor in a world gone mad. Arrested with his male lover, Rudi, by the SS, he learns on the train to Dachau that the pink triangle of homosexuals makes them an even lower form of life than Jews. To change his status he helps the guards beat Rudi to death and has sex with a dead thirteen-year-old girl. Arriving in Dachau he falls in love with Horst who is wearing the pink triangle, and when Horst is killed, Max dons his dead lover's coat, complete with pink triangle, and throws himself onto the electric fence.

McKellen had just left his first agent Elspeth Cochrane and signed with Jimmy Sharkey. According to Chetwyn, Sharkey read *Bent* and was immediately on the phone to his client advising him strongly not to do the play as it would ruin his career. *Edward II* was one thing, but this was a play with a distinct gay rights agenda. Sherman was not simply telling the shocking story of the Nazis' treatment of homosexuals, he was presenting a metaphor for what it means to be gay. When Max denies his sexual identity to the Nazis, it symbolises the pretence of generations of homosexuals, surviving in a repressive society. When he commits suicide at the end, wearing the pink triangle, it is a gesture of gay pride. For McKellen to align himself with such a message would be a step on the road to coming out publicly. Was he ready to take that step?

'Ian was terrified,' says Chetwyn.

With his star almost decided that he wouldn't do the play after all, and Sherman turning to a possible Broadway opening, Chetwyn tried one final throw. 'I got Tim Curry [who had already had hits in New York in *The Rocky Horror Show* and *Travesties*], the writer Howard Shuman, Ian and myself together in my sitting room, and we read the play through. Tim played all the other main parts.'

When the reading was finished there was a silence in the room. Then McKellen said simply, 'I have to do this play, don't I?'

But, though he did the play, it did not mean he was yet ready to come out. 'It was a thrill,' he told the *Evening Standard* later, 'to act out on stage the secret which I refused to share publicly.' And if he or his agent feared doing the play would result in him being exposed and vilified as a homosexual, that never happened.

There were a number of scenes Chetwyn thought were going to be difficult, including the necrophilia on the train to Dachau. But toughest of all was the scene in the camp itself, in which Max and Horst, standing next to each other and without touching, bring each other to orgasm simply through words. It was not so much a shock reaction they feared; it was that the audience might laugh. As much as anything else, what made that scene and the whole production work was casting Tom Bell as the openly homosexual Horst. Born in Liverpool and best known for playing tough, working-class characters on TV, Bell had been in a television production of *Hedda Gabler* with McKellen in 1974.

'Tom was absolutely at ease,' remembers Robert Chetwyn. 'At that time for a straight guy to do a gay scene like that was quite something, but he had no problem with it at all.'

As Jimmy Sharkey had suspected, Bell and McKellen both had to field press questions about their attitude to homosexuality. Chetwyn remembers Bell telling one journalist he'd always thought he owed something to the gay cause, because he got out of joining the army by saying he was gay. McKellen, on the other hand, responded nervously to Nicholas de Jongh of the *Guardian*: 'I had no hesitation in being in a gay play and to be publicly associated with a cause as well expressed and relevant to people in the modern world as this.' Gay actor to gay journalist – the article gives a flavour of the nervous 1970s, when Gay Pride demonstrations in London still never attracted more than a thousand marchers.

Bent opened at the Royal Court on 3 May 1979, the night Margaret Thatcher became Prime Minister and three weeks before Ian McKellen turned forty. The setting and plot had been kept a closely guarded secret, and the opening scenes with Max and his lover, Rudi, suggested the audience was in for something along the lines of *The Boys in the Band* – a lightweight story of what happened when a heterosexual was admitted to a gay party. The knock at the door, which produced two SS guards who cut the throat of Max's one-night stand, brought an audible gasp in the theatre. The scene of non-contact love-making between Bell and McKellen got an ovation, as it continued to do throughout the run. McKellen, with gaunt cheeks and heavy stubble, was virtually unrecognisable to those who remembered him only as the gilded youth of *Richard II*.

The month-long run at the Court was rapidly sold out, and Eddie Kulukundis, who had financed the production, began looking for another theatre. It would prove a tough search with one theatre owner said to be unwilling to soil his stage with the play. Meanwhile, it was causing an uproar elsewhere. In Parliament there were calls for the return of the censor. And the critics were unsure what to make of it. While mostly admiring the performances, many thought the play sensationalist, and agonised over whether the Holocaust was a subject for drama at all. The debate had been fuelled by the TV mini-series *Holocaust* of the previous year, coincidentally featuring Tom Bell on the opposite side of the conflict as Adolf Eichmann.

John Barber, writing in the *Daily Telegraph*, particularly disliked the play, claiming that it, 'seeks to glamorise homosexual love by presenting it as coming to valiant birth amid the most succulent horrors in recent history'. The article provoked a direct response from McKellen in a letter to the paper, pointing out that Shakespeare himself had used horror in his plays and arguing that *Bent* fulfilled an educational function in informing a younger audience about the events of the Holocaust.

It wasn't the first time he had taken on the critics directly. Not one of those actors who claim never to read their notices, McKellen had been on the receiving end often enough to have his first crack back in 1975, while he was with the RSC. He accused theatre critics then of jumbling together facts and opinions, and of concocting their notices in a well-worn style and always to the same formula. It was a well-worded attack, and one that many an actor would like to have made himself. On the other hand, British critics argue that they wield nothing like the power of a Frank Rich or a Clive Barnes in New York. For one thing there are so many different reviewers covering the same plays that notices are almost always what the biographers like to call 'mixed' – which gives the public the chance to make up their own minds.

Bent closed at the Court on 2 June. There was no theatre to go to. Still hoping for a transfer, the cast kept themselves available, and finally just over a week later, Ian Albery agreed to let them have the Criterion until November, when he planned to bring in his own production of *The Last of the Red Hot Lovers*.

With *Bent* a solid hit at the Criterion, McKellen was at Buckingham Palace in October with his stepmother, Gladys, and sister, Jean – now Jean Jones, married with two children. He had been awarded the CBE in recognition of his work as an actor. In 1979 he would also win the SWET Award for Best Actor for the third year in a row for his performance in *Bent*.

The show duly closed at the Criterion in November. McKellen remained convinced that the play was shut down because members of SWET warned Albery that a play with gay characters wasn't suitable for Christmas. Right up to the last minute they were still looking for another theatre. 'We almost got Wyndhams,' recalls Chetwyn, 'and then Ian decided he wanted to do a film and the whole thing came to a horrible grinding halt.' It was Prospect and the Piccadilly all over again. But this time the film did actually happen, and it was the one which at the age of forty was supposed finally to make a film star of Ian McKellen.

Bent opened on Broadway on 2 December 1979. McKellen wasn't there. Richard Gere was playing Max with David Dukes as Horst. But almost exactly a year later McKellen would be at New York's Broadhurst Theatre on West 44th Street in an even bigger hit, the one that would make him a theatre star on both sides of the Atlantic.

Peter Shaffer's *Amadeus* opened at the National Theatre in November 1979, just as *Bent* was coming off. It starred Paul Scofield as the scheming nonentity Salieri, who plots the downfall of his composer rival, Wolfgang Amadeus Mozart. What had got Shaffer interested in the rivalry between the two men originally was the mystery surrounding Mozart's death, and the play begins with the rumour that he was in fact poisoned by Salieri. But what made the play a *succès de scandale* at the National was Shaffer's portrayal of Mozart, played by Simon Callow, as a manic, giggling, overgrown infant with a liking for toilet humour. James Fenton in the *Sunday Times* called the play 'a nauseating load of – to use a word much loved by Peter Shaffer – shit'.

But the play was a massive hit, and a Broadway production was soon being mooted. Scofield said he didn't want to do it. Shaffer knew McKellen from the 1968 double bill *White Liars/Black Comedy*, but more importantly his was the kind of bravura acting which could carry the evening, because Salieri was the pivot of the show. Never off the stage, transforming before the audience's eyes from age to youth, frequently addressing them more in the manner of a stand-up comedian than an actor, the part could have been written for McKellen, who had grown up on those old music hall acts at the Bolton Grand, and whose one-man show already had more than a trace of the stand-up about it. Alongside McKellen, Shaffer and his director Peter Hall decided to replace Simon Callow with Tim Curry, the man who had helped persuade McKellen to do *Bent*. They also wanted ex-Bond girl Jane Seymour as Mozart's long-suffering wife. The only problem was American Equity.

It took until May 1980 to get permission for the three British actors to appear on Broadway in *Amadeus*. Meanwhile, Shaffer was rewriting the play that was still filling the Olivier Theatre in London. Eventually a new scene at the first night of *The Magic Flute* was inserted, and the final confrontation between Mozart and Salieri was strengthened. But crucially the swearing was toned down for the American audience. Zoë Wanamaker, who would become friends with McKellen when their two shows were neighbours on Broadway, remembers the pre-New York try-out of *Piaf*, another British show making the transition to Broadway that season, in Philadelphia: 'My first line was f***ing this and f***ing that, and you could hear the seats going clunk, clunk, clunk, as people walked out.' In 1980, at least, an American audience was much less willing to accept that kind of language than a British one.

Rehearsals for *Amadeus* finally got under way on 27 September in a room 45 stories above Times Square. On a health kick McKellen ate fruit salad and cottage cheese nearly every day for lunch. Hall had plenty on his mind apart from rehearsals. He'd confided to his diary that he saw the production as one of his last chances to make a lot of money out of directing. He'd also just left his wife and was conducting a passionate affair with opera singer Maria Ewing, who was in New York at the time, and whom he later married. But McKellen told an interviewer from the *Washington Post* he was enjoying himself. 'Yes, there is tension,' he admitted. 'Frustration, tension and despair. It's all right though. So long as there is never anger.' He had seen the production at the National, but tried to switch off in Scofield's most dramatic bits. He wanted to make the role his own.

Rewrites were still going on in Washington, as the play began its pre-New York run. McKellen was now on stage not just for the entire play but, at his own suggestion, while the audience was coming into the auditorium as well. He had a special pocket sewn into Salieri's cloak in which he concealed a book to read.

On 17 December 1980, nine days after John Lennon was shot dead on the steps of New York's Dakota Building, *Amadeus* opened at the Broadhurst Theatre on Broadway. Pinned up around the mirror in McKellen's dressing room were telegrams from, amongst others, Princess Grace of Monaco, Lauren Bacall and Edna O'Brien. British critic Michael Billington saw the production in New York. He particularly admired the moment in McKellen's performance, when, as he wrote in the *Sunday Telegraph*, in 'one single, sweeping movement he shed his old man's cloak with his back to the audience and turned round arms raised triumphantly aloft to appear as a handsome, tall, dark-wigged young man'. It was a million miles from The Other Place or the RSC small-scale tour. It was back to the grand gesture with a vengeance. At times it was almost pantomime: one night, later in the run, as Salieri planned another dastardly scheme against the hapless Mozart, a woman in the audience shouted out, 'Oh no!' to which McKellen replied unscripted and without hesitation, 'Oh, yes!' Simon Callow called Peter Shaffer's work the theatre of gesture, and no one really agreed with what Paul Scofield thought the play was about – the relevance of human goodness to art. But what they did believe was that it was a really exciting theatrical experience. One that could hold its own against the big guns on Broadway that season – *Evita*, *Barnum*, *Sugar Babies* and the like.

But what really mattered, as every actor on Broadway knew only too well, was what Clive Barnes thought. Would Barnes agree?

The first night performance ended. McKellen and Sean Mathias went for the traditional drinks at Sardi's, then on to a big do at the Milford Plaza. Early reviews were already beginning to appear. There was excitement in the air. Then came the all important *Times* notice: 'A total, iridescent triumph.'

And they were a hit.

It was a chauffeur-driven limo to the theatre and back every day. Zoë Wanamaker used to cadge a lift. It was showbiz parties with Liz Taylor, Lauren Bacall and Christopher Reeve. If you're in a hit in New York, even the cabbies know your name. Once he got back to England McKellen would claim to have laughed at the excesses, but while he was there he revelled in the acclaim. 'Looking back,' he wrote in an article in the *New York Times* at the height of his success, 'I realise that I always wanted to be on Broadway, right from the beginning . . . It is certainly more invigorating to be an actor here than anywhere else I know.' He took a smart loft apartment off Union Square. Zoë Wanamaker remembers the surprise birthday party in May. 'Cakes and a male stripper. The usual sort of thing. And we went roller skating for someone else's birthday. I can't remember whose.'

The Broadhurst and Plymouth Theatres on West 44th and West 45th respectively communicate through what Zoë Wanamaker calls 'a secret corridor'. The British members of the two casts could visit during the show. Jane Lapotaire, starring as Edith Piaf, was an old mate of McKellen's from Ipswich days. She had made her debut there in a tiny part in *David Copperfield* under the name of Jane Burgess. 'My time off in *Piaf* was about Ian's interval,' remembers Wanamaker, who was playing Toine. 'One night I went through the secret door to show him my photo album – I'd taken a lot of pictures at Sean's birthday party – and I got locked out. And I was banging on the door to get back in and it was a very quiet scene. Jane was really pissed off.'

It was quite a year for the Brits on Broadway. Tony nominations included the names of Ian McKellen and Tim Curry for Best Actor, Peter Hall for Best Director and John Bury for Best Designer. McKellen, Hall and Bury all won. And *Amadeus* was judged Best Play. Jane Lapotaire got the Best Actress award for *Piaf*.

The Tony Award ceremony that year was on Sunday 7 June at the Mark Helinger Theatre. McKellen and Sean Mathias were congratulated discreetly by fellow gay actors for their daring in being seen together at the ceremony. As they walked out of the theatre, there were screams. Had a pop star appeared from somewhere? McKellen looked round, expecting to see Adam Ant. But it wasn't the king of the 1980s New Romantics. The screams were for the boy from Lancashire.

The Tony Awards go out across the States on TV. For a winner there is a guaranteed audience countrywide. So when a show wins the Tony on Broadway, the management, in this case the Shubert Organisation, immediately starts making plans for a road company and thinking about movie rights. When the movie was finally made in 1984, the money wanted an American in the part, and McKellen lost out to F Murray Abraham, who went on to win the Oscar. As for the road company, McKellen was reportedly offered $1 m to take his tour de force as Salieri around the United States. He turned it down even though the advice he gave Nickolas Grace was that if you're in a hit, stay with it. At the time he told reporters it was because he still saw himself as a British actor, based in Britain, so he was going home to work. But on his return he scarcely worked for months. Like leaving the RSC in 1978, quitting *Amadeus* looks as though it had more to do with Sean Mathias, and a desire to focus for once on his personal life.

He got back just after Christmas 1981. It wasn't just the Tony in the suitcase. McKellen was bringing back half a shelfful of silverware: the Drama Desk Award, the Outer Critics' Circle Award, the New York Drama League Delia Austrian Medal, no less. But breathing familiar English air brought back McKellen's familiar English irony. 'New York's a wonderful town,' he said in a *Sunday Telegraph* interview, 'if you've got money and you're in a hit show. But being in a play in New York is actually rather like being in the village pantomime. Everybody knows it's on, who's in it and what they've done before. Half of them are hoping it's going to be a disaster and it usually is. Where a puritan like me gets worried is in wondering, after a certain time, what it's all for, who the audience is and where they've come from.'

The serious sting is in the tail – what's it for and who's it for? Before joining the RSC in Stratford, McKellen had pondered the nature of the audience he would meet, fearing a bunch of 'pernickety aficionados who had collected every Hamlet since Burbage'. In the same article for *The Times* he damned the West End audience as made up of foreigners and people who were strangers to each other, 'unresponsive and unexcitable'. As for the Broadway audience, the problem there has always been the exorbitant ticket prices, which ensure the people in the auditorium come from only one social stratum.

The people for whom McKellen has always felt a real affinity is the provincial audience – the audience who 'knows who you are, and are glad you're there'. It's the reason he's always aimed his performances at non-experts – the girl in Edinburgh who thought Laertes might win the duel with Hamlet, the ladies in Nottingham who weren't sure if they would understand but had come because they'd seen *Richard II* on the telly. It's the romantic idea of 'taking theatre to the people'. It's what lies behind the 'pioneering instinct' Trevor Nunn talks about. It's an attitude which would cause a furore in 1998, when McKellen appeared to be saying he was giving up the London stage and would only work in provincial theatre from then on. But for the boy who saw Gielgud in Manchester, it's hardly a surprising attitude. In many ways McKellen's commitment to audiences outside London has been payback for those early theatre experiences in Lancashire, which made him want to be an actor in the first place.

But the other question McKellen was asking in that 1982 interview was what it was all for. Eight shows a week as Salieri had left him physically and mentally drained and uncertain of what to do next. With the proceeds from *Amadeus* he swapped the moped, which had been his trademark around London through the 1970s, for a Mini. He also swapped the terraced house in Camberwell for a three-storey, early eighteenth-century house on the north bank of the Thames, backing onto the river. Sounds swanky, but this was not Cheyne Walk in Chelsea. This was Narrow Street in Limehouse in the East End – before the developers moved in. David Owen and Francis Bacon would become neighbours, so would Steven Berkoff and Janet Street-Porter, but in 1982 it was no more fashionable than Camberwell. But it was bigger. And this time McKellen wasn't living alone. Sean moved in.

At the Tony Awards, McKellen had said thank you to the New York audience in true showbiz style – they 'lift you so high that sometimes you feel you want to fly for them'. He had said thank you to colleagues. He had said nothing about Sean, sitting next to him all evening. Now, for once, he was putting his private life first.

The new house with its lightning-blue front door was all stripped-wood elegance and book-lined walls. A wide window, running the full width of one room, looked out onto the river. People visiting for the first time looked through it and said, 'Oh, what a pity! All those chimneys.' McKellen was defensive. He didn't find it ugly. He liked the feeling of openness with the river and the sky and the seagulls swooping by. It reminded him a bit of home – in industrial Lancashire.

The dentist's chair made the move from Camberwell. The terrace overlooking the river would soon fill up. His grandfather's eightieth birthday bench, inscribed W H McK, would find a place there. So would a vast assortment of statuettes. McKellen has admitted he never knows what to do with them all.

Not long after moving in, he was gazing out at the river one day from that terrace, when he spotted, washed up on the pebbles, the four-legged corpse of an animal. White and bloated from long immersion in water, the species was indeterminable. It could have been a calf or a lamb. It could have been a dog. Eventually the rising tide washed the horrifying object away, but for McKellen, who had never been a great eater of meat anyway, it was a decisive moment. He has been a vegetarian ever since.

Amid the domestic pleasures of decorating and cooking vegetarian food, McKellen's thoughts turned once more to work. He had already agreed to do a film for television which would open the new Channel 4 in November. But he also decided to do something to kick-start his lover's stalled career.

Sean Mathias had done a stint at the Glasgow Citizens' Theatre in 1979. McKellen had been up to see him in *The Maid's Tragedy*. But Sean was already beginning to feel that his relationship with McKellen, which was, of course, well-known in the theatre, was not encouraging people to take him seriously as an actor. He turned instead to writing, concocting a bizarre first play, which began as a pastiche of Noel Coward, before developing into a tale of murder and incest, involving a would-be playwright and his would-be actress sister. McKellen decided to play the brother. He got Janet Suzman on board as the sister, and Nigel Davenport agreed to do a turn as an ageing actor-knight who goes to bed with Suzman's character. Then McKellen began hawking the project around West End managements.

The plan was to put on Sean's play, which he'd called *Cowardice*, and another piece about cult leader Jim Jones. They didn't want fringe. They wanted a small theatre in the centre of London, and as a sweetener for this new play by an unknown playwright, McKellen was offering to do it for £200 a week. Three managements turned the whole thing down. Then the Jim Jones play fell through, but Duncan Weldon agreed to put *Cowardice* on at the Ambassador's.

The critics were savage. Before damning the play, Anthony Masters began his review in *The Times*, 'Once upon a time in the West End, the star-part play was almost a genre in itself. Playwrights often wrote them for spouses: Marion Lorne, Constance Cummings, Hugh Williams . . .' The veiled suggestion, obviously, was that Sean Mathias was another playwright in the line of those spouses – Walter C Hackett, W Benn Levy and Margaret Williams – writing a star part for his 'spouse', Ian McKellen. In fact, of course, it was much more a question of McKellen trying to promote Sean's career. At any rate, the experiment failed: *Cowardice* closed; and with the movies still not beating a path to his door in Limehouse, McKellen began to consider a return to the RSC.

At the beginning of 1984 Adrian Noble asked him to go to Stratford to play Coriolanus. It was clearly one of the major Shakespearian roles that he should play – a heroic, larger-than-life warrior who needs the grand gesture if any part does. But Sean made it quite clear that he was not going to move to Stratford or do the constant shuttling back and forth at weekends. Home and work. It's a tension that's broken up many a theatre couple.

Again McKellen decided to go for home. He was about to turn Noble down, when a counter offer arrived from Peter Hall at the National Theatre, coincidentally including *Coriolanus* in a three-play package. It was the perfect solution. McKellen joined the National Theatre, 'taking up the central place held by Finney during the 70s', as Michael Owen put it in the *Evening Standard* on 30 March 1984. For some at least he was still treading in Albert Finney's footsteps.

McKellen described his feelings about joining the National in exactly the same terms he had used to talk about the RSC. Coming back from New York, he said in an interview for *Plays and Players* in June 1985, 'I found that my base as an actor is working with a company. That's what I've mainly done – so although I've never acted before in this building, joining the National was in a sense coming home for me.' Coming home – out of the storm of the commercial world and under the sheltering roof once more of the subsidised theatre. He described the past year as 'a fallow period', and at the age of 45 was looking forward to the hard work of rehearsing and playing in repertoire. He was contracted for eighteen months until September 1985, but he was already talking blithely about staying three, four, even five years.

It was quite a turnaround. Back in 1976, when the National Theatre was making its long-delayed move to the South Bank, McKellen had been among the severest critics of Peter Hall's South Bank complex, fearing its centralising power, likening it to a siege fortress. There were those bad memories of the National under Olivier as well, when he had felt lost in a big company. As much as anything this still seems to be what McKellen feared about the National in 1984. Yes, it represented a view that London was the centre of the artistic universe, and all his instincts were against that. But more than that it was a big machine, run by the mightiest impresario of his day, in which a mere actor, however recently he had been the toast of Broadway, might disappear.

What he was wondering was whether the National was like the RSC. Did it too look monstrous from the outside but break down into smaller units from the inside? With the division of the enterprise into five separate groups, one of them the McKellen/Petherbridge company, the attempt to form such smaller units would be made. But it was always going to be harder on the South Bank, because the basic difference between the National and the RSC is simply that the National is in

London and the RSC is in Stratford; actors live in London; so National Theatre actors go home after the show; RSC actors go to the pub. That's how the RSC in its best years has been able to create a sense of company, in a way that the National has never really managed.

Thomas Otway's *Venice Preserv'd*, directed by Peter Gill, was McKellen's first show on the South Bank. Not often revived, the play still carried the weight of Peter Brook's legendary production at the Lyric Hammersmith in 1953, starring John Gielgud and Paul Scofield. Stepping onto the Lyttleton stage for the first time, McKellen gave an uncharacteristically restrained performance as Pierre, the Scofield part. Indeed there were those who thought he should have been playing Michael Pennington's more showy role of Jaffier, the man torn between love and duty. The production entered the repertoire on 12 April 1984. Scheduling gave McKellen time for a quick week's holiday, and then he was into rehearsals for Platonov, the feckless hero of *Wild Honey* which, for many, would be McKellen's finest performance.

Wild Honey is a real collector's item. Never performed in his lifetime and discovered mouldering in a safe deposit box in a Moscow bank vault sixteen years after the playwright's death, this is Chekhov's first play. The manuscript was clearly unfinished and contained suggestions for changes. It was missing the front page, so no one knew what it was supposed to be called, and it ran for six hours. Apart from that it was all ready to be performed.

A number of previous attempts had been made to stage the play, cut in various different ways and usually called *Platonov* after the main character. In 1961 Rex Harrison appeared in a version at the Royal Court. In the audience was 32-year-old director Christopher Morahan, then just breaking into television. Morahan directed Harrison in what was more or less the same version of the play for TV, but that monumental manuscript continued to obsess him. In the early 1970s he began talking to playwright Michael Frayn about making a new version of the play.

Frayn was ideal for the job, quite apart from his talents as a playwright – he was fluent in Russian. Indeed he'd served as Russian interpreter in the army. But it was not until 1983, after the huge success of his best-known play, *Noises Off*, that the project became a go. Frayn cut the play to three hours and called it *Wild Honey*, a line in the script.

And the holiday? Well, Morahan and McKellen were taking a week in Moscow before rehearsals began.

Morahan said the trip wasn't exactly research, but it was part of an attempt by director and star to overcome the problem which always bedevils British Chekhov. It's too British. Typically, Trevor Nunn had made his cast do two weeks research before *Three Sisters* in 1978. A trip to Moscow was altogether more pleasant. In authentic Stanislavskian style McKellen tried to absorb what the great Russian actor, director and teacher called 'sense memories' – the mud on his boots, the spring sun on his face, the sense of reawakening after the long Russian winter. Near the beginning of *Wild Honey* Platonov comes on stage with an armful of spring flowers to greet the return of his old flame Sonya who has just got married. At the National stage management found flowers growing wild in the car park near the stage door, and picked them fresh each day – what McKellen wanted to add was his memory of real Russian flowers in a real Russian spring. He wanted to bring reality on stage.

They also went to watch a rehearsal at Stanislavski's old company, the Moscow Arts Theatre. Was there a secret here that would help an English actor play a Russian convincingly? They were rehearsing *Uncle Vanya*, so at least the playwright was right. But apart from a secretary writing a verbatim account of everything that was said, the rehearsal looked pretty much like any other: the director gave notes, the actors puzzled over what they meant . . .

Back in the National Theatre rehearsal rooms, work got under way. Frayn had concocted a script which at times seemed to owe more to his own comic writing or Feydeau than to what British audiences had come to expect from Chekhov. Certainly there were dark moments, but at times the play had the frantic air of farce. For McKellen the key was to be able to play in a range of styles within the same character. This meant the playing was sometimes naturalistic, sometimes it had the pace and phrasing of light comedy, sometimes it needed the precision and energy of farce and sometimes, as he put it in *Drama* magazine, 'a dash of the heavy tragic'. Where the mature Chekhov might combine all these elements into the same scene, the script of *Wild Honey* had the actors alternating styles abruptly from one scene to the next. Through it all McKellen celebrated having a real Russian speaker there in Michael Frayn and none of the usual problems of wondering what the original had said.

Morahan and McKellen had had a look at the country first hand. For the rest of the cast the director produced quantities of photographs and reproductions of paintings of pre-revolutionary Russia for them to pore over. McKellen was only too well aware that the production would not stand or fall on his star performance. Chekhov is not like that. As he put it in *Drama* magazine, 'Actors climb up to Chekhov like a mountain, roped together, sharing the glory if they ever make it to the summit.'

Meanwhile designer John Gunter was creating a stunning set which would use mirror effects to create an impression of acres of shoulder-high grass, a fireworks display and an on-coming train to flatten the hero at the climax.

What cast and production team came up with by opening night was what Michael Billington in the *Guardian* called 'a farce with the smell of sulphur'. As Platonov, the schoolmaster once talked of as the next Byron and now descended into the role of local intellectual and serial womaniser, McKellen was at his most brilliant and inventive. The part allowed him a wonderfully funny and affecting transition from the man privileged to tell the rest of the village unwelcome truths, through the farce of his attempted rendezvous with Anna, to the drunken guilt and self-loathing which leads him eventually to suicide beneath John Gunter's train. 'It says everything for the performance,' wrote John Barber in the *Daily Telegraph*, 'that one comes out laughing but feeling "poor devil".'

McKellen's attempt at combining such a wide range of acting styles worked brilliantly. The SWET Awards had been renamed that year as the Laurence Olivier Awards, but whatever they were called, McKellen was there. He won Best Actor in a Revival for the Chekhov and the production picked up nine top drama awards in all. Frank Rich's notice for the *New York Times*, which called the play melodramatic and thought McKellen 'strained' in the drunk scenes, might have given them pause, but didn't. Plans were soon afoot for a Broadway transfer.

With a season already in preparation for the McKellen/Petherbridge company, McKellen started rehearsals for *Coriolanus* at the beginning of October 1984. He was taking on a daunting challenge. Coriolanus is a noisy part. Shakespeare's portrait of Rome's greatest warrior aristocrat involves a lot of ranting at the plebeians which, depending on the director, can involve shouting over a large group of other actors. There's stage fighting too, though unlike Hamlet and Macbeth the main fight is earlier in the evening, which is good news for the actor. But the bad news was that the production was intended for the Olivier Theatre, acoustically a pig of a place, where actors can feel they have to shout and exaggerate to reach an audience of 1,100 who seem a long way away. Add this to the leads he was already playing in *Venice Preserv'd* and *Wild Honey* and the planning meetings with Edward Petherbridge for the new company, and it becomes clear why McKellen has often been called a workaholic.

He was at the gym first thing every day. This was more than just an attempt to stay fit. Coriolanus's fights with Aufidius, played by Greg

Hicks, would be staged with both actors virtually naked. Hicks was fourteen years younger than McKellen and something of an expert in Japanese Butoh and Brazilian Capoeira, both hybrids of martial arts and dance. It would be no good if Caius Marcius of Rome, who wins the name of Coriolanus by beating Aufidius and his Volsces at Corioli, looked like some kind of middle-aged wimp.

The production would turn out a major draw at the National Theatre and another personal success for McKellen, but its creation, through rehearsals and the preview period, which had to be specially extended, was tortured.

Problems began on the first morning of rehearsals. Most of the cast assembled outside Rehearsal Room One, waiting for the director, Peter Hall, and the stars to arrive. The actors introduced themselves, finding out who was playing what. One young man, just a year out of drama school said, 'Hi, my name's Sean Bean and I'm playing First Citizen and understudying Ian McKellen. Except I'm not doing it. I'm going home.' And with that the 25-year-old Sean Bean turned on his heel and disappeared down the echoing corridors of the National Theatre. He and McKellen would have to wait until 2000 and *The Lord of the Rings* before working together. As for First Citizen, Geoffrey Burridge played it in the end.

Then there were the costumes. The director and stars duly arrived. Designer John Bury unveiled his drawings. Bill Moody, playing one of the citizens, remembers the whole cast's reaction as a muted, 'Oh, dear!' 'They were sort of eclectic, if that's the word,' he explains. That meant a mixture of classical and modern. McKellen was particularly unhappy about his. 'It was a rather nondescript mustardy-coloured thing that buttoned up around the neck,' remembers Jacqueline Fletcher, who was observing the production as part of her M Phil on the Elizabethan/Jacobean playwright John Marston at the Dutch University of Utrecht. Discussions over that mustardy-coloured thing would grow heated and reach a spectacular conclusion at the first preview.

But probably what caused the most trouble was Peter Hall's determination to bring a hundred members of the audience on stage. Hall's assistant director, Alan Cohen, explains the idea behind the production against the background of the miners' strike of 1984–5, then convulsing the country: 'Peter and I talked a lot about creating an arena for political debate in relation to what was going on in the country. We wanted a kind of cauldron, a kind of hot area where debate could take place, and we thought that by encircling it with the audience, it would give it that feeling of the Senate in Rome.'

Tyrone Guthrie had used amateur actors to swell the ranks of the crowd but this was something different. This was ordinary members of the audience. And they weren't simply going to sit there on stage either, as the audience did for Michael Frayn's *Copenhagen* in 1998. The plan was for the production to begin with a riot, mirroring what people were seeing on their television screens every evening, and the cast would encourage the on-stage audience to get up out of their seats and take part. On that first day it sounded risky but interesting. No one realised just what the result might be until previews began.

In the meantime, McKellen was beginning the process of creating another Shakespearian hero. He told some of the other actors he found Coriolanus's arrogance and his hatred of other people difficult to understand because it was something he couldn't find anywhere in himself. So, as ever, he looked for a modern equivalent – and found it in an unlikely place. Tennis player John McEnroe had just won Wimbledon for the third time that summer. McKellen found a clue in this brilliant sportsman. Were Coriolanus's tantrums, when faced with the common people, an equivalent to McEnroe's on-court antics with the umpire?

McKellen dug deeper. In the play the only person who has any control over Coriolanus is his mother, Volumnia, played by Irene Worth. After the common people exile him from Rome, it is she who persuades her son not to take revenge by sacking the city at the head of a Volscian army. Was Coriolanus the greatest mummy's boy of all time? He began to experiment in rehearsal with bringing out the childishness of his response to his mother, transforming this all-conquering fighting machine into a moody adolescent whenever he was with her. As with all his great Shakespearian performances it was a psychological insight, coupled with some connection to the modern world, which produced the magic.

But, according to Jacqueline Fletcher, not all members of the company were finding rehearsals so productive. Wendy Morgan as Coriolanus's wife had most of her scenes with Irene Worth. Morgan was struggling to get the attention of the director. 'Irene rehearsed every scene as if she was the only person in it,' recalls Fletcher. Fight director Malcolm Ransom was unhappy too. McKellen and Hicks were coming on OK, wielding their heavy swords and shields, but the big battle was not going so well. Michael Bogdanov had grabbed many of the younger, fitter actors for his dramatisation of *The Ancient Mariner*. Ransom was left with older actors and even actresses to pad out the numbers. One of those older actors, Frederick Treves, who was playing elder statesman

Menenius, was struggling to learn his lines, and confided to Jacqueline Fletcher sadly one day, 'I think this is going to be my Shakespearian swan song.' He was also having trouble adjusting to Peter Hall's demands on the speaking of Shakespearian verse.

During the early weeks of rehearsal, Hall liked to work from behind a lectern, more like the conductor of an orchestra than a theatre director. The comparison is illuminating, because Hall's approach to the speaking of Shakespeare is to see it very much as a musical score. And, though a musical score still offers room for variation and interpretation, basically you either play it right or you play it wrong. As Hall himself wrote in *Exposed by the Mask*, 'We wouldn't accept wrong notes in Mozart.' The attention to verse form and structure is based on the ideas of William Poel as handed down to Dadie Rylands and thence to Hall and Barton and Nunn at Cambridge. Nunn's particular talent in rehearsals for *Macbeth* had been to leaven that rigour with psychological exploration and what Nick Grace called 'pure showbiz'. He also had the knack of not over-directing his stars. By contrast, in an interview in the *Independent* in March 1989, McKellen called both Barton and Hall 'didactic' directors.

Jacqueline Fletcher overheard one example of the didactic method in a rehearsal during previews. Hall was directing Frederick Treves. 'I told you, Freddie,' said Hall, 'it's not a full stop there, it's a comma.'

'Freddie was looking terribly sheepish and apologising,' recalls Fletcher, 'and it was the umpteenth time he'd been corrected on that.

'This thing about Peter Hall directing punctuation seems to be absolutely true,' she concludes.

On the other hand, assistant director Alan Cohen explains the impact Hall had on him; and, unlike Jacqueline Fletcher and some members of the cast, he characterises rehearsals for *Coriolanus* as 'a very happy time'. Hall said he would teach Cohen everything he knew about Shakespeare. 'It was a moment,' he says, 'like a door opening in my life. I learned about how to find the truth in the text and how to make the iambic pentameter understandable. You programme the iambic into you and then you can breathe. The opening time in rehearsals is about teaching the actors how to do the text. Older actors who have done a lot of Shakespeare but not with Peter have to unlearn what they've done, and that's a real problem.'

The difficulty is, of course, that some actors, particularly experienced actors, will see a director presenting himself as a teacher as overly 'didactic', the word McKellen himself uses. McKellen's also said that he doesn't like directors who arrive at a production with all their ideas worked out. Rehearsal should be a process of discovery with actors and director working in collaboration. The director as teacher is quite a different role.

But Alan Cohen denies Hall has a dictatorial style of directing: 'It's a complete fallacy! Anybody can say anything to him and they can try anything in rehearsal. For a lot of directors that's a threat, when an actor says, "No, hang on, I'm not happy with that" – and Ian does a lot of that – but for Peter that's not a threat. They had an excellent working relationship,' he concludes. 'They trusted each other implicitly.'

But Bill Moody, who was in the cast and therefore closest to what the actors were thinking, remembers having lunch one day with McKellen and others in the National Theatre canteen. LWT were in, recording a South Bank Show about McKellen. 'It just would be nice to get a bit of bloody direction,' he was saying to the assembled table, and Bill was nodding his head in agreement.

'Then I look up,' remembers Moody, 'and realise the camera's turning over right on us and may be picking the whole thing up.'

With the play in performance McKellen would ask for notes from his fellow actors. The situation wasn't made any easier by the fact that Hall was taken ill, and missed part of rehearsals altogether. McKellen and Hicks began rehearsing on their own, developing the key scenes between Coriolanus and his arch rival Aufidius, the very scenes which had first brought McKellen national attention at the Nottingham Playhouse. It was McKellen's idea to borrow at least one element of the Tyrone Guthrie production. 'They went for the homoerotic interpretation,' explains Bill Moody.

As they neared preview time, it was clear to everyone that the production was not ready and the decision was made to postpone the press night. Jacqueline Fletcher remembers spotting McKellen in the Green Room, the actor's bar, backstage one evening just before previews started. 'He was sitting on a stool up at the bar all on his own,' recalls Fletcher, 'and he had a bottle of champagne in a bucket in front of him, and he didn't come over to talk to anybody and no one went over to talk to him, and he just looked so unhappy. He's usually an upright person and he was slumped, and he just looked so miserable.'

Of course, he may just have been tired, and if he was uncertain about the production that would hardly be unusual. Over at the McKellen/Petherbridge company Sheila Hancock learned to expect a complete collapse of confidence from McKellen two days before opening night, and found herself wondering if he was all right if he didn't suggest cancelling. But there certainly were major problems still with Coriolanus.

The sand on which they were to fight didn't arrive until the day before the first preview, and disagreements about that costume had still not been settled.

At McKellen's insistence the 'mustardy-coloured thing' had been ditched. He had persuaded director and designer that he should be wearing modern clothes at the start of the show. He wanted to appear first as a typical young man about town, before revealing himself later as a sword-wielding warrior. The mixture of periods was deliberate. Hall and Bury wanted to create a timeless production which would allow Shakespeare's story to resonate with current events in the coal fields. But by the morning of the first preview McKellen still didn't have a costume. He and designer John Bury went out shopping in the afternoon. Bury returned to the theatre without McKellen and without a costume. That night only McKellen and his dresser knew what he was going to wear for his first dramatic entrance up stage centre through the on-stage audience. Alan Cohen was sitting with Peter Hall in the director's box.

'He came up over the back in this brilliant white suit with shades on. Peter and I sat up at the back of the audience and gasped.'

Jacqueline Fletcher had thought the whole production low on energy throughout rehearsals. She elaborates on McKellen's costume and describes the galvanising effect of his entrance that night on those already on stage: 'He had this fantastic white cashmere, belted overcoat slung around the shoulders and a blue shirt and tie with his sword nonchalantly slung over his shoulder. It was the most amazing moment, and you could see on stage everyone was shocked, and suddenly the tension and the energy were there, and everyone was acting like mad. All of the energy came back into it – it was an absolutely wonderful moment.'

The white suit stayed. But McKellen wasn't finished with his experiments. He used the extended preview period to try out new ideas on the audience. Up there on the Olivier stage with 1,100 people watching, the actors are in charge – if they've got the nerve; the director can't get up and say, 'Hold on, I don't like that.' They were about halfway through the preview period. Peter Hall was no longer watching every performance, but leaving his assistant to take notes and then rehearsing with the company through the day. Jacqueline Fletcher was watching with fight director Malcolm Ransom and Alan Cohen from the director's box. They had reached the final scene. Coriolanus was about to be killed by the Volsces who think he has betrayed them. As he began the speech, 'Cut me to pieces, Volsces, men and lads . . .' McKellen started to tear off his clothes. 'We just went, "What?!" ' recalls Jacqueline Fletcher. 'And Alan said, "What the f***'s he doing?" '

The jacket came off. Then he started to unbutton the trousers. And that's where the problems began. McKellen was wearing ankle boots with straps, and his trousers wouldn't go over them. Continuing with the speech, he sat down on the stage, removed the boots, pulled off the trousers, and stood up wearing only his loin cloth for the final moment when he was killed in a volley of rifle fire.

It is the stuff of which actor's nightmares are made. You are on the stage at the National Theatre and suddenly, without explanation,, you are removing your clothes, something you have never rehearsed.

What McKellen had decided was that Coriolanus knows he is about to die, even desires his death, but psychologically he would not want to die in the Volscian uniform he is wearing. Like the white suit, the strip stayed in. After that preview the sequence was rehearsed and by press night it was perfect. But what is revealing about McKellen the actor is that he was perfectly willing to try it out first in front of an audience and without rehearsal. Fearlessness: 'F*** off, I don't give a shit! No nerves.'

After all the problems and delays *Coriolanus* finally had its press night on 15 December 1984. McKellen went on to win the *Evening Standard* Award for Best Actor, though some of the critics were as harsh as they had ever been about his vocal delivery. Benedict Nightingale's review in the *New Statesman* was headlined 'Booyaahayaaee', a phonetic rendition of what Nightingale accused the actor of doing to the simple word 'Boy' in the final scene. Of course, the reason why McKellen placed such emphasis on the word, the reason why Coriolanus in his interpretation is so enraged by Aufidius calling him a 'boy of tears' is that that is exactly what Coriolanus knows himself to be. It is the lack of emotional maturity in the man which makes him what he is.

But one problem the actors and many in the audience had with the production never went away – those members of the public on the stage. 'We used to get [people] sitting there with Antony Sher as Richard III T-shirts right in front of Ian,' remembers Bill Moody. McKellen himself was deeply unhappy with the arrangement, and it must say something for the strained relationship between him and Hall that he expressed his dissatisfaction in the form of a memo, rather than a personal word. At the RSC he'd had the ear of the general. At the National it was memos at dawn. Hall wouldn't budge, though he himself seems to have thought the device only really worked when the show played two performances at the Herod Atticus in Athens, the ancient Greek theatre carved out of the rock of the Acropolis. With no time even for a complete run-through, the actors rose to the challenge of playing to 6,000 people in the open air. At the end the audience stood and cheered for ten minutes. It was quite a finale.

One comment everyone involved in *Coriolanus* makes – and you hear it again and again from those who've worked with McKellen since *Sir Thomas More* in Nottingham – is this: 'He's great at leading a company.' That means being the one to remember the birthdays of cast and crew, the one to organise trips and outings, if you're away from home. But it means more than that. Alan Cohen explains it this way:

'A leader of a company is like a captain at football – like Roy Keane – who can make a huge difference to a team. Not necessarily by saying anything but just by their presence. By how they walk. If you see the captain of the team walking off with his head between his shoulders looking miserable and depressed, then everybody else will do the same. So a company leader doesn't walk around with his face drooping on the ground because he's miserable with some aspect of the production. It's his job to set an example to the company.'

So far so much Head Boy of Bolton School. But Cohen has more to say about McKellen, particularly during the rehearsal period of *Coriolanus*, when everything was not always sweetness and light. 'You'd have a cup of tea in the middle of the morning and Ian would make everyone a cup of tea from the machine. And I've worked with an awful lot of people who wouldn't do that. There was no question of him waiting for the stage management to bring him a cup. In fact, he went out one day and came back with two new coffee machines because the company was getting so big with all the people observing. He'd be first to the bar, first with his hand in his pocket. And he's got no highfalutin ideas about himself and that's a big part of being leader of a company.'

Both Jacqueline Fletcher, who was supposed simply to be observing the production, and Alan Cohen, who was assisting the director, finished up on stage with McKellen during the course of previews for *Coriolanus*. The experience made quite an impression. Indeed, what they have to say is probably more illuminating because they are not professional actors.

During the previews, Peter Hall asked Jacqueline Fletcher to go on one night in the crowd scenes to report on how bringing the audience out of their seats was working. It was the end of Act 3, when the plebeians have banished Coriolanus from Rome, and he issues the most ringing of his many denunciations of the mob: 'You common cry of curs, whose breath I hate/As reek of the rotten fens, whose loves I prize/As the dead carcases of unburied men/That do corrupt my air . . .' and so on. Pressure of time in rehearsals had meant the speech had not received a great deal of attention. 'Ian was looking around the crowd,' Fletcher recalls, 'and I suppose he saw a familiar face. Perhaps because he was finding the speech difficult, he thought it might help to latch onto a familiar face, but he delivered that whole speech to me. And it really scared the wits out of me. I really felt like taking a few steps backwards – the vitriol that came out, the sense of hatred that came out was quite remarkable and I kept wanting to break eye contact because I felt horrible. But at the same time I felt that if I do that, I'm letting him down somehow, so I didn't. Gosh it was scary.' That's the power, the energy, the focus of McKellen on stage.

Alan Cohen went on in even more extraordinary circumstances after an older member of the company, who was understudying and doing the fights, died suddenly during the flu epidemic that winter. With several other actors also down with flu, Cohen suddenly realised as the performance was beginning that there was no one to fight McKellen in the second scene. 'I threw on a costume and ran on,' Cohen remembers. Naturally, McKellen was unfazed, and thoroughly enjoyed himself, muttering under his breath as he prepared to kill his adversary, 'I've always wanted to get a director into this position.' But, returning as part of the crowd, Cohen began to get an insight into McKellen's method as an actor – one which he had not had from the director's box.

Coriolanus doesn't have soliloquies like Shakespeare's great tragic characters, but McKellen still seemed to be finding a way to address individual lines to individual members of the audience without removing himself from the scene on stage. 'That has a kind of cumulative effect through the evening,' says Cohen, 'as more and more of the audience become in tune with him, so that by the end of the evening over a three hour play every single person in that audience thinks he's Ian's best friend, because he's spoken directly to them. It's a rare, rare gift.' It's an ability to reach out to an audience and include them in what's happening on stage. It's more obvious in soliloquy or in a one-man show like *Acting Shakespeare*, but it's most obvious in those music hall stars that McKellen admired so much back at the Bolton Grand, when Josef Locke held an audience spellbound through a long Thursday matinee.

And McKellen would be back doing *Acting Shakespeare* sooner than he expected. A triumphant coda was planned for his two years with the National Theatre. *Wild Honey* was to transfer to Broadway. Once again American Equity raised its head, and no other member of the British cast was allowed to join McKellen in the USA. The loss of the likes of Brewster Mason, Abigail McKern, Basil Henson and, most of all, Charlotte Cornwell as Anna Petrovna looked a tough one to sustain from the outset. So McKellen took a rare holiday in Antigua – definitely not research this time – and then headed for the States.

In October 1986 they got a muted response at the Ahmanson in Los Angeles, but there was still time to fix things before Broadway. Ten to fifteen minutes was cut from the London version, and the style was shifted more towards comedy. The tone was set by the poster, which had swapped the NT's smoky train emerging from a Russian forest plus the names of every member of the cast, for a picture of McKellen with his trousers falling down, which would have looked over the top outside a Ray Cooney farce. Where the play had been a wonderful ensemble event in London, in New York it was a star turn with a supporting cast that some reviewers felt wasn't up to the job.

They opened at the Virginia Theatre on 18 December. McKellen was staying with friends. 'The contract says I'm here for nine months,' he had observed warily in an *Evening Standard* interview a week earlier, 'but ... you know what it's like in this place.' It was just as well he didn't rent an apartment. The show lasted 28 performances. Roped together to ascend Mount Chekhov, this particular cast had plunged into a crevasse.

So, rather than go back to London with his tail between his legs, McKellen set off on a one-man odyssey around the United States, performing *Acting Shakespeare* wherever he could find an audience. In Washington he played to 1,800 a night in a vast touring theatre. In Boston he wound up in a converted synagogue which had last been used for male strippers. Cleveland offered a brand new theatre. In Columbia he did supper theatre, entertaining the diners. It was back to that childhood fantasy of setting up in a tent, doing the show and then moving on.

He did 200-odd performances over eight months, though there were often breaks between engagements. But the most important date, the one that would transform Ian McKellen's life, was San Francisco. Because in San Francisco he got talking gay politics to Steve Beery, Terry Anderson and his lover, Armistead Maupin, author of *Tales of the City*. And between them they would persuade the 49-year-old British actor to take the biggest step of his career.

7. LET'S TALK ABOUT ME . . .

Working in the USA always seems to bring on a crisis in Ian McKellen. In 1982 he came back from a year on Broadway, uncertain of what direction to take in his life and career. He moved in with Sean Mathias and took, for him, something of a sabbatical from acting. In 1987 he returned from his one-man US tour of *Acting Shakespeare*, asking himself whether acting was an honourable way of life at all. 'Or is it too ridiculous,' he wondered in an interview for the *Independent*, 'to dress up and pretend and show off in front of people if you're a grown up?'

It's a crisis of conscience which afflicts many actors at some point in their careers. In McKellen's case it had been brought on by those conversations with Armistead Maupin, Terry Anderson and Steve Beery. The latter had been the lover of Harvey Milk, the first openly gay politician in America, at the time when he was assassinated in San Francisco. Maupin, Anderson and Beery were now devoting much of their time to persuading gay celebrities to come out of the closet. They pointed out to McKellen the lack of openly gay actors. Shouldn't he be leading the way? The press had been tiptoeing round the issue for years. A very early interview in the *Observer* in 1966 had said that McKellen shared the flat at 25 Earls Terrace with 'a teacher' without specifying the sex of the teacher. This was Brodie, of course. As far back as 1977 the *Sunday Telegraph* magazine had published an article called 'What Makes Men Attractive?' suggesting that in some cases it was because they were 'unobtainable'. Mug shots of Rudolf Nureyev, Norman St John Stevas, David Hockney and Ian McKellen appeared alongside. A feature in the *Guardian* in 1982 by Michael Billington revealed that he was sharing his new house on Narrow Street with a man. But it was all hints and suggestions. Nothing had been openly stated by the press or by McKellen himself – though he liked a tease every now and then.

Richard Digby Day, Frank Dunlop's assistant back at Nottingham, remembers an occasion in November 1969, when the *Richard II/Edward II* tour reached Cardiff, where he was by now director of the Welsh Theatre Company: 'He insisted on me being invited to a party that was being given by the Lord Mayor of Cardiff for the Prospect Theatre Company, and then he made me walk arm in arm with him down the stairs of the Mansion House in Cardiff.'

But a young star actor teasing a few dignitaries in Cardiff is a different matter from Ian McKellen CBE coming out nationally. In 2005, when the Director of the Royal National Theatre is openly gay, and leading actors and directors like Simon Russell Beale, Antony Sher and Greg Doran make no secret of their homosexuality, the decision McKellen was trying to make looks insignificant. But look at Hollywood and you get a completely different picture. In Hollywood, even in the early 21st century, openly gay actors are extremely rare. If you're a screenwriter or a director or an agent, OK, but if you're an actor, everyone will tell you, 'Keep quiet.'

The gay actor's fear is simple – coming out of the closet will end his career. Once they know he is homosexual the public will either a) be repelled and avoid any plays or films in which he appears, b) not take him seriously in heterosexual roles, or c) he won't get any parts in the first place, because producers will fear public responses a) and b). That was the fear McKellen was facing in 1988, as he arrived back in England, still undecided about what he should do. Events were to force his hand.

The year 1987 had seen actor Stephen Fry produce *Hysteria*, a comedy benefit for the Terence Higgins Trust, an organisation set up in 1983 and named after the first man to die of AIDS in the UK. The Government had recently launched its 'Don't Die of Ignorance' cam-paign, complete with doom-laden imagery and sepulchral voice-over from John Hurt, designed to shock the nation into practising safe sex. The Terence Higgins Trust was looking to open the London Lighthouse just off Ladbroke Grove as a residential and support centre for people with HIV. Only they didn't have the money to complete the work. So, despite having just played it 200 times across the length and breadth of the USA, and despite having said he would never do the show in London, McKellen agreed to revive *Acting Shakespeare* yet again to raise funds for the project.

David Kernan's Show People donated their services as management; the Playhouse Theatre on Northumberland Avenue offered a reduced rent; every penny of the proceeds from the eleven-week run was to go to keeping work going on the London Lighthouse.

Acting Shakespeare was made up of extracts from the plays, arranged around a potted biography of the playwright, with anecdotes from his own and others' experiences as a Shakespearian actor. Peter Kemp in the *Independent* called it 'a prodigiously accomplished theatrical cabaret'. McKellen had kept the casual dress of the show's original incarnation at the Edinburgh Festival, and his first entrance, running through the audience and jumping up onto the stage, emphasised the same atmosphere. But over the years the show had become extremely slick. He did Falstaff and Hal from *Henry IV*, as they impersonate the old king.

He did a very moving Mistress Quickly, describing Falstaff's death. He played both Romeo and Juliet. He even incorporated an extended exegesis on Macbeth's 'tomorrow and tomorrow and tomorrow . . .' which would not have disgraced a John Barton seminar. Then, as the audience left, he was at the stage door with a bucket, collecting donations. 'I don't want to hear it rattle,' he told theatre-goers, 'I want to hear it rustle.'

The show opened on 11 December 1987 and played for eleven weeks. They were to be eleven extremely eventful weeks in the life of Ian McKellen.

At the beginning of January 1988 he was doorstepped at the stage door by a gay activist, distributing leaflets about Clause 28 of the Conservative government's Local Government Bill. The clause aimed to ban local authorities from 'promoting homosexuality' or presenting 'pretended family relationships' in the classrooms of state schools. Many might agree that actively 'promoting homosexuality' should be no part of a local authority's remit, but the clause appeared to limit a school's ability to teach sex education to its pupils and could even be construed as making it illegal for a local library to stock books by gay authors or for a local authority to fund a theatre that put on a play by a gay writer. Described to McKellen by government whip Tristan Garel-Jones as 'red meat thrown to our right-wing wolves', opposition to Clause 28 would become a rallying point for British gays, and for a broader group which called itself the Arts Lobby. McKellen was soon a leading member of the Arts Lobby, and an already busy week got a lot busier.

On Sunday 24 January he was speaking at a rally for people with AIDS in Hyde Park in the afternoon and presenting an award at the Laurence Olivier Awards in the evening. It was an opportunity for another political speech, and a roar of approval went up from the audience when McKellen denounced Clause 28. The following day the Arts Lobby staged a well-publicised protest against the Clause outside the Playhouse Theatre. Standing in line for the photographers alongside McKellen were Melvyn Bragg, Michael Cashman, Eleanor Bron, Terry Jones, Sheila Hancock, Lenny Henry and John Schlesinger. A message of support was delivered from the Oliviers.

But Wednesday was the big day. Before the evening performance of *Acting Shakespeare*, McKellen had been invited to take part in a live debate on Clause 28 on Radio 3's arts programme, *Third Ear*. Peregrine Worsthorne had written an editorial in the *Sunday Telegraph* arguing that homosexuals brought intolerance on themselves because of their 'proselytising cult'. McKellen was there to argue the case against him.

The situation contained some irony in that Worsthorne had already publicly declared that he had had a youthful gay affair with George Melly while at school. As the debate grew more heated, and Worsthorne mounted another attack, referring to gays as 'them', McKellen finally came out with it: 'Let's not talk in the abstract. Let's not talk about "them". Let's talk about me.'

It was not quite as dramatic as it might have been. In fact, a week earlier McKellen had described himself as 'gay' on a programme on the BBC World Service. Presumably nobody had been listening. But some people must have been listening to Radio 3 that Wednesday evening, because McKellen's announcement was almost at once hot news. An appearance on *Wogan* shortly afterwards, on which he told Terry Wogan's vast TV audience, 'I've been a homosexual all my life,' was the clincher.

In the meantime and before all this, there was what for many people is the toughest part of all – coming out to the family. First port of call was the village in the Lake District where stepmother, Gladys, by now in her 80s, was living. McKellen drove her out into the countryside, the hills he had loved since he was a boy. Trying to avoid giving her too much of a shock, he warned Gladys he had something important to tell her. But when he'd finished, his stepmother seemed anything but shocked. In fact, she claimed always to have known he was gay. So far so easy. Next stop was sister Jean, a married teacher with two children. In an *Evening Standard* interview, McKellen recalled her response: 'I wish you'd told me earlier because I have a gay friend who's going through a lot of problems. I would have loved to have talked to you about it and I couldn't. I didn't feel you wanted to.'

So none of the shock and disapproval McKellen had feared all those years from his family materialised. In fact, having come out to his stepmother and sister, he found he felt much closer to what remained of his family. Another gay activist says this about his own experience of coming out: 'It makes you look back over your whole life before, and think things could have been so much better.' So could there have been that closeness earlier?

Of course, there were two members of his family that McKellen couldn't tell – his mother and father. The secrecy he'd maintained so long had been a divide between him and his family – a divide which death meant could never now be wholly bridged. In January 1991, looking back over his life, McKellen told Robert Hewison, 'I despise the Ian McKellen of the first forty-nine years of his life.'

And there was a great irony to his having finally come out as an openly gay man, because the relationship with Sean Mathias was over.

In fact, McKellen would later claim that part of the reason he delayed coming out was so as not to out Sean at the same time.

The disaster with *Cowardice* had not put Sean off writing for the theatre but, wisely, he'd decided to switch his attentions to fringe theatre. *Infidelities* had been Perrier Pick of the Fringe at the Edinburgh Festival in 1985. He followed that success up the following year with *A Prayer for Wings* which won a Fringe First Award, transferred to the Bush Theatre in London and was hailed as the work of a major new Welsh playwriting talent. Thirty-one years old in 1987, with some success but still nothing to match the fame of his lover, Sean had decided it was time to strike out on his own.

Some friends saw him as the villain of the piece, the younger man deserting his older lover. But McKellen, at least some years after the event, was more philosophical. He had never seen the relationship as a marriage, intended to last for ever. 'There is something about two people of the same gender living together which is utterly different from a man and a woman living together,' he told Lynda Lee-Potter. 'I don't think of it as a marriage. It's two people who decide to share their lives, not necessarily for ever.' Many long-term gay couples find a formula in which the partners allow each other to take a series of other sexual partners, but remain living together – an open marriage in effect. For McKellen that was never an option. 'Promiscuity is not something I've ever indulged in,' he declared in the same interview. 'Promiscuity seems to me just too much hard work.'

Sean Mathias has offered insights into McKellen which reveal some of the personal tensions in their relationship. He's called him pernickety and obsessive. He's also called him childlike. Retaining the child's ability to see things anew is a great gift for an actor who wants to bring something fresh to the classics, but Sean seems to have found it maddening to deal with as a person. But, despite Sean moving out, their working relationship and indeed friendship would continue, and McKellen would continue to advance the career of the younger man whenever he could, sometimes to the detriment of his own reputation.

'Coming out is a bit like finding Jesus if you're a Christian,' says David Allison of the gay campaigning group Outrage! 'Suddenly the blinkers are removed, life seems so much better, freer, more relaxed. You're not looking over your shoulder all the time to see who's listening. You're not worried about walking into a gay bar or taking a gay book out of a library.'

McKellen echoed the sentiment back in 1988, telling *Gay Times* he felt, 'buoyant, self-content and deeply happy'. And there was the fervour of the religious convert there too – perhaps not surprising for someone with McKellen's background. In fact, he seems to have seen the campaigning work into which he now threw all the energies he had previously devoted to acting as being part of his rapprochement with his family. There were generations of missionaries and preachers in his ancestry – nonconformists who believed that you had to walk the walk as well as talk the talk. McKellen had admired them, but never followed in their footsteps, having abandoned organised religion many years back. Now he had found his own kind of missionary work, preaching tolerance and acceptance of homosexuals.

He was soon treading the corridors of power, attempting to persuade ministers of the folly of Clause 28. He saw his Cambridge contemporary Michael Howard, then local government minister and since leader of the Tory party. He saw Baroness Cox, later deputy speaker in the House of Lords and then a strong supporter of the Clause, and left with her agreement to become patron of an organisation to promote public understanding of homosexuality. But nobody changed their minds. One campaigner remembered McKellen returning from another unsuccessful meeting almost in tears, feeling he had personally let the gay community down. He seems to have believed he could change government policy single handed.

In February the run of *Acting Shakespeare* came to an end. McKellen had raised some £500,000 for the London Lighthouse, and they responded by naming a public room after him. He took a brief time-out from campaigning for a trip to Yugoslavia to make a video for gay pop duo the Pet Shop Boys' latest single, 'Heart'. The actor's turn as Dracula helped lift the song to number one in the charts. The same month he was training to be an AIDS counsellor. 'I don't like saying he's a saint,' one campaigning colleague told the *Independent* in February 1988, 'but I can't think of any horrible things about him.' The Pet Shop Boys would repay McKellen by agreeing to play live at an anti-Clause 28 benefit at the Piccadilly Theatre in June. The show was called *Before the Act*.

In the end there was some minor change. An amendment, put forward in the House of Lords by Viscount Falkland of the SDP (now the Liberal Democrats), did seem to lift the most obvious threat to the arts. McKellen was widely credited with the success, such as it was. But, despite three lesbians abseiling into the chamber from the public gallery during the final debate, on 24 May Section 28 of the Local Government Bill passed into law. As a final protest four campaigners invaded the studios of BBC Radio 4's *Today* programme. The debate about whether such direct action or McKellen's lobbying work behind the scenes was more effective in promoting the gay rights agenda would remain a topic of heated dispute among gay activists.

In March 1988 McKellen hit the road again, doing *Acting Shakespeare* in a series of Sunday night one-offs all over the country. Again all the proceeds were going to charity, either AIDS organisations or a new name – Stonewall.

Michael Cashman, then an actor in *EastEnders* and one half of the famous first gay kiss on British TV, told *Gay Times* in May 1996 the original idea for Stonewall came from him. 'When I first suggested it would be good if there was an organisation to lobby and campaign to prevent something like Clause 28 happening, Ian looked at me as if I was completely mad. When somebody else made exactly the same suggestion about six weeks later, he took them seriously.'

Specifically brought into being by Clause 28, Stonewall and other gay rights organisations which followed were also a reaction to a perceived heightening of homophobia in British society. HIV and AIDS infection rates were steadily mounting in the UK through the late 80s and 90s, and the disease was still being called 'the gay plague'. In August 1989 George Gale, a columnist in the *Daily Mail*, suggested all homosexuals were likely to spread AIDS and were therefore incipient murderers. It was a time when gay people felt the need to come together for self-protection and to assert their rights under the law.

The name of the new organisation came from a clash between police and homosexuals in America in 1969, which has passed into gay legend. New York police carried out a raid on a gay bar in Greenwich Village called the Stonewall Inn and, when trouble ensued, for the first time gay people resisted arrest and fought back. There has been a Gay Pride march in New York every June since to commemorate the event. Within a year the Gay Liberation Front was founded in the US, starting the modern gay rights movement. However, calling the organisation which McKellen and Cashman were setting up Stonewall had its ironies, because this was no direct action group. In Stonewall's own words, 'Their aim was to create a professional lobbying group that would prevent such attacks on lesbians, gay men and bisexuals ever occurring again and to put the case for equality on the mainstream political agenda by winning support within all the political parties.' In other words it was to be a continuation of the polite meetings McKellen had had with Michael Howard and others, not abseiling into the House of Lords or interrupting Sue Lawley mid-news.

Not everyone was impressed. Not long after Stonewall came into existence, more radically minded homosexuals, preferring to call themselves 'queer', set up an organisation devoted to direct action called Outrage!. David Allison, a member of Outrage! explains, 'It was modelled on the American gay rights group Queer Nation, which held very theatrical demonstrations – not just marches but carefully staged events – a very media savvy campaign.'

Outrage! staged queer kiss-ins and weddings, as well as outing ten Church of England bishops in 1994. Emphasising the distance between them and Stonewall, one Outrage! campaigner speaks of 'rejecting the assimilationist and conformist politics of the mainstream lesbian and gay rights movement'. David Allison is more accommodating, believing that McKellen has actually achieved more for gay rights through his dealing with 'the movers and shakers' than has Outrage! founder Peter Tatchell with his 'more in your face approach'. With typical moderation McKellen has always believed there was room for both approaches.

As for the distinction between gay and queer, David Allison calls it 'a quasi-theological thing', suggesting a distinction without a difference. 'Some people,' he says, 'see the word "gay" as associated with the more commercial side and "queer" is the more political side. But a lot of people have problems with the word "queer" because they've heard it as an insult their whole lives and they don't understand the idea of trying to take it back.' But quasi-theological or not, the division between people campaigning for homosexual equality in different ways would turn a couple of years later into personal attacks on McKellen himself. Angela Mason, who became Stonewall's executive director in 1992, told Tilly McAuley, 'I think sometimes he has been hurt by some of the extreme criticism.'

Stonewall's campaign focused on achieving equality under the law for homosexuals. But McKellen also saw it as part of his personal mission to encourage other well-known people in Britain out of the closet. Actor Simon Callow was already out. Indeed he had probably been the first actor voluntarily to out himself in his book *Being an Actor* in 1984. Antony Sher did follow McKellen's lead in 1989, declaring himself in a press interview, and receiving a surprise phone call of thanks from McKellen, whom he didn't know, the following Sunday in Stratford.

But not everyone was so eager to try what McKellen described in *Gay Times* as 'a delightful experience'. Nigel Hawthorne, who didn't come out publicly until 1995 at the age of 65, protested that he and partner, Trevor Bentham, opened the annual fête in the village in Hertfordshire where they had lived together since 1979, and that if the vicar knew they were a gay couple, it would be dreadfully embarrassing for all concerned. Sir John Gielgud gave money quietly to Stonewall, but absolutely refused when McKellen asked him if he would make his contributions public. Pressed by McKellen to reveal once and for all whether he was gay or straight, Alan Bennett replied that this was like asking a man crawling across the Sahara whether he would prefer Perrier or Malvern water. After a couple of years of this, there were those – gay and straight – who thought McKellen was becoming a gay bore. Certainly no article about McKellen since 1988 has been complete without a retelling of the coming-out-on-live-radio story, and every chat show appearance has come in two parts – the acting section and the gay section.

McKellen is unapologetic. He is well aware of the dangers of celebrities sounding off about every issue under the sun. But acting and being a gay man are two things he knows something about. So why shouldn't he talk about them?

But back in 1988, amidst all the campaigning – and he was soon throwing his weight behind campaigns to save the rediscovered Rose Theatre and remove VAT from theatre tickets – there was still the little matter of acting to be considered.

McKellen had come out in the full belief that it could mean the end of his acting career. But he had decided that if the public wouldn't accept him as a gay man, then his career wasn't worth having. To test the water he chose not a return to the subsidised safety of the RSC or National but the toughest route of all, the commercial West End, where success or failure is measured in raw box office receipts. The play was Alan Ayckbourn's latest, a typically bleak comedy called *Henceforward*, set in a London of the future where law and order has totally broken down. McKellen was to play Jerome, a composer who is comfortable with his electronic music and his robot servants, but profoundly uncomfortable with real people. The part turned out to be a thoroughly unhappy experience for McKellen, but not for the reasons he expected.

Part of the problem was that he was taking over the role from someone else. Barry McCarthy had already played the part successfully in Scarborough and on a five-country British Council tour. But producer Michael Codron thought they needed stars for London, so in came his favourite actor Ian McKellen, and Jane Asher, who was doing a comic double as an obedient robot in the first act and Jerome's wife in the second. Alan Ayckbourn, directing his own play, could never under-stand why rehearsing a part which he knew worked with the audience was such heavy going with McKellen.

In his biography *Alan Ayckbourn – Grinning at the Edge*, Paul Alan gives his view of the problems between star and playwright: 'When Ayckbourn faces a problem he can't solve he seems to cut himself off from everything other than the basic formalities of a relationship, and McKellen became more and more frustrated at being unable to uncover a part in the way he was used to, digging for more meaning in the text and searching for a key to the character.'

But Ayckbourn isn't Chekhov and he isn't Shakespeare. Many actors will tell you that his plays are essentially machines for generating laughter and that the actors are cogs which must turn efficiently in the machine. Digging for extra layers of meaning and character doesn't work. Yes, there's usually a dark subtext somewhere, but ultimately everything is sacrificed to the gag. When McKellen wanted changes to the script to clarify some character point, Ayckbourn refused point blank because he knew the change would upset the rhythm of the lines and spoil the laugh.

Michael Simkins, playing the social worker Mervyn, was in his eighth Ayckbourn production. McKellen was in his first. In an interview with the *Independent* Simkins likened Ayckbourn the director to 'a sheepdog that slowly hounds you into the pen he wants'. With Mike Alfreds at the National McKellen had discovered his delight in absolute freedom on the stage. The director as sheepdog was something else.

Jane Asher, who had worked with McKellen back in 1973 when the Cambridge Theatre Company's production of *The Recruiting Officer* was filmed for TV, reported rows about props and costumes and particularly about how the play had been done before. She also focused on the central problem of *Henceforward*, which is that although Jerome is the main character, he doesn't get the laughs, which can be a bitter pill to swallow for a star actor.

The play opened on 21 November 1988 at the Vaudeville Theatre to generally excellent reviews, though McKellen's performance was not greatly admired. It was six years since he'd done a modern play, and even then *Bent* and, even more so *Amadeus*, had been period pieces. In the next seventeen years he did not appear in another new stage play, and it's a general criticism of McKellen as an actor that on stage he has never been as convincing in a modern setting as in period drama.

Geoffrey Banks visited backstage at the Vaudeville and found his old pupil and friend thoroughly out of sorts and complaining that Ayckbourn should never be allowed to direct his own plays because he was far too protective of every line. A couple of years later at the National McKellen confided to Brian Cox how boring he had found doing the play, lending credence to tales that McKellen wandered the stage of the Vaudeville Theatre during performances of *Henceforward* muttering, 'Boring, boring,' under his breath.

Henceforward may not have been an enjoyable job personally for McKellen, but the success of the play in the West End, as well as his casting as John Profumo in the film *Scandal*, certainly suggested that his career had not been harmed by coming out. From that point on, his life would become a balancing act between acting and campaigning, with the two frequently coming together. On 25 June 1989 he played Max again in *Bent* at the Adelphi Theatre for one night only as a benefit for Stonewall with an all-star cast including Ralph Fiennes, Richard E Grant, Alex Jennings and Ian Charleson who had already been diagnosed with AIDS. Directing was Sean Mathias. Such was the success of the evening that McKellen approached Richard Eyre at the National Theatre about a full-scale revival of the play, and Eyre rapidly slotted in thirty performances for the New Year in the Lyttleton, as well as setting in motion plans for a transfer to the West End. Once again Sean Mathias directed. Despite Sean having moved out of the house in Narrow Street, McKellen wanted to keep his friendship; inviting him to direct at the National Theatre was also giving his career a massive boost.

The original director of *Bent*, Robert Chetwyn, the man who had nurtured McKellen as a young talent at Ipswich rep and directed his *Hamlet*, was less than impressed. 'I didn't feel the need to do it again,' he claims. 'I felt I'd done what I could with it. But no one even bothered to invite me, and I did find that a bit hurtful.' When Sheridan Morley's review in the *International Herald Tribune* referred to him as 'the late Robert Chetwyn', insult was added to injury. 'I know I'm often late,' Chetwyn pointed out to the critic when they ran into each other at a function not long afterwards, 'but I'm still alive.'

The revival of *Bent* began previews at the Lyttleton on 5 January 1990. The following day Ian Charleson died. McKellen, Richard Eyre and other actor friends flew up to Scotland for the funeral. The death of Ian Charleson crystallised for many actors the impact AIDS was having on the theatre, and with *Bent* playing on the South Bank there was a feeling that the National Theatre was responding to a national issue in the way that it should. Most critics thought the production inferior to the original. Michael Cashman, they felt, didn't measure up to Tom Bell's harrowing portrayal of Horst, and the Lyttleton Theatre, along with Sean Mathias's direction, rendered the whole evening somehow underpowered. Michael Coveney in the *Observer* thought McKellen pulled off 'brilliantly the difficult feat of making Max both despicable and pitiable', but there was much more comment in the press on how appropriate it was that the National should be mounting this statement about gay survival at a time when homosexuals were perceived to be under threat both from disease and an anti-gay government.

After the National, the production ran at the Garrick until 21 April with the cast slipping in an extra Sunday performance on 9 April with proceeds going to the Royal Free Hospital to care for those with AIDS and to clinics in Bucharest looking after babies with AIDS. The whole production had been half theatre and half campaigning/fundraising, exactly the balancing act McKellen was by then looking to achieve. Michael Cashman went on to abandon acting altogether, becoming a Member of the European Parliament in 1999. McKellen was asked by one gay group to stand for parliament following the battle over Section 28. 'I considered it,' he told James Rampton of the *Independent*. 'I thought it would be fascinating to see how the political process actually worked. But then I said to myself, "Suppose I actually got elected – wouldn't that be dreadful?" ' He continued his balancing act instead.

But his high profile as a campaigner was still not appreciated by all, and divisions rose spectacularly to the surface in 1991 when the New Year's honours list included a knighthood for one Ian Murray McKellen. McKellen had agonised, albeit briefly, about whether to accept. The call had come when he was on tour with the National Theatre in Paris. Director Richard Eyre was summoned early on the morning of 23 November 1990 to the apartment belonging to film director Tony Richardson, where McKellen was staying. He arrived to find McKellen both anxious and elated.

'I've been offered a knighthood,' were his first words. 'Do you think I should take it?'

The problem was, of course, that it was the very same Conservative government which had pushed through Section 28, headed by the arch demon herself, Margaret Thatcher, that was now offering a knighthood to one of its most tireless critics. Indeed, McKellen noted the irony that okaying his honour must have been one of Thatcher's final acts as she was being deposed by her own party.

Eyre gave the nod. 'He was relieved,' he wrote in *National Service: Diary of a Decade*, the diary of his tenure at the NT, 'but being Ian wouldn't show his elation.'

McKellen also telephoned Sean Mathias and Michael Cashman. They gave the go-ahead as well. It could only boost the profile of Stonewall and give further proof that coming out as a gay man need not harm your career. After all here was one becoming a knight of the realm. When the announcement appeared in the papers, some in the gay community were

Above left The RSC at last: as Romeo opposite Francesca Annis in 1976 – 'Thus with a kiss I die . . .' (© Rex Features)

Above right The legendary 1976 *Macbeth* with Judi Dench at The Other Place in Stratford, just after the murder of Duncan. Many still think this McKellen's finest performance. (© Rex Features)

Left Back at The Other Place in 1989 as Iago, cradling Imogen Stubbs's Desdemona in his arms, shortly before Othello kills her. (Joe Cocks Studio Collection © Shakespeare Birthplace Trust)

Right In the original production at the Royal Court in 1979 McKellen and Tom Bell make love without touching in the key scene from *Bent*. (© John Haynes)

Below In the film version of *Bent* in 1997, directed by his ex-lover Sean Mathias (centre), McKellen had a cameo as Uncle Freddie while up-and-coming star Clive Owen (right) played the part of Max. (© Allstar/Cinetext/Orion)

Left With Melvyn Bragg during the making of Ian McKellen's 'Diary of a Year' for *The South Bank Show* in 1985.
(© Rex Features)

Below Marching at a gay rights parade with playwright Larry Kramer, author of *The Normal Heart*, the first play to draw attention to the AIDS crisis.
(© Rex Features)

Above In the run-up to the Oscars, McKellen hosted US TV's *Saturday Night Live* in drag on 16 March 2002, kissing anchorman Jimmy Fallon on the lips. (© Rex Features)

Below Waving to the crowd at the gay Pride London parade 3 July 2004, with London Mayor Ken Livingstone (right). (© Corbis/Paul Hackett)

Left McKellen broke cinematic convention, speaking straight into camera for the soliloquies in the film of *Richard III*, directed by Richard Loncraine in 1996. (© Corbis)

Below left After *Richard III*, Hollywood finally beckoned. Director Bryan Singer cast McKellen as the old Nazi Kurt Dussander in *Apt Pupil* in 1998. (© Corbis)

Below right As gay film director James Whale in *Gods and Monsters* in 1998, McKellen was playing a role closer to himself than ever before. (© Corbis)

Above 'I always seem to find myself attached to unavailable men,' joked former White House intern Monica Lewinsky at the London premiere of *Gods and Monsters,* with McKellen and Boy George. (© Rex Features)

Below As Magneto in *X-Men 2* (2003), using his powers to escape the specially constructed plastic prison. (© Rex Features)

Left Gandalf in *The Lord of the Rings* trilogy turned McKellen into the international star friends say he had always wanted to be. (© Rex Features)

Below left Peter Jackson in trademark shorts directs Gandalf the White on the set of *The Lord of the Rings*. (© Rex Features)

Below right Walking up the pink carpet at the premiere of Richard Eyre's film *Stage Beauty*, 23 August 2004. The beard was for *Neverwas*, filming in British Columbia the following month. (© Rex Features)

delighted, re-christening the new theatrical knight Sir Ian as 'Serena'. Others were disgusted.

Radical filmmaker Derek Jarman, a prominent supporter of Outrage!, wrote to the *Guardian* to protest. Theatre critic Nicholas de Jongh and Simon Watney, a founder of Outrage!, suggested some toning down of the first draft of the letter, but what appeared in the paper on the morning of 4 January 1991 was angry and personal enough.

'As a queer artist,' wrote Jarman, 'I find it impossible to react with anything but dismay to his acceptance of this honour from a government which has stigmatised homosexuality . . . maybe Ian McKellen will use his knighthood to try to influence the government. But I'm not at all certain – I think it's a co-option and allows anyone to say, "The Tory party isn't so bad: it's not really anti-gay. After all it gave Ian McKellen a knighthood." ' Jarman concluded with the personal question, 'Why did you accept this award, Ian? It has diminished you.'

McKellen supporters mobilised immediately for a reply. The initial idea seems to have come from Antony Sher. Certainly it was he who phoned Ned Sherrin to get him on board. The carefully worded letter they concocted began with that 'quasi-theological thing', picking up on Jarman's opening:

'As Gay and Lesbian artists, we would like to respectfully distance ourselves from Derek Jarman's article. We regard [McKellen's] knighthood as a significant landmark in the history of the British Gay Movement. Never again will public figures be able to claim that they have to keep secret their homosexuality in fear of it damaging their careers. Ian McKellen provides an inspiration to us all, not only as an artist of extraordinary gifts, but as a public figure of remarkable honesty and dignity.'

The letter had eighteen signatories, including Simon Callow, Michael Cashman, Stephen Fry, Alec McCowen, Cameron Mackintosh, John Schlesinger, Antony Sher, Martin Sherman, Ned Sherrin and Nicholas Wright, not all of whom were out at the time.

Jarman, of course, had more than earned the right to his opinion, having been diagnosed HIV positive in 1986 and becoming one of the few public figures to talk openly about his illness. A leading member of Outrage! and a perennial controversialist, Jarman famously called Rudolf Nureyev a sad little man from Siberia and Simon Callow a bumbling old vulgarian, but he reserved his real vitriol for Stonewall. Denying that sexual preference made a community in the first place, he dismissed the lobby group as a bunch of assimilationists kowtowing to authority. And king of the assimilationists was Ian McKellen. He pointed out that McKellen was accepting his honour in the same year as the romantic novelist Barbara Cartland and Manchester Chief Constable James Anderton who had once referred to the HIV positive as wallowing in a 'cesspit of their own making'. Still more ironically, McKellen's original antagonist on Radio 3's *Third Ear*, Peregrine Worsthorne, also got a knighthood that year.

David Allison, who knew Jarman as a regular attender at Outrage! meetings, thinks the filmmaker's antipathy to McKellen ran deeper than political differences. 'I think there may have been some kind of personal rivalry there in artistic terms,' he says, with McKellen again a figure of the establishment with his ties to the RSC and National Theatre and Jarman the maverick outsider, shooting his movies on a shoestring budget. Jarman would later make a proposal to Channel 4 for a film called *Pansy* in which he satirised McKellen as Sir Thespian Night. Sadly the film was never made.

The storm over the knighthood blew over quickly enough. George Melly wrote to the *Standard* arguing both sides of the case. Lindsay Anderson wrote to Jarman personally, congratulating him on his stand. But most people seemed to be on McKellen's side. Lisa Power, Secretary General of the International Lesbian and Gay Association, put it to journalist Robert Cheshyre in August 1992 like this: 'I don't believe in the honours system, but if there are people who pay attention because someone has a handle to his name, let's use it.'

And that is surely the point – the same point made by those eighteen signatories to the *Guardian*. As the respectable face of gay activism, McKellen has access to those in power. As a knight of the realm he is still more respectable and some people may listen to him more. But perhaps more importantly, and this is the line he would take himself, he offers a role model for young gay people, coming out to their parents and friends, who can say, 'Well, look, Sir Ian McKellen is gay. So it can't be that bad, can it?'

Later McKellen himself developed mixed feelings. Part of him seems to wish he'd joined the likes of Michael Frayn, Alan Bennett and Albert Finney, all of whom for various reasons turned down a knighthood, and also Vanessa Redgrave, who refused to become a Dame. But that's typical of the man – part ex-head boy, part the outsider who never wanted to work for the RSC in the first place.

'The joke is that there could never be a less knightly person than Ian,' Trevor Nunn told the *Sunday Telegraph*. But that McKellen has had access to the corridors of power there is no doubt at all. On 6 February

1991 he was at the Home Office meeting John Patten to discuss Clause 25 of the Criminal Justice Bill, which proposed to reclassify certain homosexual acts as rape. Then on 1 July the politicians came to the actor, when Prime Minister John Major visited the National Theatre to see *Napoli Milionaria*. Afterwards he and Norma had dinner with McKellen and other members of the cast in the National's Richardson Room. At McKellen's request Lady Soames, chair of the National Theatre board, sat him and Major side by side.

As far as these kind of official functions ever are, it was a relaxed occasion. McKellen offered Major vocal coaching on the strict understanding that he didn't use it to win the next election. Then he seized his opportunity. 'Would now be an appropriate time to express some of my concerns on gay issues?'

'Why not come to Downing Street?' was the response.

So he did.

On 24 September 1991, with costume and props for the occasion – raincoat and briefcase – Sir Ian McKellen arrived for his meeting with the Prime Minister at 10 Downing Street. As soon as they were seated, McKellen produced a copy of the Pink Guide to London which, among other things, identifies the homes of famous homosexuals. Major nervously asked why Number 10 was on the front cover, and McKellen explained that one of his predecessors in office, William Pitt the Younger, had been an undeclared gay. He then raised the full range of issues that Stonewall had identified as of pressing concern if homosexuals were to achieve equality under the law – the age of consent, the laws on gross indecency, soliciting and procuring, a review of police conduct, the status of gays in the armed forces and registered partnerships. McKellen also suggested that Major's beloved Citizen's Charter outlawing discrimination should include discrimination on the grounds of sexuality. Major wasn't interested in specific policies. His aim, he said, was to find out more. Coincidentally, his next meeting that day was with French Prime Minister Edith Cresson who had recently declared that 25 per cent of the male population of the USA, Germany and the UK was homosexual.

Major received a tide of critical letters after the meeting. Some of his own backbenchers were none too happy about their leader dallying with a declared homosexual. But Conservative backbenchers were not the only ones unhappy with McKellen's meeting with John Major. Derek Jarman demanded to know why the actor had gone alone to 10 Downing Street to put the gay case. Who and what gave him the right to represent all homosexuals?

McKellen countered that he had been representing no one but himself. But he agreed the test of the meeting's success, if any, would be what was in the Conservative manifesto for the 1992 election. In the event there was nothing. However, Major did agree to a debate on equalising the age of consent for homosexuals, announcing a free vote on 31 May 1992. Naturally, McKellen was in the public gallery for the debate. The bill was proposed by Edwina Currie, former minister in the Department of Health and MP for South Derbyshire. Parliament Square was blocked by 5,000 activists, and when the Commons opted for eighteen rather than full equality, violence on the streets ended in eight arrests and a police sergeant being knocked unconscious as protesters tried to storm the Commons.

Other changes followed. In 1994 homosexuality in the forces was decriminalised, though gay servicemen and women remained subject to discharge. The following year McKellen would be in the public gallery again as a legal challenge to the ruling was mounted in the High Court.

Still trying to combine performing with campaigning, McKellen revamped his one-man show for an arts festival accompanying the Gay Games of 1994 in New York. He gave the show the punning title *A Knight Out*. Like a cross between *Words Words Words* and *Acting Shakespeare*, the show was essentially a compendium of extracts from past performances and readings from other texts. As an encore he even included a dramatic rendition of the Beaufort Scale's surprisingly evocative definitions of weather conditions from 'Force Two. Light breeze. Wind felt on face,' through to the full King Lear of 'Force ten. Who-oole gale! Trees uprooted!' But where *Acting Shakespeare* was held together by the narrative of the playwright's life, *A Knight Out* was held together by a narrative of McKellen's life as an actor and gay man, and all the extracts linked in some way to the gay theme. There was *Edward II* of course. There were the two Aufidius scenes from *Coriolanus*. There was James I's letter to his gay lover. But the moment which aroused most controversy was when McKellen took a copy of the Bible and tore out Chapter 18 verse 22 of Leviticus which runs, 'You shall not lie with a man as with a woman. It is an abomination.'

When it reached Britain in November 1994, the show was condemned by the church as profane. Scottish Tory MP Sir Nicholas Fairbairn demanded the actor should be locked up. A member of the London Muslim parliament damned the action as a reflection of a morally bankrupt society. The audience thought differently, greeting the ripping of the Bible with rapturous applause. McKellen went on to reveal that he also regularly tore the offending page from Gideon Bibles in his US hotel rooms. 'I don't want it in the drawer,' he said in a *Times* interview in May 2003, 'burning its way into my mind while I'm trying to get a good night's sleep. I know I shouldn't do it, but I feel so much better for having done it.' He sounds conscious of the schoolboy naughtiness of the action – the sort of stuff the Captain of Bolton School would never have got up to.

A powerful account of the difficulties homosexuals have faced through history and a plea for acceptance and understanding, *A Knight Out* would reappear off and on for the next eight years, fitted in between other commitments. He took it as far afield as South Africa, playing the Market Theatre in Johannesburg just months after the first free elections in the country brought Nelson Mandela to power. He took it as close to home as the new St Paul's Arts Centre on the Isle of Dogs, a mile downriver from his home in Limehouse. But what the audience found most fascinating about the evening was what it revealed of McKellen himself. He told stories of his uncertain childhood, of the realisation at the age of twelve that he was gay and his anxieties as he waited to see if he was changing sex. He was funny about his unrequited passion for Derek Jacobi at Cambridge. He was bullish about his status as the first openly gay actor knight. But A E Housman's lines written to Oscar Wilde as he started his sentence in Reading Gaol in 1895 resonated as loudly as anything. Housman describes the experience of being homosexual in a world where it was a crime:

And how am I to face the odds
Of Man's bedevilment and God's?
I a stranger and afraid
In a world I never made.

For all his feeling 'buoyant, self-content and deeply happy' in the aftermath of coming out, there remains in everything McKellen has to say about growing up gay in Lancashire in the 1950s a deep sense of hurt, the hurt in Housman's poem, a hurt that has never really gone away. His parents had taught him to stand up for what he believed and above all to be honest. But he had never been honest with them about this central part of his nature, about what he called in the *Independent* in December 2003 the 'terrible personal burden' that he was carrying. 'How can this not leave you scarred?' he asked rhetorically in a *Times* interview that same year.

So there's regret, and there's a measure of guilt there too – guilt at not having stood up to be counted sooner. For McKellen had come to believe that feeling it was necessary to hide his homosexuality meant that he hadn't liked who he was, that he had himself been homophobic for the first 49 years of his life.

Coming out transformed every aspect of Ian McKellen's life. There is a sense in which everything about the man is either before or after that 1988 radio show. There are those who believe it led him to cut off aspects of his former existence, including friends and even ex-lovers. His first long-term lover, Brian Taylor, observes, 'We were together for seven years. But it's always Sean Mathias he talks about, not me.'

One mutual friend points to that crucial turning point in 1988: 'Really what happened was that Ian cut everything off when he decided to come out, and he was making a clean sweep and aiming in a totally other direction, so Brodie had to go.'

What is certain is that, in McKellen's own estimation, coming out transformed him as an actor. The Other Place in 1976, Mike Alfreds in 1985 and coming out in 1988 – those are the experiences which created McKellen the mature actor. Small theatres taught him to focus a performance without resort to the grand manner; Mike Alfreds taught him to improvise in performance and keep a production dangerous and alive; and coming out?

In April 1969, twenty years before he came out publicly as a gay man, McKellen described the attraction of acting to journalist Paul Sheridan like this: 'To pull the wool over an audience's eyes with make-up and performance, that's a kind of magic because you have made a mystery of yourself.' He called the make-up, which had been such an integral part of his most successful Cambridge roles, 'ointments of deceit'. The following year he was describing to the Illustrated London News his admiration for the music hall artistes he had watched from backstage at the old Bolton Grand: 'Being able to step on a stage and do something totally at variance with one's personality seemed a very exciting accomplishment.'

So acting was about mystery and deceit and disguising who you are. Or was it? Because in the very same 1969 interview he was saying, 'I have had the experience many times during the rehearsal of a play when the director has called out, "That's it. That's exactly right," and I've known that at that moment I was giving away a bit of myself, had not been able to stop it.' So McKellen always knew that for him acting was not at its best about mystery and deceit and disguising who you are, it was about what Peter Hall calls the revelation of self through text.

Laurence Olivier built stage characters from the outside. He liked to talk about the actor as a skeleton: 'Bone, just bone onto which he places and moulds the flesh [of a character]', as he puts it in *On Acting*. For Olivier getting into character was a covering up, a disguise. For the 'Olivier from Wigan' it was the other way round. The process of rehearsal for McKellen was a stripping away of outside layers until the actor can reveal in performance the part of himself, which is like the character he is playing. Acting is 'an ability to expose yourself, to tell the audience things about yourself even you don't really know,' he told *Harper's and Queen* in April 1976. He'd proved he didn't mind taking his clothes off on stage. In fact, he'd proved that he was utterly fearless on stage. The problem was that before 1988 there was a core to his innermost self that he wasn't prepared to expose. It explained, he now realised, why his Hamlet had not been the success he had hoped for. To play Hamlet the actor needs voice and body to be in perfect condition. That much he'd had in 1971. But at its best the part is really about allowing an audience to see into the actor's soul, to find out who the actor is as much as who Hamlet is. Ian Charleson's painfully truthful account of the part of Hamlet, which McKellen watched on the night of 13 November 1989, was made in the shadow of Charleson's own death and only came about because the role had brought on physical and mental exhaustion in the original Hamlet, Daniel Day-Lewis. Seeing Charleson on stage had made McKellen realise that he'd failed in 1971 precisely because he wasn't prepared to allow an audience fully to know who he was.

Charlotte Cornwell has worked with McKellen both before and after his coming out. She was in *Wild Honey* in 1984 and she took over from Clare Higgins in *Richard III* in the States in 1993, as well as playing Katrine Stockmann in *An Enemy of the People* in 1997. In 1998 in an interview with *USA Today* she spoke of the 'tremendous emotional shift in his work' which had happened after coming out, adding, 'It has been a treat to watch it happen.'

It didn't work in every role, just as the grand manner could still return. But his new willingness to allow an audience to see into his innermost self would transform his performances, in particular his screen performances. Or, as he would put it to James Rampton in December 2003, 'If I can be Gandalf or James Whale in front of the camera, it's because I can be Ian McKellen away from the camera.'

8. BACK TO SHAKESPEARE

With a less than happy six months in *Henceforward* behind him, in the summer of 1989 Ian McKellen went back to his spiritual home, the tin hut in Stratford called The Other Place. Trevor Nunn had summoned him once more to return to Shakespeare. It was thirteen years since the two men had created a piece of theatre history there with *Macbeth*. McKellen had been doing his one-man show *Acting Shakespeare*, but he hadn't tackled a new Shakespearian role since *Coriolanus* closed in September 1985. As for Nunn, he had finally left the RSC in 1987 after ten years as Artistic Director and another nine years running the place jointly with Terry Hands. For the last eight years Shakespeare had often taken a back seat for him to directing big musicals like *Cats* (1981), *Starlight Express* (1984) and *Les Misérables* (1985). And Nunn had become a rich man. In 1986 gross profits from two companies in his name had reached £2.4 m. He was also on his second marriage – to Sharon Lee-Hill – with a son of eight by Janet Suzman, and two daughters of three years and five months.

But after the success of *Macbeth* the two men had always had another project in mind for The Other Place – *Othello* with McKellen as Iago. The problem was who should play Othello. The part was written for a white actor, Richard Burbage, who probably wore black make-up, and for 200 years or so that was the way things stayed. In 1825 the black actor Ira Aldridge played the role, but the production never reached London, blocked by the pro-slavery lobby. Then in 1930, with Peggy Ashcroft as his Desdemona, Paul Robeson played Othello in London, reprising the role in Stratford in 1959, a production McKellen saw and hated. But the part continued to be played usually by white actors in black make-up, most famously by Laurence Olivier in 1964. In 1989 Nunn was sure this would not do.

Partly his reasons were political. Nunn no longer believed it was acceptable for a white actor to black up and impersonate a black man. Partly they were to do with the integrity of the play. If Shakespeare had intended Othello to be a black man – and though some have argued the Moor is an Arab, constant references in the text to blackness seem to suggest that he did – then shouldn't a black man play the part if the right actor could be found? Partly his reasons were typically practical. The play requires a physical relationship between Othello and Desdemona. With a white actor playing the Moor, he told journalist Alex

Renton, 'If they touch each other, Othello comes off on Desdemona.' By which he presumably meant a transfer of black make-up.

Now, in 1989, with the tin hut just about to be demolished, Nunn had finally found his Othello. Jamaican born Willard White was an opera singer who had starred in Nunn's 1986 Glyndebourne production of *Porgy and Bess*. He was widely described as one of the greatest bass voices in the world, but he had never performed in Shakespeare before. Nunn was sure he could do it. When White spoke – two octaves lower than everyone else – heads swivelled, even if he was only asking for a cup of tea. The man's presence on stage was formidable. In the confines of The Other Place, Nunn knew he would be monumental.

As Desdemona, Nunn cast 28-year-old Imogen Stubbs, who had been at the RSC in 1986 and was also making a name for herself as a screen actress. Determined not to succumb to the conventional portrayal of Desdemona as a passive victim, Stubbs brought a strength and passion to the role which matched Willard White's towering Othello.

It was McKellen's Iago, however, that everyone felt ultimately dominated the production. *Times* theatre critic Benedict Nightingale thinks that of all McKellen's performances, this was the one 'theatre historians will surely be discussing in a hundred years'. But it was the casting of Emilia, Iago's wife, a relatively minor role, which did as much as anything to make the production what it was.

'I agreed to do it,' says Zoë Wanamaker, 'because it was Trevor, and I'd had such a good time working with him on *Once in a Lifetime*' – the play for which Wanamaker had won the 1979 Laurence Olivier Award as Best Actress. Emilia is not the size of part that an actor of her clout would normally accept; her presence could have had the effect of artificially skewing the production, and in a way it did, but the result was an illumination of the play. This wasn't simply because there was a heavyweight actress playing the part, it was because of the water she displaced in rehearsal.

She recalls her preparations for playing Iago's wife: 'I'd done a lot of reading about battered wives and women who deny that their husbands are murderers or don't know that they are and are in denial about their husbands. I had a very strong idea of what the relationship was like from reading books about people like Myra Hindley who did it out of love or passion.' This was the kind of detailed research many leading actors will carry out in preparation for a major role. But for Emilia? One of the reasons Shakespeare is difficult is that the cast is so big for most of his plays. It's not just that you can't get good actors to play the smaller parts – though that is a problem – it's that Hamlet has put in months, even years of preparatory work on his own and in discussion with the director, and then, when the play gets into rehearsal, the director devotes most of his attention to Hamlet. Whereas the ambassador, Voltemand, turns up on the first day, is told where to stand, and that's about it. Even if he's done a whole lot of research on the part, even if he thinks he knows things which will give this production of *Hamlet* insights which have never before been discovered, no one is going to listen to Voltemand in rehearsal, because he's Jack Nobody just out of drama school.

But Zoë Wanamaker's ideas about the relationship between Iago and Emilia get listened to because of who she is, and Iago and Emilia move to the centre of the play. They don't displace Othello and Desdemona, but Shakespeare's most domestic tragedy becomes a terrifying portrait of the disintegration of two marriages – one which has been hollowed out at the core years ago by jealousy, the other which is destroyed by the same 'green-eyed monster' before our eyes.

McKellen and Wanamaker did the same for Iago and Emilia as McKellen and Judi Dench had done for the Macbeths thirteen years earlier. They revealed the truth about their marriage. The defining moment was the short scene in Act 3 when Emilia gives Iago the fatal handkerchief – Othello's first gift to Desdemona, which Iago will use to convince the Moor that she is unfaithful to him with Cassio.

'I was very nervous of working on that scene,' remembers Zoë Wanamaker. 'I mean Ian's a very sexy man for heterosexual women like myself. I find him very attractive. He's got the most beautiful hands – the most stunning pair of hands. Hands mean a great deal to me and he's got very strong, beautifully proportioned hands – very nice to hold.' The fact that Wanamaker found McKellen sexy raised the temperature of their on-stage relationship, and made the power of that scene much easier to achieve.

Before she handed over the handkerchief, which she knew perfectly well her husband would use for some nefarious purpose, Wanamaker's Emilia hesitated. Then, with the object of his desire finally in his grasp, McKellen gave her a shockingly brutal kiss, passionate and loveless, which she accepted with surprise, excitement and desperate gratitude. In that moment the whole sexual history of their marriage was revealed – Emilia's frustrated desire, the fact that she still wants a man she knows is corrupt, even evil, his inability to give love at all and the horrible truth that he can now only summon sexual desire for his wife via his lust for Desdemona.

The psychological emphasis of this kind of approach fitted exactly what Trevor Nunn wanted to achieve. For this production he had decided to abandon the RSC method with Shakespearian text, the method he and Hall and John Barton had been preaching for nearly thirty years, and to replace it with absolute naturalism. Gone was the importance of marking the end of the verse line, observing the caesura and playing the rhythm of the iambic pentameter. He took his cue from the way the part of Iago is written which is hardly in verse at all. 'Iago speaks in torrents of prose,' he observed in the *Independent* interview with Alex Renton, 'which are extraordinarily arrhythmic and vernacular. It won't unlock until it's tapping naturalistic juices.' So the production was surrounded with precise, naturalistic detail, placing it believably into a real army camp with the constant sound of cicadas in the background to emphasise the heat and exoticism of the location. But much more importantly the emphasis was more than ever before on psychological motivation. 'Trevor knew the psychological background of every character on stage,' observes Zoë Wanamaker. 'He always knew a motivation for each character, which made it terribly exciting.'

The approach suited McKellen, of course, because, as always, he was looking for psychological motivation. Coleridge's famous formulation that Iago is intended by Shakespeare as an embodiment of 'motiveless malignity' is still around. It was still being trotted out in the 2004 *South Bank Show* about the performance history of *Othello*. But McKellen's Iago should have put an end to this once and for all. As always, he began from a detailed reading of the text, trying to forget what others thought about the play, trying to see it as a script that has just been newly delivered by the playwright. What he found was that Iago makes clear in soliloquy his reasons for driving Othello to murderous jealousy: he has been passed over for promotion and he thinks Othello may have had sex with Emilia, his wife. He also tells the audience that he lusts after Desdemona. Shakespearian scholars from Coleridge onwards have dismissed these motives as inadequate. 'All right,' the theory goes, 'Cassio has been made Othello's lieutenant instead of Iago, but what possible reason could Iago have for believing Emilia had committed adultery with the Moor?' But that is precisely the point of the play. Jealousy is not subject to reason. What this production made clear is how easily jealousy can poison any relationship – not just Othello's and Desdemona's. The marriage Wanamaker and McKellen created was an image of what that terrible poison can do to two people over a period of many years. McKellen's meticulous reading of the text then, combined with Zoë Wanamaker's research and Trevor Nunn's desire to get away from rhetoric and approach Shakespeare wholly naturalistically was what made this Iago so remarkable. Add to that the ability to reveal himself in a role which McKellen thinks coming out had given him, and the intimacy of the setting which allowed detailed naturalism to reach every member of the audience, and it begins to become clear why the performance was so good.

But, of course, there had always been another dimension to a great McKellen Shakespearian performance – the contemporary model. Where was the John McEnroe which lay behind Coriolanus? Or the Dalai Lama which gave rise to Richard II? Or the Jack Kennedy hidden in Macbeth? McKellen said that he looked into himself for Iago's psychology, that he found the character's envy and jealousy in his own experience. But what about the physical detail of his characterisation of the ultimate non-commissioned officer (NCO) in the army – the little tin box from which his roll-ups emerge; the practised routine of lighting the cigarette and blowing out the match; the half cigarette saved for later; the clipping of the soldierly moustache – where did all that come from? Old school friend Michael Shipley thinks he knows.

Back in the 1950s every summer for speech day the boys of Bolton School put on a gymnastics display on the sports field. They drilled each morning through the summer term in preparation. The man who put them through their paces was an ex-World War I soldier named Archie Sayers. 'It was uncanny,' says Shipley, 'some thirty years later, to see the man brought back to life. Ian had his moustache, his physical mannerisms, the way he held his arms, his voice – everything.'

There were two more pieces in the jigsaw which went to make McKellen's Iago. First was the technical command he now brought to Shakespeare, to those 'torrents of prose' Trevor Nunn had identified. Cicely Berry, still Director of Voice at the RSC, remembers the 35-year-old who came up to Stratford to play Romeo and compares him with the McKellen who took on Iago. 'There was a far greater confidence with the words. He really found the abrupt changes and corners in the language.' And secondly, as Berry puts it, 'With Iago, you've got to make the right kind of contact with the audience which Ian is very skilled at.'

Alan Cohen at the National Theatre spoke about how McKellen made contact with every member of his audience in the wide open spaces of the Olivier Theatre. Take that skill into The Other Place or the Young Vic, where the production played in London, and you have an actor who can draw an audience inside the arid, horrifying landscape of Iago's mind. For what is extraordinary is that the audience sees the events of the play entirely through the mind of the villain. They laugh with him and they are disgusted by him; they can't help admiring his cleverness and part of them even wills him to succeed. They are left implicated in what he does in a way that makes the impact of the play so much greater. But there are problems with the relationship Iago has with the audience – problems which all Othellos find out in the end.

Rehearsals had had their tensions. Nunn and McKellen's friendship and working familiarity gave them a special relationship. And the director and his leading lady were finding each other more than just professionally interesting. 'It was the beginning of Trevor and Imogen's infatuation,' explains Zoë Wanamaker. 'I don't think they did anything about it. But this was the start.' The couple would marry in 1994. 'Both Oxford and Cambridge types, of course,' Wanamaker goes on, 'which always sends me running to the *Daily Mail* or the *Sun*, because I feel intellectually inferior. I think Willard was very nervous and Trevor was very helpful towards him and so was Ian, but after a while most Othellos and Iagos suddenly realise . . .' Her voice tails off. What most Othellos and Iagos suddenly realise doesn't happen until the audience arrives. Laurence Olivier played Iago in 1938 and, having thoroughly upstaged Ralph Richardson's Othello for the entire run, he became convinced that Shakespeare had written the part of the Moor of Venice to 'fix' Richard Burbage. Olivier was very nervous of playing it himself. The problem lies partly in the relationship Iago has with the audience which puts him in a stronger position than Othello, and partly in the way the lines are structured. Othello roars and bellows a dozen lines of orotund iambics and Iago pricks his balloon with 'Is't possible?' and the audience laughs.

'Willard would feel very undermined,' says Zoë Wanamaker. 'I don't think Trevor and Ian were aware of it to begin with. I don't think it was a problem to begin with. But I think it may have become a problem when we went to the Young Vic and we didn't see each other all the time. I think it was sorted out, but I think Ian had to placate him to some extent.'

In fact, White was impressive as Othello, particularly for a man who had never played Shakespeare before. But he was ponderous in his delivery, signalling changes of emotion and thought, trying to explain lines to the audience, where McKellen knew from all his work with Cicely Berry that you don't need to. You let Shakespeare speak for himself through you. All the same this was by no means a star turn from McKellen. It was a wonderful ensemble of just twelve actors, including stalwarts like Clive Swift and, as Roderigo, a young Michael Grandage, who would later gain greater fame as a director, following Sam Mendes as artistic director of the Donmar Warehouse.

An important part of the success of the production was the design by Bob Crowley. The uniforms, reminiscent of the American Civil War, lent resonance to the presence of a black general in command of white troops, and made each reference to slavery and slaves, of which there are a number in the play, jump into focus. In a symphony of half glances and raised eyebrows Nunn and his actors also inserted a racist subtext into the exchanges between the sailors at the beginning of Act 2.

Virtually sold out before it opened, the production played a month in Stratford, a short season at the Young Vic, and then it was gone. Compared to the extended life of the 1976 *Macbeth* sadly few people actually got to see it, but the working lives of top opera singers are arranged a lot further in advance than even the most successful actors, and Willard White's availability was limited. McKellen won the *Evening Standard* and Critics' Circle Awards as Best Actor for his Iago and the Laurence Olivier Award jointly for Iago and Max in the revival of *Bent*; Trevor Nunn won best Director and Zoë Wanamaker Best Supporting Performer. And they made a video. And, like the video of the 1976 *Macbeth*, it captured many of the strengths of the production and stands up well to repeated viewing.

Receiving his statuette at the *Evening Standard* Awards ceremony on 14 November, McKellen offered thanks, but said that having seen *Hamlet* at the National Theatre the previous night, he thought actor of the year was Ian Charleson. The National Theatre was back in McKellen's life.

On 21 August 1989 Richard Eyre was almost exactly a year into his tenure as artistic director of the South Bank complex, now renamed the Royal National Theatre in honour of its 25 years of existence. Eyre announced a new group of associate directors. There were familiar names there like David Hare and Bill Bryden. There were rising directorial stars Declan Donellan and Nick Hytner. There was a woman – Deborah Warner. And there were two actors. One was Michael Bryant, a fixture on the South Bank since 1977. The other was Ian McKellen.

There were plans afoot for the revival of *Bent*. But more importantly there were plans afoot for what would be in many ways the apotheosis of McKellen's career as a stage actor and the beginning of his late arrival as a screen actor. It would be the biggest tour ever undertaken by the National Theatre. It would be the most ambitious and (probably) final theatrical tour for the actor who had made his name that way twenty years earlier. They would visit cities throughout the UK as well as Japan, Germany, Italy, Spain, France and Ireland. By special request of the British Council they would be the first theatre company into the new Cairo Opera House. McKellen was producing. The play was *Richard III*.

The hand of history was heavy on them: the massacre in Tiananmen Square in June meant plans to go to China were dropped; then the fall of the Berlin Wall in November meant adding dates in East Germany, Romania, Czechoslovakia and Russia. The hand of the sponsors, Guinness, was pretty heavy too. The Irish leg had to be switched from Dublin to Cork because Dublin's Abbey Theatre had done a deal with rival brewers Murphy's. And at the last minute Moscow had to be dropped after the Russians couldn't pay the hotel bill. But it was still a monumental enterprise with 55 people, including 27 actors and three trucks to carry the sets and equipment.

The initial idea had not been *Richard III* at all. McKellen had seen and admired Deborah Warner's 1987 RSC production of *Titus Andronicus*, notorious for audience members fainting at the graphic depiction of violence, starring Brian Cox. He wanted her to direct him in a second outing as Coriolanus, plus another play of her choice, in which he agreed to play whatever part she wanted. Warner said she wanted to do *King Lear* with Brian Cox as Lear and asked McKellen to play Kent. He agreed and, not wanting to do two Shakespeares, started looking for a modern play which could use the same actors as *Lear*. He couldn't find one. Only Shakespeare would cross-cast with Shakespeare – not so surprising when you remember that the plays were originally written for the same group of actors. Eventually he decided on *Richard III*, a part people had been saying for years he should play. With Warner deciding she couldn't direct that as well as *Lear*, McKellen asked Richard Eyre to step in.

The decision to do *Richard III* had not been an easy one. McKellen had always resisted the part, finding offensive the apparent equation the play makes between physical deformity and evil. In the wake of coming out and his new-found political work, such political incorrectness seems to have been particularly worrying. It is the same reason he has never wanted to play Shylock. For McKellen, rub it how you will, *The Merchant of Venice* remains an anti-Semitic play. It was Pieter Rogers, a friend since Chichester days, who persuaded the actor to take another look at *Richard III*. If he hadn't, there might have been no *Richard III* tour, no film and, very possibly, none of the movie career that film helped generate.

Then there was the rest of the casting to decide on. 'I wanted a group whose commitment to one another as a company would be reflected in their work on stage,' said McKellen in an interview for the *Sunday Times* in July 1990. 'The first question I asked every actor was whether they would understudy.' They were precisely the criteria which had been the basis of the Actors' Company. McKellen himself understudied the small part of a herald in *King Lear*. But the real reasons the other actors had for joining the tour varied. Clare Higgins, for instance, playing Queen

Elizabeth and Regan, said her main reason was simply that she'd never worked with McKellen and desperately wanted to. Peter Jeffrey on the other hand, at sixty the senior member of the company, was eager to play Gloucester and Clarence and to visit some of the parts of the world they were going to.

Rehearsals got under way on 19 March 1990 with champagne and orange juice laid on for the first morning by Ian McKellen. With the company committed to a year together he knew how important it was that they bonded, and he also knew they needed a company leader. It would be McKellen, the same 'Troupe' who had led Prospect and the Cambridge Theatre Company and the Actors' Company and the RSC small scale tour, who led the way.

Clare Higgins, for one, found early rehearsals quite intimidating. 'In *Richard III*,' she explained to *Plays and Players*, 'I had this twenty-minute scene with him and I thought, How can I seriously go on stage with Ian McKellen and battle it out?' But eventually she found McKellen's experimental method of rehearsing liberating, and began to adopt his constant search for spontaneity and change herself.

But preparations were not without their frictions. Thirteen weeks of rehearsal were scheduled with Eyre and Warner taking it in turns. But it wasn't long before disagreements arose, and some of the actors found it hard to adjust to the very different methods of the two directors. Deborah Warner waited for the actors to invent and then selected what she wanted from that. Richard Eyre, by contrast, had the details of his production worked out minutely beforehand. Within a month Brian Cox was writing in *The Lear Diaries*, a record he kept of both productions, 'Perhaps it's only in my imagination, but I feel there's a sort of race on between the two productions.'

Just to make the race more interesting, McKellen was keeping himself busy in the evening with the West End transfer of *Bent*. A typical day saw him up before nine a.m. to read the paper, and off to the National in the rusty, V-reg Honda, which had replaced his Mini; half an hour of answering the considerable volume of mail generated by *Bent*, then rehearsal; lunch in the NT canteen, which had finally added a vegetarian option; then more rehearsal; over to the Garrick for the evening show – on-stage for the entire two and a half hours, including lugging real granite boulders around; a quick shower afterwards before the dressing room filled up with friends and well-wishers; back to Narrow Street by 11.30; watch *Newsnight* – taped on the VCR – then sleep.

Quite a day. And the fact that it's a heavyweight current affairs programme, largely devoted to political news that he's watching at the end of the day is a measure of the man. *Bent* closed in April, but just to keep the day full, he fitted in a month at the Haymarket in the Alan Bennett *Talking Heads* solo, *Chip in the Sugar*. But that's a workaholic for you, and besides the Bennett was another boost for Sean Mathias who directed.

Small wonder that Brian Cox finished by calling his co-star 'a monk of the theatre', because that kind of twelve to fourteen-hour working day had frequently been the norm for McKellen over the past thirty years, squeezing out all possibility of a life outside work. By contrast, Cox finished the tour sure that he wanted to devote more time to his private life, a realisation which would unfortunately come only following the break-up of his relationship with Irina Brooke, Peter Brooke's daughter. Richard Eyre, meanwhile, was finding his star heavy going. A week of rehearsals found him admitting in his *Diary* that he felt 'slightly wary of Ian. He monitors his effects and orchestrates them very carefully.' Searching for external effects – it's a criticism you'll still hear of McKellen's stage acting, however much he himself feels coming out or working in small theatres has changed him. After two weeks things were no better. 'Ian is particularly exhausting,' wrote Eyre in his *Diary*. 'It's difficult to divine his true feelings and he fusses around and over-decorates.'

For Eyre it was a particularly difficult rehearsal period. His father was dying, and he felt tired and low much of the time. 'Ian was remorseless,' he told Robert Cheshyre in August 1992. 'He would go on and on about parts of the show that weren't right.' But gradually director and star were learning to trust each other. 'He has a doggedness to get things better,' Eyre concluded in the same interview. 'He's a perfectionist, and I love that.'

By the middle of June with previews just a fortnight away, Eyre had totally changed his tune about McKellen. 'I'm proud of the work,' he noted in his *Diary*, 'and am loving working with Ian, who's become a real collaborator and friend. Everything that I was interested in has matured in the production.'

But the problem was, as with Mckellen's *Hamlet*, that while director and star may be on the same page, others in the cast may feel they've not been shown the script. When rehearsals got under way, McKellen and Eyre had already had three months talking about the production. But Brian Cox, for example, seems to have begun rehearsals with no idea of what Eyre was planning. With ballroom dancing lessons and voice classes on pukka English accents dominating the first week or so of rehearsals, he was guessing it was to be 1930s and he turned out to be right. But it was a slip in the communication that could never have happened at the Actors' Company, and as far as the accents were concerned it would have a lasting effect. Some members of the cast never mastered the cut-glass English which Eyre wanted. Cox, for instance, a Glaswegian, acknowledged 'deeply psychological reasons' for his inability to come to terms with the accent, and McKellen finished up with a strangulated croak, like Edward Fox as Edward VIII, while others, who were supposed to be of the same class, didn't. It was a classic instance of the gap between star and supporting cast.

Between them Eyre, McKellen and the designer – Bob Crowley again – had come up with an imaginary version of Britain in the 1930s with Richard taking over as an Oswald Mosley-like fascist dictator. The key moment was just before the interval, when Richard and his followers change into fascist uniform and he greets the crowd with a stiff-arm salute. In the second half the back wall was adorned with a huge, nude portrait of an idealised Richard, painted in the mythic/heroic vein beloved of the Nazis, with withered arm miraculously healed. Eyre insisted on the penis being redone, claiming it was out of proportion, though McKellen maintains it was drawn accurately from life. Large or small, when the tour reached the USA, the penis disappeared altogether under a full suit of armour. Somebody felt the Americans would find the nude McKellen too much, though, of course, they had seen the real thing at BAM back in 1974.

Updating *Richard III* to the 1930s worked brilliantly in some ways and not in others. The scenes of dark-suited, paranoid men in dimly lit meeting rooms made the politics of the play clear and vivid. But the sudden intrusion of armour and swords on the battlefield, not to mention 'a horse a horse, my kingdom for a horse', was hopelessly anachronistic. And when Richard was winched into the air on a platform to address a Nuremberg-style rally, it looked as if Eyre would rather have been directing *The Resistible Rise of Arturo Ui*, Brecht's parable of the rise of Hitler, transposed to the Chicago gangland. In *Playing Shakespeare* John Barton says the great danger with putting Shakespeare into modern dress is that 'it can reduce rather than resonate'. In other words a play which has something universal to say about, say, tyranny is reduced to a patronising spelling out of narrow historical parallels. Barton prefers 'timeless' productions, set in no one period in an attempt to say something about all periods.

As for McKellen's Richard, the performance certainly grew through its long life. Critics on the opening night missed the devilish humour which is usually an aspect of the part. Most Richards beckon the audience in, encouraging them to enjoy their Machiavellian scheming. McKellen's

Richard began by being chilling and wholly unlikeable. He discovered or perhaps succumbed to the humour in the part as he went on, blowing his nose loudly into his handkerchief as he feigns tears at the imprisonment of his brother Clarence, which he himself has ordered, allowing the audience a guilty relish for his villainy.

The willingness to keep working on the part was what Richard Eyre came particularly to admire in McKellen the actor – something Robert Chetwyn had spotted as long ago as 1963 in Ipswich. 'The great thing about him is that he keeps reinventing it, but he doesn't f*** about,' Eyre told America's *Theater Week* two years into the production's life. 'Often when you hear people say a certain actor never does the same thing twice, your heart sinks, because it implies that the actor is impatient. With Ian, he just accumulates, discards and refines.'

There was all the detail one expects from a McKellen characterisation, some of it a clear continuation of his Iago – the fastidiously buttoned-up uniform, the clipped speech. There was the bravura theatricality of demonstrating Richard's dexterity with his one good arm. Every cigarette was lit with studied unconcern using only one arm. In the scene with Lady Anne, again using one arm only, he stripped off the entire top half of his uniform to present his bare chest to Eve Matheson's knife. The ring he gives Anne was sucked from the finger of his good hand in a moment of delightful *grand guignol*. But the characterisation was at its strongest in the psychology McKellen found to underpin a part which can descend very easily into campy villain-acting.

He took his cue from his mother, the Duchess of York, played by Joyce Redman, and her clear distaste for her disabled child – 'He was the wretch'st thing when he was young' – to create a man who has been poisoned inwardly. 'Richard is not a psychotic figure,' he told *In Theater* in July 1998. 'He seems to me to be responding to the lack of love in his own life.' It is precisely the same approach he took to Macbeth and to Iago. These are men who do wrong, but they are driven by human motivations. They are not monsters.

Typically too, the psychology of his interpretation centred around a few individual moments, when the humanity of the character leaped suddenly into sharp relief – like Richard II's 'need friends' and Iago's 'I hate the Moor'. When Lady Anne spat at him in disgust as the murderer of her husband, the sudden, real pain in 'Why dost thou spit at me?' illuminated a whole history of mistreatment this Richard had endured because of his deformity.

McKellen also brought out a terrible hatred of women in Richard. 'Why this it is when men are ruled by women' was spat out viciously.

He flinched at Anne's attempt to help him up, while her yielding to his wooing produced a deep disgust rather than the glee some Richards display. The loss of this approach though was a desexualising of Richard. Where Antony Sher's 1984 Crookback slid his wooden crutch between Lady Anne's legs after she spat at him, McKellen recoiled. And with Eve Matheson finally on the floor, clearly in a sexually inviting position, McKellen's Richard notably failed to pounce. The difference is interesting since Antony Sher's *The Year of the King*, an account of the creation of one of his most famous roles, makes it clear that he worked from exactly the same psychological premise as McKellen – the absence of love and a mother's rejection.

After a gruelling eighty performances in ten weeks at the Lyttleton, during which matinee days could involve *King Lear* in the afternoon followed by *Richard III* in the evening, the whole circus was airlifted to Tokyo's high-tech replica of the Globe and the tour was under way. There were highs and there were lows. Brian Cox, his relationship with Irina Brooke under severe strain at home, found playing both Buckingham and Lear more than he could stand, and began trying to extricate himself altogether from *Richard III*. But McKellen was tireless. He addressed meetings of Japanese businessmen alongside both the Japanese Prime Minister and the British Foreign Secretary, Douglas Hurd; he dined in embassies; he attended sponsors' dos; he led company outings to the Giant's Causeway in Northern Ireland and the red-light district in Hamburg.

It wasn't until Madrid that things turned nasty.

The hotel was horrible, and the touring allowance of pesetas wasn't there when the company arrived. But that was just the start. The technicians at the Teatro Nacional, where they were due to play, were on strike. There was no way the British technicians were going to do anything which looked like breaking a strike, and some of the actors were worried too. So after a company meeting Deborah Warner and her two leading players went out to look for another venue. Back at the hotel resentment was soon rising. Some members of the company didn't feel they had been properly consulted about moving the performances elsewhere. After two months on the road a week's holiday seemed a better idea.

When Warner, Cox and McKellen returned with talk of transferring to an abattoir, a whole series of grievances surfaced in a meeting which went on until five in the morning. In particular the spear carriers in *Richard III* were sick of having to stand at attention for fifteen minutes during McKellen's confrontation with Queen Elizabeth – the scene Clare

Higgins had been so worried about in the first place. The contrast with Nigel Havers's enjoyment of the first two scenes of *Richard II*, when he stood with his banner and watched McKellen in action, is striking. Cox began to wonder whether his public complaints about having to play Buckingham had raised the general level of whingeing to its current state and eventually decided to stick with *Richard III* to the bitter end. Safely back on the South Bank, Richard Eyre confessed to his *Diary* that he felt 'relieved but guilty' to be missing the whole thing.

McKellen brought all his skills as company leader to bear. Cox felt he showed remarkable statesmanship. Realising that there was a feeling abroad that decisions were being made over the heads of the more lowly members of the company, he handed over the decision of whether to do the shows in Madrid to them. In the end they did a run-through of *Richard III* and half of *Lear* without an audience, and tempers cooled, but it had been an unpleasant experience for McKellen. Memories of the Actors' Company had come back to haunt him, when Margery Mason accused him of behaving like a star in rehearsals before Wimbledon.

So why do it? Why deal with all the hassle? Because there were more low points to come, like the Cairo Opera House, where nothing worked, and Bucharest, where the flight was diverted and they had to travel miles overland by coach. Though there were high points too, like the meeting in Prague with playwright President Vaclav Havel, who said he had been inspired to go back to writing by seeing their *Lear*, and a single extraordinary performance of *Lear* to the maximum security mental patients of Broadmoor Hospital. Why the endless touring?

A lot of actors can't stand it. In his *Lear Diaries*, Brian Cox declares himself at one extreme with, 'When you die instead of purgatory you actually go on tour.' Most actors will do a tour if there's nothing else on offer. But for 22 years, as the NT trucks drew up back at the South Bank for Christmas 1990, Ian McKellen had been doing it because he wanted to. Was it still that childhood fantasy of running away to join the fairground? Was it the 'pioneering spirit' Trevor Nunn talked about, the desire to take theatre to the parts theatre doesn't usually reach, the moral imperative that the National Theatre should really serve the nation and the world – not just the London middle classes?

Some actors like the irresponsibility of touring. 'Touring doesn't count,' goes the old theatre saying, meaning that while you're in Aberdeen or Tokyo you can sleep with who you like irrespective of the spouse back home. Plus you can run away from boring basics like cleaning your flat and paying your bills. 'I am free of financial and other responsibilities and I enjoy it,' McKellen told Joy Leslie Gibson back in

1979. Other responsibilities? No family. That's what he meant. And perhaps that's where we get to the heart of it. Twelve years later in an interview with the *Sunday Times* he was calling touring 'a passion', and why? 'Partially because I live alone. It's like a family, and you get the chance to be close friends with fifty people.'

This is the man who lost his mother as a boy of twelve, whose father died when he was first becoming a star, and who until 1988 had always felt an unbridgeable gap between himself and his family anyway because of the secret of his homosexuality.

'Many theatre people find the outside world uncongenial,' McKellen told Robert Cheshyre, shifting the thought to a comfortable psychological distance. 'Here they are at ease with one another; the welcome they get is overwhelming.' It's the theatre as a place of safety, a place where he feels welcome, a place where 'to be gay [is] not extraordinary or a difficulty.'

Brian Cox sums it up. He admired McKellen as an actor and a man. He felt competitive with him. He came to the conclusion that he could never give up a home life to the extent that McKellen had. 'He likes to be part of a group,' wrote Cox in *The Lear Diaries*. 'I think he likes touring because he feels he is part of a family.'

But amidst the chaos in Cairo of flying machinery that couldn't cope with the set, McKellen had told Cox he would never tour again. Not quite yet – but an era was coming to an end.

Meanwhile, back on the South Bank, along with his knighthood McKellen had just been made Cameron Macintosh Visiting Professor of Theatre at Oxford and was planning his inaugural lecture. Except that in the end he decided he didn't want to give lectures at all or even acting master classes, he wanted something altogether more high-minded; he wanted a debate with the students about what theatre in Britain is for and what it might become in the future. He had also picked up the Laurence Olivier Award as Best Actor yet again for Richard. And Richard Eyre had persuaded him, somewhat against his better judgement, to take on the role of Gennaro in a comedy by Eduardo di Filippo, set in Naples during and after World War Two, called *Napoli Milionaria*.

Previous National Theatre productions of di Filippo plays like *Saturday, Sunday, Monday* and *Filumena* had gone for a rather uncomfortable, Italian-accented English. *Napoli Milionaria* was billed as 'a version by Peter Tinniswoode', which meant the language and the accents had been transported to the north of England. The set design, however, was a highly detailed and authentic recreation of the back streets of Naples.

Gennaro is the husband and unwilling accomplice of a Neapolitan black marketeer, played by Clare Higgins. Sporting a soup-strainer moustache, McKellen had a very funny scene in the first half when he had to play dead in a bed full of contraband. A genuine ensemble piece, Peter Kemp in the *Independent* called it 'a communal triumph', though many had their doubts about the second half of the play which became more serious, and seemed to be trying to make points about the moral impact of dealing on the black market. Isabella di Filippo, the playwright's widow, saw the production in August, liked it and declared herself unnerved by the resemblance between McKellen and Eduardo. But McKellen seems to have retained his reservations to the end, saying the whole thing rather reminded him of the predictable structure of the well-made plays cranked out week on week at the Bolton Hippodrome when he was a lad.

Antony Sher was at the National too doing *The Resistible Rise of Arturo Ui*, while McKellen continued in *Richard III* and *Napoli Milionaria*. McKellen had telephoned Sher to congratulate him on coming out in 1989; now the two actors, both memorable Richard IIIs, became friends. Passing in the maze of corridors backstage, in which actors searching for the Cottesloe have been known to get lost and miss their entrances, McKellen would joke, 'Oh, damn . . . what's my first line again?'

McKellen was already looking for a way to bring Sean Mathias to the National to direct him in the title role of Chekhov's *Uncle Vanya*. They decided to ask Sher to join them as the doctor, Astrov, and he was only too delighted to work with an actor who had always been something of a hero. Richard Eyre, on the other hand, was less than happy about the package. Sean had done the revival of *Bent*, but this was something different. McKellen's ex-lover simply didn't have the track record to warrant directing Chekhov in the Cottesloe. According to Antony Sher's autobiography *Beside Myself*, Eyre took the two actors on one side and told them, 'I'll line up any director in the land for you.'

McKellen was not to be persuaded. Though Sher later maintained it was the right decision – and the production went on to garner five nominations for awards, including Best Director – some thought this latest attempt to boost Sean's career was a step too far. 'I think Ian lost a lot of respect for that,' offers one colleague. '[But] you can't blame Mathias for taking the opportunity.'

For McKellen there is more to it. Yes, he may be advancing his friend's career, but he also believes Mathias is good at directing *him*, precisely because he knows him so well. For many actors and directors there would either be a fatal cosiness in such an arrangement – a mutual admiration society which allows actor and director to become lazy and uncreative – or conversely, as McKellen put it in the *Washington Post* in December 2001, they might have to 'get through a lot of personal stuff before they can get down to being professional'. In fact, both men claim their way of working together falls into neither trap. Mathias says they have a kind of shorthand. McKellen elaborates. 'It rather alarms other people, because, you know, he cuts straight through, says, "Stop it!" or something. To say it to anybody else might appear to be a bit rude.' And when does he say stop it? Mathias explained to journalist Chip Crews, 'He [McKellen] has a tendency to indulge and to be mannered and to be showy. An actor can play to the qualities that the audience is seeking.' As a director then, McKellen believes Mathias is what Guthrie or Nunn or Barton have been for him – someone who won't allow him to get away with a box of tricks; someone who demands truth; someone who demands his best. There remain those who disagree, and think McKellen has returned to Sean so often as a director because he finds him so easy going.

In *Beside Myself* Antony Sher gives a fascinating description of McKellen in action in early rehearsals for *Uncle Vanya*. Like Nick Grace on *The Alchemist* back in 1977, he notes the way McKellen jumps in and tries things out straight away, but doesn't fix anything too soon, keeping his options open. 'He's an actor to his fingertips,' writes Sher. 'From day one, he's there performing, needing to entertain the director, the other actors, stage management, anyone who's watching. He'll interrupt a scene to invent some comic business, people will laugh and applaud.'

Sher admits he found this way of rehearsing irritating at first. But he was soon won over by what he calls McKellen's 'irresistible charisma'. And he was amazed to see Vanya appearing almost at once before his eyes, as McKellen brought in clothes, spectacles, props to rehearsals. On the other hand he also notes that even in 1991, in the wake of coming out, when he saw himself as so much more open and truthful as an actor, McKellen still found it hard to get in touch with his emotions in the service of the part.

And it was real emotion they were after. McKellen was finding the surface of Vanya easily, but what lay beneath was more difficult. At the end of Act 3, Vanya fires a revolver at the retired professor he envies and despises. That is the moment which reveals the character's suppressed anger. McKellen has admitted he has always found it hard to express anger in real life. For *Uncle Vanya*, he had to find real anger in himself before he could play Vanya's. That's the way Chekhov works. 'On the second night he really exploded,' Mathias told journalist Robert

Cheshyre. 'It was amazing, and became the key to the greatness of his performance.' Real emotion was closer to the surface in a McKellen performance perhaps than it ever had been. To his own surprise during the course of the run, he found himself crying on stage for the first time in his career.

In April 1992 a largely recast *Richard III* returned to the Lyttleton Theatre. Brian Cox had had enough of *Lear*, but McKellen, the man who warned Nickolas Grace against 'throwing hits away', was going to play this one to the hilt. Slipping on carpet slippers for the flight – his usual trick – McKellen was off across the pond once more, courtesy of Northwest Airlines who underwrote shipping and travelling expenses for this, the final leg of the tour.

A week before opening in New York, bookings were only 60 per cent at the Brooklyn Academy of Music. McKellen hit the interview trail, as he always does, and by opening night they had set a box office record. The obligatory first night party was thrown by Tina Brown, British editor of *Vanity Fair*. Among the New York glitterati sat Henry Kissinger. Richard Eyre tried to draw him out about similarities between his or Nixon's politics and those of Richard III. Kissinger steered the conversation safely back to medieval England.

After Brooklyn there were three and a half months of dates in vast theatres across the USA, ending up in September at the Royce Hall in LA. More than twelve years later, McKellen could still summon a shudder at the name, as a fan at a movie screening brought up memories of seeing his Richard III there. 'Very difficult theatre,' he muttered. 'Could you hear anything?'

It was the old economics of touring rearing its head again. For all the sponsorship money, this huge-scale tour could only break even if they played vast theatres, designed for opera and music rather than plays. And vast theatres meant a return to the grand gesture. The *Washington Post* complained of a 'lame production' and 'ranting cast', but McKellen makes no apology for the scale of performance he offered. The truth and detail that looks so good at The Other Place in Stratford won't reach past the tenth row in a 1,900-seater in St Paul, Minnesota. He acknowledges the long-standing criticism of his overacting, still speaks most fondly of characters created for studio theatres, but adds with a practicality old Frank Greene would have applauded back in Bolton School Hall, 'People near the back may have been rather grateful that they could hear.'

Presenting the 1992 Tony Award for Best Actor in New York to Judd Hirsch for *Conversations With My Father*, McKellen was introduced as 'the world's greatest classical actor'. But he was already close to the point where he had had enough. Back in Cairo he'd told Brian Cox he would never tour again. As he finished playing Richard III for the last time on 27 September 1992 in the echoing vastness of the Royce Hall in LA, he was heard to say, 'I'm not doing any more theatre.' McKellen was 53 years old. He had a knighthood and several hatfuls of awards to show for his career as a theatre actor, but he was going to have one last shot at what he'd always felt was missing from his career – the movies. He headed for Montana to make a Western.

There was still the one-man show, and in the next few years amid a string of supporting roles in movies, he would return to *A Knight Out* at regular intervals, but it wasn't until 1997 that Sir Ian McKellen was back on a stage in London. And it took Trevor Nunn to lure him back.

For all the talk of McKellen himself succeeding Richard Eyre at the National or other bold appointments, in the end the board went for a safe pair of hands, the man who had already run the RSC for nineteen years – Trevor Nunn. For his inaugural production in September 1997, Nunn asked his old friend McKellen to return to the Olivier Theatre as Dr Tomas Stockmann in Ibsen's *An Enemy of the People*. In the event McKellen turned up two days late after the shoot overran on his latest screen role. But if that was a symptom of where his professional focus was now located, it did not show up in the contract he'd signed with Nunn. McKellen was committing himself to three plays – the Ibsen, which would do a short season in Los Angeles (not a tour) in 1998, a revival of Nunn and John Caird's RSC *Peter Pan* for Christmas and a new play by a major British dramatist which in the end didn't materialise. The new play would have been a departure for McKellen. He had not touched one since *Henceforward* in 1988. But Ibsen and hamming it up as Captain Hook were neither adventurous choices for the National nor for McKellen personally.

Journalist John Walsh of the *Independent*, visiting rehearsals for *An Enemy of the People*, declared himself astonished at McKellen's approach to the part, as the actor concocted from hints in the script a rich past life for Stockmann, packed with detail about what had happened to the man before the play begins. But McKellen was simply going through the standard Stanislavskian motions he and Nunn always adopted. The problem was the scale of the production envisaged by Nunn and his designer John Napier. To fill the Olivier Theatre, and in due course the Ahmanson in Los Angeles, Napier had built a massively elaborate set which attempted to transform Ibsen's tale of a truth-teller exposing the lies on which a community has built its prosperity, into a great public play. 'It looked like a musical,' is the succinct critique of Zoë Wanamaker who was in the first night audience. And many of the critics thought McKellen was back to his old, worst ways. John Gross in the *Sunday Telegraph* described McKellen 'twitching, gesticulating, fiddling with his collar', or, according to Kate Kellaway in the *New Statesman*, he was 'breathless, hyperactive, with a chattering laugh'. And most telling of all, and a sure sign that the actor was straining to scale up his performance for the perceived difficulties of the Olivier Theatre, 'ramming home every character trait as if his life depended on it', as Robert Gore-Langton put it in the *Daily Express*.

At Christmas McKellen took on the role of Captain Hook in *Peter Pan*. But the long piece he wrote about the production for the *Guardian*, in which he moaned about real cuts and bruises inflicted by the crocodile's spiky teeth, suggested the experience was proving less than delightful. 'You try chasing young Peter up the rigging of the Jolly Roger ship in two-inch heels with a metal hook on your hand,' he concluded. Certainly some first night audience members, while enjoying Claudie Blakley and Daniel Evans as Wendy and Peter, found McKellen's Hook oddly subdued, failing in what he was usually best at – building up the villain's relationship with the audience.

Returning from *An Enemy of the People*'s Los Angeles run in August 1998, McKellen walked into the kind of storm in a teacup that the British theatre likes to brew up every once in a while. Nunn wanted him to stay with the National. McKellen wanted to be free for possible movies in 1999. So at a press conference at the Criterion Theatre in September he announced to the assembled national media that rather than signing up at the National or committing to any theatre work in London, he was heading north for a four-month season at the West Yorkshire Playhouse. He billed it as a return to his own theatrical roots, which no one could really argue with. What caused the fuss were his remarks about audiences in London.

McKellen had been worrying about who was out there in the dark ever since he started turning down offers to join the RSC back in the 1970s. As early as 1976 he had expressed his reservations in a *Times* interview about the London audience: 'half of them foreign, all strangers to each other'. He said much the same thing to the journalists at the Criterion, commenting also with particular reference to Trevor Nunn's *Oklahoma!*, which he had seen the night before, on the absence of black faces in the London audience. He then went on to say that what he liked about the provincial audience was their homogeneity. They were local people with a connection to each other who might be expected to have a collective response to what they saw, making the actor's job of communicating with them that much easier and more rewarding. He concluded in response to Amanda Mitchison's question about when he might be seen next on the London stage, 'I think it is possible I may not be seen on the London stage again.' It was partly the actor's standard anxiety response – 'I may never work again' and McKellen said later it was a joke but the big guns of the London theatre were not amused.

'They [journalists] know, he knows and I know that he will not appear on the London stage again until he appears on the London stage again,' opined Peter Hall in the *Sunday Telegraph*. Richard Eyre in the same article said, 'It's fantastically sentimental. Why does he imagine the Leeds bourgeoisie is hugely different from the London bourgeoisie? I don't know why he has to dump on London in order to justify his emigration. Is it such a massive act of martyrdom to go to Leeds?' And McKellen *has* appeared on the London stage again – but not much. And not for any of the big name directors whose noses seemed just a little out of joint as he headed north in September 1998.

Ironically after all the trouble, the West Yorkshire Playhouse, with its two auditoria, its bookshop, café, restaurant and live music is the nearest thing to a National Theatre of the north. Jude Kelly had been running the Playhouse as artistic director since its inception in 1990, and she was slated to direct McKellen as Doctor Dorn, a supporting role in Chekhov's *The Seagull*, and as Prospero in a voodoo version of *The Tempest* in the New Year. In between McKellen would take on Gary Essendine, the star part Noel Coward wrote for himself in *Present Laughter*. At McKellen's insistence, they adopted the Mike Alfreds method of not setting moves for Chekhov. He might not have been producing, but a star of McKellen's magnitude couldn't be ignored by any director. He also had a fair bit to do with the casting. Clare Higgins from the original *Richard III* company was there. So was Claudie Blakley from *Peter Pan*.

Playing on a traverse stage in the Courtyard Theatre, the West Yorkshire Playhouse's 350-seat studio, McKellen seems to have enjoyed *The Seagull*. Dorn is a good part, which won him the Barclay's Theatre Award for Best Supporting Performance, but it isn't over-taxing, which is just as well because he was busy through the day, rehearsing *Present Laughter*.

As one might expect from Coward, Gary Essendine is an old-fashioned star part, hogging centre stage and all the best lines from carefully delayed entrance to final curtain. And under Malcolm

Sutherland's direction, McKellen came up with an old-fashioned star performance. The plot is virtually non-existent. It's simply an everyday story of a star theatre actor's life. Played by Sir Ian McKellen, a star contemporary theatre actor, it was a demonstration of perfect phrasing, wonderful pace and effortless breath control, with a cultured snarl and consciously mannered delivery not unlike the older Peter O'Toole. Perhaps the limbs still occasionally looked just a little dislocated from the torso, just as critics had complained all the way back in Coventry; perhaps there was an absence of sexual chemistry with the women; but the voice, once called an oboe, was now definitely a bassoon. And if he grunted and muttered his way through everyone else's lines, pulling focus in a way that not every fellow actor would have found easy to forgive, the audience still lapped it up.

The problem was it could actually have been interesting, rather than just a Cowardly night out. This was a chance to reinvent the play. Like Gary Essendine, or Sir Noel Coward for that matter, Sir Ian McKellen is a star, answering fan mail, dealing with hangers-on. Played as himself, Gary Essendine might have told us something about contemporary celebrity. Done in the wake of his huge success as Gandalf rather than just before it, it could have been even more interesting. As it was, we got McKellen the boulevardier, working within the conventions of teach-yourself-light-comedy and, as the play descends into unconvincing farce, so McKellen descended into a moustache-twirling Lesley Phillips impersonation.

There was much worse to come. Prospero was not a part McKellen had ever particularly wanted to play. He felt daunted by the long, expository speeches to Miranda in the second scene, hurdles over which many a Prospero has stumbled. He wasn't happy with having a Caliban who had already successfully played Prospero elsewhere. But Jude Kelly wanted the greatest classical actor of his generation to do Shakespeare in her theatre, and McKellen agreed. Feeling tired from the high-energy acting of Coward, McKellen struggled through rehearsals. One friend reports him as having been 'very unhappy', adding, 'I think he . . . wanted out.' There were dark tales, as from the stage of *Henceforward*, this time with McKellen reported as 'striding around the stage kicking people'. Certainly it's hard to see how any Prospero could be entirely happy dressed in what looked like an old gardening hat and a see-through plastic mac.

The Tempest closed on 27 February 1999. The trip back to his theatrical roots had been not altogether a happy one. 'It has been one of the most tiring jobs I have done and that probably means that I won't be doing it again,' McKellen told David Ward of the *Guardian*. For once he took a break, and seemed almost shocked at how much he enjoyed it. If a decent film part came along, OK, but he had decided not to go anywhere near a stage for the rest of the year. In the event it would be longer than that. And the film parts that did come along would transform his life, and mean there would be little theatre in the new millennium. *X-Men* and *The Lord of the Rings* were just around the corner.

9. THE BIG SCREEN

McKellen the stage actor has had it easy. Not for him the long periods of unemployment punctuated by a bit on the television and a voice-over, which is the majority of actors' experience of the 'crowded profession'. Never out of work, his career built steadily through rep to the West End. Then the theatre world fell at his feet in 1969 where, give or take a couple of cavilling critics, it has remained ever since. McKellen the screen actor has led a rather different life. Coming out of Cambridge he made the conscious decision to do an apprenticeship in repertory theatre and not go chasing TV parts. In the mid-1960s he had started to dip his toe into television, but it wasn't until 1966, when he was already making a name for himself on the West End stage that McKellen made his first feature film.

The Bells of Hell Go Ting-a-Ling-a-Ling featured Gregory Peck, playing English in a tale of war-time derring-do with McKellen as his faithful lieutenant. They shot in the Alps in August. But whether it would have proved an auspicious big-screen debut will never be known because the snow arrived early in Switzerland that year, the movie was closed down, and McKellen went home with £4,000, which helped keep him comfortable through the next few years of theatre jobs.

The abortive start to his film career rather set the tone for the 1960s. There were the failed screen tests for *Barbarella*, *Star!* and *Ned Kelly*, and there were the ill-judged movies which disappeared without trace like *A Touch of Love* and *Alfred the Great*, both released in 1969. The only things McKellen did on screen during that time which are of real interest now are recreations of his stage performances in *The Promise* (1969), *Richard II* (1970), *Edward II* (1970) and *Hamlet* (1972). Not that they necessarily work that well – the performances look stagy on the small screen – but they do give an inkling of what the stage original might have been like. In 1974 he added *The Recruiting Officer* to the list.

His first agent, Elspeth Cochrane, said she had trouble persuading him to do screen work at all, especially television. His first part on the small screen – two lines in a 1964 BBC series called *Kipling*, which involved sitting up a tree on Ham Common in the rain – hardly encouraged him to take it seriously. And though the occasional better TV part followed, like leads in a BBC *David Copperfield* (1966) and Rattigan's *Ross* (1970), McKellen seems to have retained the old school actor's attitude that screen work was necessary simply in order to boost your pulling power at the theatre box office.

In 1970, at the age of 31, he was still telling interviewers he'd like to find out at some stage if he was any good on film. He saw his first film roles as apprenticeship parts, like the years in rep; now he was waiting for someone to offer him a lead. A couple of years later he seemed to have given up on the medium altogether. 'Films are absolutely the worst of all,' he stormed in an *Evening Standard* interview. 'The actor is never told anything. It is so insulting, so rude and so despicable. I would be glad to not only cut them off but cut their heads off.'

It was less the movies he had made, than the ones he hadn't, which caused the change in attitude. *Ned Kelly* had looked in the bag after the screen test. He'd worked out for three months, learned to ride, and then read in the newspaper that Tony Richardson had given the part to Mick Jagger. *Star!*, Robert Wise's biopic of Gertie Lawrence, looked a sure thing too after the crew applauded his screen test. He got down to the last two for the role of Noel Coward. Daniel Massey got that one, plus an Oscar nomination.

But though publicly he may have turned his back on films in the 1970s, and though his huge success on the stage reached the US as well at the beginning of the next decade with *Amadeus*, friends and colleagues all agree he was desperate to crack the movies as well. Was it simply because the business said, 'You can't have it,' so he wanted it all the more? Was it money? There are those who have written about McKellen who claim he is inordinately interested in money, but a succession of old bangers and houses in unfashionable parts of London hardly suggest they're right. Status perhaps? A British stage actor, however fêted, doesn't approach the celebrity of a minor Hollywood star – any more for that matter than an American stage actor does. At the beginning of the 1980s, for all his stage success, a journalist from *Woman* magazine was still writing, 'Ian McKellen is Ian Mc-who? to all but the country's slim group of theatre-goers.' And people were still mixing him up with the kilted crooner, Kenneth McKellar.

Was it just the simple desire to be the best, to prove himself able to succeed in every department of the actor's craft? Or immortality? Stage performances come and go. Film performances are there for as long as the celluloid lasts. Or was it competitiveness? Albert Finney, Alan Bates, Tom Courtenay and Anthony Hopkins were all successfully combining theatre and screen. Michael York and David Hemmings were movie stars. Jacobi had made it on TV with *I, Claudius*. His contemporaries were leaving him behind. Why? At the very end of the 1970s it became clear.

Director Christopher Miles, brother of Sarah Miles, saw the last night of *Bent* in the West End. With a budget of £3 m and locations lined up in Mexico and Italy, he was in pre-production of a film based on a biography of D H Lawrence by Harry T Moore called *Priest of Love*. What he was looking for was an actor who actually looked like the author of *Sons and Lovers*. Thin and hollow-cheeked as Max in the concentration camp, McKellen certainly looked as if he could be suffering from the tuberculosis which killed Lawrence. The next day Miles called Jimmy Sharkey, McKellen's agent, and asked to see him. One look at the actor's blue eyes, and that was it. Lawrence had blue eyes; McKellen had blue eyes; he was the man for the job. At the age of forty, Ian McKellen finally had a crack at a leading role in a major film.

In the theatre it would be the kind of extended rehearsal period he had got used to at the RSC that would come next. But films aren't made that way. He read the book. He found it stodgy. He fell back on externals. He had the blue eyes. With his hair cropped and dyed and a little triangular beard he did bear a fair resemblance to the man. He went on a crash diet to make himself look more tubercular. But what about inside? A phrase in the book about the author bounding into a room caught his attention. 'I imagined he had a lot of surplus energy and a lot of things gnawing away at his innards,' he told Michael Billington. It seemed like a useful clue for an actor. For McKellen on screen it was disaster.

Still searching for some inkling of how to play the man, McKellen approached the screenwriter, Alan Plater, at the pre-filming cast party at Stanley Seeger's Mayfair address. Seeger, an American millionaire, had put up the entire budget of the film. 'What would Lawrence be doing?' he asked Plater.

'Just sit in a corner and watch,' came the reply. Since that was what Plater himself seemed to be doing, McKellen decided to base the character on him. His preparations for playing the role had become increasingly desperate, and on screen that's exactly how McKellen comes across – desperate. Always with a tendency to over-energise on stage, resulting in those twitchy feet and mangled vowels, he over-energises on screen as Lawrence, twitching and fidgeting and looking for the most part thoroughly uncomfortable. At the same time, in an apparent attempt to play down for the camera, the whole performance is oddly muted. His friendship with Janet Suzman, then Mrs Trevor Nunn and playing Frieda Lawrence, helps a bit. He looks relaxed in bed with her, but the relationship only erupts at moments of violence. Suzman plays with some welcome panache; Ava Gardner adds old-fashioned star quality; Penelope Keith does her usual thing as the Honourable Dorothy Brett. But Miles and Plater help not at all, taking the audience on a kind of travelogue to a range of 'authentic' locations without appearing to have any idea of how to photograph them. The story is entirely without dramatic structure, relying on ill-assorted flashbacks and cuts to an all-purpose Colonel Blimp figure from John Gielgud, designed to represent repressive old England. Presumably panicked in post production, music has been laid on with a shovel.

There are moments which hint at something better. Nearly an hour and a half in, the film finally stutters into life, as McKellen and Suzman discuss the manuscript of Lawrence's latest, *Lady Chatterley's Lover*. In the darkened bedroom, quizzing Frieda about women's sexuality, McKellen's Lawrence actually might be a creative artist for the first time. The deathbed scene is affecting too. Playing the final stages of tuberculosis, McKellen is forced to use less energy, but maintains his intensity. But for the most part the whole enterprise looks like the fatal combination of a director who doesn't know how to tell a story and a star who doesn't know how to carry a film. The most interesting aspect of the film is spotting the visitors to the set – Penelope Keith's husband Detective Constable Rodney Timson as a tourist in Mexico, Sarah Miles as a film star signing autographs and – as her assistant in a very dashing white suit and a ludicrous hat – that's a 23-year-old Sean Mathias.

With the failure of *Priest of Love*, McKellen's screen career went back into the doldrums. He was in an Anglo-American TV version of *The Scarlet Pimpernel*, cast as Chauvelin opposite Jane Seymour's Marguerite Blakeney and Antony Andrews's Sir Percy, in 1982. He played a Jewish professor taken from Auschwitz by a couple of Nazis to exorcise a demon called Molasar in Michael Mann's bizarre *The Keep* in 1983. In 1985 he did a no-budgeter called *Zina* for Ken McMullen, and the following year, while at the National Theatre, he fitted in a cameo in Fred Schepisi's movie of *Plenty*, filming only on Sundays in the British Foreign Office as Sir Andrew Charleson. Through it all he retained a slightly pathetic enthusiasm, telling Tim Pulleyne of the *Guardian* in 1985: 'I'm more excited now when a film script comes through the letter box than when I'm asked about a play.'

But at the beginning and end of the 1980s McKellen did have two important screen roles. The first was by far his most successful TV part. The second was yet another missed opportunity on the big screen.

Back in 1965 a young actor named David Cook had played a tiny role at the St Martin's Theatre in *A Lily in Little India*. His main duty was understudying Ian McKellen. Cook had had periods out of work like most actors, and turned to writing with some success. His third novel, *Walter*, which told the harrowing story of what happens to a mentally handicapped young man after both his parents die, won the Hawthornden Prize for imaginative literature in 1978. TV producer Nigel Evans, with a track record of making tough documentaries about handicapped people, including the shocking *Silent Minority*, thought the book would make a movie. He sold the idea to Jeremy Isaacs, boss of the brand new Channel 4, due to go on air for the first time on 2 November 1982. David Cook started work on the screenplay.

Himself a native Lancastrian, Cook had McKellen in mind as he wrote the screenplay. At 42, McKellen was really too old for the part, but make-up and a boyish haircut could deal with that. The finished script was sent to McKellen in New York, as he was coming to the end of the run of *Amadeus*. For an actor who likes variety in his work, it could not have arrived at a better time. To go from the glitz of Peter Shaffer's Broadway hit to the gritty, neo-realism of *Walter*, shooting in a derelict wing of the old Royal Free Hospital in Islington with a supporting cast of real handicapped people, was about as great a contrast as could be found. Add to that the fact that Isaacs had decided *Walter* would screen on Channel 4's opening night, inaugurating the prestigious Film on 4 slot, and the part looked better still. There was even an old Cambridge friend directing – Stephen Frears. According to producer Nigel Evans, the film wouldn't have been made if McKellen had said no. He said 'Yes'.

Playing a severely mentally handicapped man was going to be the greatest challenge of McKellen's screen career so far, and this time he prepared thoroughly. Extended work with ex-nurse David Parsons and with the author, who had based the story on his own experiences of working in a mental hospital in the 1960s, produced ideas for Walter's physicality – the unfocused, wandering eyes, the shuffling walk, the head tilted a little to one side. But what about inside that head? That was harder. The book gives the reader access to Walter's confused thoughts. A film can't do that. But if the viewer was to empathise with the man, McKellen had to make them understand what the world looked like from his point of view. Rereading the book, he was taken by a comparison of the thoughts in Walter's head to 'fish darting about in a goldfish bowl, too slippery to grasp'.

The result of this careful preparation, combined with the skilful direction of Stephen Frears and the cinematography of Chris Menges, schooled in the semi-documentary style of Ken Loach on *Kes* (1969), is one of the high points of British television. All possibility of sentimentality is squeezed out of the story by the casual brutality with which his workmates treat Walter and an outstanding performance from Barbara Jefford as the religious maniac mother who regards her offspring as 'one of Jesus's mistakes'. First Walter's father dies, then his mother. He moves his beloved pigeons into her room and, while the birds deposit their droppings on the corpse, he sits waiting to see whether Jesus will return her to him, as he prays, or take her up to heaven. Eventually he is carted off to a relic of the Victorian asylums, where the mentally ill are mixed with the mentally and physically handicapped, and a paraplegic dwarf sexually assaults him on his first night in the vast dormitory. In the morning Jim Broadbent's world-weary nurse orders Walter to clean excrement off the quadriplegic in the bed next to him. But Walter and the film survive this descent into *grand guignol*. He finds a role looking after the most severely handicapped and disturbed patients, and the film broadens its focus to say something about society's treatment of the unfortunate and the survival of human dignity.

McKellen is utterly convincing throughout. His Walter conveys incomprehension, terror and anger at the way his workmates tease him. He goes from screaming hysteria at his mother's rejection of his slobbering kisses to childlike bliss at her caresses. He fondles and nuzzles his father's pigeons, as if he has indeed spent his entire life as a bird-fancier. His terrible grief, screaming and sobbing over his mother's corpse as he's dragged away to the asylum, is harrowing in the extreme and entirely devoid of any sense of being an externally created effect – a criticism so often levelled at his moments of high emotion on stage. Even the dislocated limbs, exaggerated here, become an integral part of a complete physical and mental characterisation.

So where does the performance come from? How has he moved from the unease of Lawrence to the total immersion in Walter? Of course, it's a lot to do with the quality of the script and the excellence of the director. Stephen Frears, who would break through internationally a couple of years later with *My Beautiful Laundrette*, before going on to quality hits like *Dangerous Liaisons* (1988), *The Grifters* (1990) and *High Fidelity* (2000), was the first top rank film director McKellen had worked with. But the brilliance of the performance is also to do with the nature of the role. Walter's Lancashire vowels are McKellen's own, but apart from that, the character is a complete disguise – internally and externally. The very extremity of the role is what frees McKellen from the tension and anxiety which had blighted his screen acting. Walter is not self-revelation, something which McKellen had found so hard for so long. Because his very mental processes are so utterly at variance with the actor's own, Walter is closer to the disappearance of self.

Walter caused quite an uproar on the first night of Channel 4 – which was the whole idea, of course. There were phone calls of complaint; there were letters to the press. 'Channel 4's *Walter* touched a new low in television obscenity,' offered the Reverend E Ward on the letters page of the *Daily Mirror*. And when the sequel, *Walter and June*, was aired in May 1983 the whole furore broke out again, as McKellen's Walter had sex with Sarah Miles's mentally ill June. But most of the serious critics loved it, and McKellen won an award as Royal Television Society Performer of the Year. 'I don't think I really considered until we started work that this might be anything other than an ordinary part,' he told the *Daily Mail* at the time. But the experience of working with the mentally and physically handicapped people Frears recruited to play the other inmates of the nightmarish asylum had quite an impact. 'My perception of human beings has been changed in two weeks,' McKellen went on, 'and that doesn't often happen with a part.'

That was the high point of the 1980s for McKellen the screen actor. But it was TV. And British TV at that. So as far as the American movie world was concerned, it didn't exist. And McKellen's improvement didn't last, because the following year he was back to B-picture hell with *The Keep*. But at the end of the decade McKellen did finally get what looked like a decent part in a decent film. The result proved that *Walter* had been something of a false dawn.

Stephen Woolley of Palace Pictures had spent six years trying to raise money to make a film about the greatest political sex scandal of the 1960s. In 1963 secretary of state for war John Profumo, married to the film star Valerie Hobson, was forced to resign after lying to the House of Commons about his relationship with a good-time girl named Christine Keeler. Keeler had been having sex with the British war minister and the Russian naval attaché, Eugene Ivanov, at the same time – and in 1963 'Russian naval attaché' meant 'spy'.

It seemed an obvious subject for a commercial movie, but Woolley was having trouble selling his idea. The original plan was for a four-and-a-half-hour television mini-series, but the BBC didn't want it, and none of the ITV majors wanted it, and pretty soon Woolley was convinced it was political interference that was preventing his film from being made. Eventually he went to the bank and borrowed half the £3 m budget himself, and 270 minutes on the small screen turned into 110 minutes on the big screen. Something was gained, but more was lost.

No one seemed to want to play Jack Profumo. Donald Pleasance was said to be first choice, then there was talk of David Suchet. McKellen says that, having come out as gay at the start of 1988, he took the part to prove he could be convincing as a heterosexual. But the reason actors didn't want to play Profumo may have had less to do with politics and more to do with Michael Thomas's script. To get the story down to feature length, the film was concentrating on what the makers saw as the central and tragic character of the story, not Profumo but Stephen Ward, the society osteopath who introduced Keeler and her friend Mandy Rice-Davies to London society and who was said to have provided girls for all the top drawer risqué parties of the time.

Arrested as a pimp when the scandal broke, Ward took an overdose of sleeping pills and died on the last day of his trial.

John Hurt was already on board as Stephen Ward. The Right Reverend Jim Thompson, the Bishop of Stepney, wrote to Hurt and McKellen asking them to reconsider taking part, saying that Profumo and his family should be left to live their lives in peace. Since his resignation Profumo had devoted himself to voluntary work in the East End and Thompson was not the only one to think he had rehabilitated himself for his indiscretion of 25 years earlier.

John Hurt responded publicly to the bishop in the *Evening Standard*, 'He's not being very bright.' McKellen wrote to Profumo himself, inviting an exchange of views, but received no reply. With Joanne Whalley, who had aroused Michael Gambon and the rest of the nation in *The Singing Detective*, as Christine Keeler, and Bridget Fonda stepping in as Mandy Rice-Davies after Emily Lloyd pulled out, the film began shooting in June 1988. It would turn into a film acting master class from John Hurt.

Wholly at ease with the camera, drawing the viewer to him with his stillness and suggesting inner processes with those haunted eyes, Hurt made a fine job of Ward, turning what might have been a sleazy exploitation film into an unlikely tragedy. If Michael Caton-Jones as director had tightened the story up and injected a little more variety of pace, the film might have been really good. As it is, *Scandal* is pitched uneasily between farce and filth and political drama, with an orgy scene bunged in for good measure. For his part, McKellen has a nightmare. Sporting a hairstyle which makes him look like a Klingon and which he himself admitted in a *Time Out* interview of October 1996 made him 'the laughing stock of five continents', he wanders uneasily around the periphery of the plot, which is not his fault, making his lust for Joanne Whalley less than convincing, which is. Hurt makes him look wooden, awkward and downright amateurish.

Scandal did respectably at the box office, but after his outing as Jack Profumo no sane filmmaker would ever trust McKellen with a leading role in a major movie. He himself seems to have thought that was it, telling *Observer in London* in August 1989, 'It's a slight mystery as to why bigger film roles haven't come my way, but now I've been left behind.' He was fifty. He'd missed the boat as a movie juvenile long ago. Now he'd just proved he couldn't play leading character parts either. He disappeared back into the theatre. For three years there were no more screen roles at all, and in the end it would take do-it-yourself on a scale which made the Actors' Company look like something at the end of the pier, to bring McKellen the successful leading part in a film he had always wanted.

On 1 June 1992, the National Theatre's stage production of *Richard III*, starring Ian McKellen, reached New York. It was the final leg of a massive world tour, but McKellen was not ready to let go of the part yet. Kenneth Branagh had proved there was a modern audience for Shakespeare on film with his *Henry V* in 1989. More importantly he had had the temerity to challenge head-on Olivier's famous 1944 version and bring it off. So why shouldn't McKellen take on Olivier's equally iconic 1955 film of *Richard III*?

Richard Eyre told him if he really wanted to play Richard III on screen, he'd have to write the screenplay himself. So through the fifteen-week tour of the USA which followed, that is precisely what McKellen did. Retaining the fascist 1930s setting of the stage production and taking his cues for the location of scenes from Bob Crowley's design, McKellen produced a draft which he showed to Eyre. Depending on who you believe, Eyre said he wouldn't direct it because he couldn't be away from the National Theatre for so long, or he said he wouldn't direct it because he thought the screenplay was rubbish. But in any event, the lack of a director was the least of McKellen's worries. Money was the real problem – money and his own lack of experience of movie making. With typical determination – or perhaps stubbornness – he set out to remedy both deficiencies.

When the play closed in Los Angeles, McKellen turned his back on the theatre for a full five years, apart from brief outings for his one-man show. He threw himself into an endless round of meetings with the movers and shakers of the movie world in an attempt to raise finance for his *Richard III* and an endless round of small movie parts. The film roles paid the bills. They also gave him a chance to learn everything he could about the whole process of making films – after all, he was to be writer and executive producer on this one, not just an actor. Taking minor movie roles also meant he was never committed to a long-term contract, so that as and when finance came through for the film, he would be free to start. Maybe he was too old to become a matinee idol

– he'd never really had the looks for that anyway – but he could still prove himself as a lead actor in a film, even if he had to create the film himself.

In the next four years McKellen made nine films for television or theatrical release. There were tiny cameos, like his day on Arnold Schwarzenegger's *Last Action Hero* (1993), during which he wandered New York's Times Square in a bald wig and white face paint as Death. There were some real turkeys, like *The Shadow* (1994), in which he camped it up with Tim Curry in a mad scientist routine, and *Jack and Sarah* (1994). There was historical hokum like *Rasputin* (1995) with McKellen in a nice uniform as the last of the Russian Czars and *Restoration* (1995) as Robert Downey Jr's quasi-comic servant with a quasi-Suffolk accent. There was a real life drama close to McKellen's heart, *And the Band Played On* (1993), in which he played a gay activist dying of AIDS in the early days of the epidemic. He got a Cable Ace Award and an Emmy Nomination for his portrayal of Bill Kraus in that one, but it was only TV, so once again nobody paid a great deal of attention in Hollywood. The same goes for the Golden Globe Award he got for *Rasputin*. He even got to play himself in Fiona Cunningham-Reid's *Thin Ice* (1995), set around the Gay Games in New York in 1994, for which McKellen had created *A Knight Out*. And along the way there was some real quality in John Schlesinger's BBC film of *Cold Comfort Farm* (1994) and Fred Schepisi's *Six Degrees of Separation* in 1993. And also along the way, McKellen began to learn about making films.

For instance, in the first in the sequence of supporting roles in Maggie Greenwald's off-beat western, *The Ballad of Little Jo*, shot in Montana in 1992, the effects McKellen believes coming out had on his acting at last begin to show on screen. He looks comfortable in his skin. As the deeply unlikeable Percy, who attacks a whore who won't go down on him and then tries to rape the heroine, Jo, a woman passing as a man in the American west, he is learning how to draw the camera to him like John Hurt.

On *Six Degrees of Separation* he makes a hash of the accent as the South African Geoffrey. But watching Stockard Channing tone down her stage performance for the camera taught him lessons which could be valuable for *Richard III* – if he ever found the money.

And in *Cold Comfort Farm* he makes the most of his chances as the hellfire preacher Amos Starkadder. Though Schlesinger complained furiously about the stingy BBC budget, he made a good shot at capturing the subtlety of Stella Gibbons's classic comic novel, shooting mostly around his own home village of Robertsbridge in Sussex. Freddie Jones and Eileen Atkins are both on great form and a 21-year-old Kate

Beckinsale is charmingly prim as Flora Poste. For Amos, McKellen drew on what he remembered of his own grandfather, William H McKellen's preaching style. He booms and thunders magnificently to the Quivering Brethren, climaxing with a great cry of 'there'll be no butter in hell!' Being a preacher, it's really a chance to give a stage performance on screen, but even so it's very funny. Only the Sussex accent tends to slip and slide around the British countryside.

On 18 May 1993, at the Cannes Film Festival, McKellen proudly announced plans for the making of a film of *Richard III*. Anthony Hopkins and Dame Maggie Smith were both possible starters. An as yet unnamed American actress would play Queen Elizabeth: McKellen had conceived her as a kind of Wallace Simpson figure, the American divorcee whose relationship with Edward VIII led to his abdication in 1936. He would play the lead role himself. Of course, it didn't really mean anything. Cannes is largely about trying to whip up interest for possible films and selling films that have already been made. McKellen found no backers.

Two years later, directors and cast members had come and gone; Hopkins had been courted unsuccessfully for Buckingham; Patrick Stewart had been announced as Clarence; Marisa Tomei had been mooted as Lady Anne; Al Pacino was said to have asked McKellen for a part and been turned down; Anjelica Houston was on board as the Queen – probably. Meryl Streep had been approached: McKellen jokes that he asked her if she could do an American accent! Alex Cox and Julien Temple had been possible directors; Nic Roeg was said to have flirted with it. As for the money, that finally seemed to be in place. UA-MGM were on board, along with Mayfair Entertainment and British Screen. The BBC had put up the final 10 per cent for terrestrial TV rights. The film was on.

Then it was off. On 31 March 1995, with pre-production under way, the *Daily Mail* announced that the BBC had pulled out. The cast began to peel away immediately. Stewart and Houston took other jobs, and McKellen was talking about giving up and going back to the theatre. Sean Mathias was directing Judi Dench at the National in Stephen Sondheim's *A Little Night Music*. Could McKellen cope with the singing well enough to play opposite her as Frederick? What a reunion for the Macbeths nearly twenty years on. Send in the Glamis . . .

Then, at the last moment, Rupert Murdoch's BSkyB agreed to step in, and *Richard III*, the movie, was on again.

At the helm was Richard Loncraine, director of some 420 TV commercials, as well as *Brimstone and Treacle* (1982) and *The Missionary*

(1983). Loncraine was most definitely not a Shakespeare man. He didn't go to the theatre, and he didn't like Branagh's Shakespeare films. But looking at McKellen's script, a severely cut version of the play with clear echoes of 1930s gangster pictures, Loncraine thought there was new ground to be found. He and McKellen worked solidly for three months on the script. 'I stick up for Shakespeare and he sticks up for cinema,' was McKellen's description of their working method in an *Independent on Sunday* interview.

Realising that the £6 m budget was cutting it very fine, Loncraine had set himself to woo leading actors into taking part in the film for much less than the going rate. Tim McInnerny, best known for the *Black Adder* series, was contacted about playing Catesby and invited to Loncraine's house. He describes the director's method: 'First of all there were cups of tea and being introduced to the family, which was totally disarming. Then he spent an hour talking about me and not auditioning at all in any shape or form and I began to realise that what he was doing was attempting to persuade me to play the role, which is of course terribly flattering. It may have been genuine or a brilliant mind game, but it certainly worked because I'd said "Yes" before I left his house.'

The method worked equally well on Maggie Smith, Bill Paterson, John Wood, Nigel Hawthorne, Jim Broadbent and Kristin Scott Thomas. But the American distributors were adamant that they had to have American stars. Loncraine dug out his old address book.

Back in 1983, after the release of *The Missionary*, he had received a phone call of congratulation from none other than Warren Beatty. Beatty had been married since 1992 to Annette Bening. As far as Loncraine was concerned, she was top choice to play Queen Elizabeth. Time was short. Without an American star, the funding would collapse again. Cutting through the usual channels of agents and managers, he phoned the number Beatty had given him twelve years earlier. Warren answered himself and, within days, Bening had read the script and agreed to do it. Then, on the strength of the friendship he and McKellen had struck up during *Restoration*, Robert Downey Jr agreed to play the tiny part of Queen Elizabeth's brother, the Earl of Rivers. To accommodate his nationality, the character was renamed Earl Rivers. Loncraine admitted Bening was nervous about filming Shakespeare: 'Rightly so,' he told Peter Guttridge in November 1995. 'I'm very nervous: I got through more underwear in the first week than most people do in a lifetime.'

The joke is typical, and exemplifies his sometimes iconoclastic approach to shooting the film. If Fred Schepisi had coaxed from Stockard Channing a performance more suited to the screen, Loncraine's methods with McKellen were rather different. At the least sign of his star slipping into a rhetorical manner, he would burst out in broad cockney, 'What's all this bollocks? Ian, what are you doing? We don't want any of that theatrical crap!'

Actor and director had established a level of trust which facilitated the tight schedule the budget demanded. And money remained a problem even during the shoot. In fact, at one stage cash ran out to a point where producer Stephen Bayly had to take drastic action. 'The story I got,' relates Tim McInnerny, 'was that Steve put a second mortgage on his house over the weekend.'

There were a few lighter moments during the shoot. One sunny day the star suddenly appeared in the doorway of his trailer wearing nothing but his underpants, struck a bathing beauty pose and cried out in his campest voice, 'Not bad for fifty-six!'

'And it wasn't either actually,' comments McInnerny who was among the surprised onlookers.

But the pressure told on McKellen, who returned his acting fee to pay for another day shooting the climactic battle scenes, and most of the time seemed obsessed with the job – if he wasn't in the shot himself, he was either behind the camera or in a meeting. Tim McInnerny sums up, 'My memory is of Ian being a rather solitary figure. He would occasionally have a laugh and joke with people but there was no staying up late and having a good time. It seemed a question of getting through it before he collapsed.'

And get through it they did, co-opting a range of buildings around London as locations. St Pancras became a seaside palace; the basement of County Hall stood in for royal chambers and a hospital morgue; and with a little digital trickery the battle of Bosworth Field was fought outside Battersea Power Station.

The film opened to considerable critical excitement on both sides of the Atlantic (in December 1995 in the US and April 1996 in the UK) and went on to be the London *Evening Standard* film of the year. McKellen won the European Actor of the Year award, was nominated for a Golden Globe and was rumoured to be just a few votes short of an Oscar nomination. But looking at it now, *Richard III* only seems a very partial success. The best scenes are the ones which worked best on stage – the shadowy interiors peopled with paranoid politicians. But generally, despite its Oscar nomination for costume design, the film lacks a visual style. It needs darkness and a sense of the oppression of the 1930s architecture featured so prominently. On the other hand, it manipulates its locations cleverly, and manages to hide the low budget, except for the final battle scene when Loncraine struggles to fill the frame with two tanks and a bonfire and a great deal of Battersea Power Station. Crucially what it finds no answer to is the perennial problem of Shakespeare on film – how do you scale performances down appropriately for the camera without scaling down the impact of the play? Because the impact of the play comes through the language. Here, the language loses most of its form and pressure and size, so all the characters and the relationships between the characters are eviscerated.

McKellen, for his part, in trying to scale himself down for the camera, blunts the edges of his characterisation, losing detail and subtlety, so that the misogyny of the stage version's 'shallow changing *woman*' is reduced to the conventional '*shallow, changing* woman'. And Richard turns from the psychological study he'd attempted on stage back into the medieval 'vice' figure from which he sprang.

Annette Bening, despite a panning from the British press, actually makes a pretty decent fist of it, but no one in the starry cast has the right level of intensity. So, in place of the punch of the language, we get the familiar Hollywood punch of explosions and quick cutting, but without the resources to make them work.

Loncraine and McKellen had set out to make a film that would draw an audience that didn't usually go to Shakespeare. Limited success at the box office suggests they did not succeed. It would be left to Baz Luhrmann's radical reimagining of *Romeo + Juliet*, released in the same year as *Richard III*, to capture the holy grail of the youth market. That film opened wide in the US and made serious money. Looking back on his own film a few years later, McKellen seems to have felt it lacked the gravitas he'd hoped for when he started. Certainly for Ian McKellen in Shakespeare on screen a viewer is much better off with the DVD of *Macbeth* or *Othello*, both transferred to the screen by Trevor Nunn.

In 1997 McKellen put in appearances in two more films that had very limited life in the cinema. On location in Cornwall for Beeban Kidron's *Swept from the Sea* he shared a house with Rachel Weisz. Like many young actors, male and female, she found him an avuncular figure – 'very easygoing and easy to live with, like a student,' she told *Hello* magazine. She also enjoyed his cooking. In fact, the two struck up a friendship which saw Weisz, already a rising star, take on the tiny part of a prostitute in Sean Mathias's crack at turning *Bent* into a movie, which was McKellen's other screen outing in 1997. Now much too old for Max – the part went to Clive Owen, with Lothaire Blutheau as Horst – he had a one-scene cameo as the closeted Uncle Freddie. But over in Hollywood, *Richard III* was beginning to take effect.

Though it may only have screened in four cinemas in the USA, the critical success of *Richard III* established McKellen for the first time as a major player in the movie business. It left him with no desire whatever to repeat his experience as screenwriter and executive producer. In fact, his response to the completion of the film was a resounding, 'Never again.' But it did open the way for the unlikely movie stardom which has come to him in his seventh decade. In that sense, *Richard III* stands as one of the most expensive calling cards in history.

One Tinseltown director who saw *Richard III* was Bryan Singer, who had had a major hit with *The Usual Suspects*, released in the US roughly four moths before *Richard III*. Singer was casting his latest project, a screen adaptation of the Stephen King novella *Apt Pupil*. There had been a previous attempt to film the story which had run over budget and been closed down back in 1987. Nicol Williamson had been playing the leading role of the Nazi war criminal, Kurt Dussander, who is living under another name in a quiet American community until a high school boy discovers who he is. It may have been partly the British casting in the earlier film which had Singer looking at McKellen for his own version, but after the fascist iconography of *Richard III*, it was also probably inevitable that Hollywood would offer him Nazis.

Singer thought McKellen was too young to play the 75-year-old Dussander. Then it transpired the director had also recently seen *Cold Comfort Farm*, which John Schlesinger had had transferred at his own expense to 35mm for theatrical release. Singer had liked the film. But he hadn't recognised the actor playing the ancient Amos Starkadder. It was what Hollywood loves – someone who's done it before. McKellen had been a convincing quasi-Nazi and a convincing old man. Put them together and you've got Kurt Dussander. Normally chary of anything that smacks of repeating himself, McKellen thought the part too good to refuse. After all, it was his first Hollywood lead.

The film is a potentially very interesting variation on a winter/spring story. Brad Renfro plays the high school student, Todd Bowden, who develops a fascination for the Nazis, spots a man in his neighbourhood who closely resembles one of the pictures in his books about war criminals, and proceeds to track him down. Rather than exposing the old Nazi, Todd wants graphic accounts of what he did in the concentration camps, and the film then turns into an investigation of who is corrupting and manipulating whom.

As the old Nazi, Kurt Dussander, McKellen treads a difficult line with some skill. His face aged by make-up artist Daniel Parker who had done Richard III's face, he potters, heavy footed and stiff legged, around his low-rent house, avoiding any temptation to play for audience sympathy. Invited to dinner with Todd's parents, he turns on a lethal charm in what is probably the film's most chilling sequence, showing the surface plausibility of a man the viewer knows to be a monster. The German accent comes and goes occasionally, and he doesn't noticeably attempt the much harder task of a German who has lived in America for forty years. But he deploys a wonderfully asthmatic, wheezing laugh, and the extended duologues with Renfro are compelling. For most of the film's 111 minutes, McKellen resists the plot's attempts to push him into melodrama. Only when Todd insists on him dressing up in a Nazi uniform and marching, and the clothes somehow ignite his old Nazi self, does the film start to slip into something a good deal less convincing.

The problem with the film is that the plot is wildly implausible. The idea that a fourteen-year-old should be able to track down a Nazi war criminal so easily, where the combined forces of law and order have failed, is unbelievable, and the coincidence which precipitates the film's crisis, in which Dussander ends up in a hospital bed next to an ex-concentration camp inmate, is ridiculous. The boy is also under-motivated. In spite of a fair amount of screen time for the rest of his family, there is no insight into what has generated his fascination with Nazism.

More interestingly, there seems to be a gay subtext to the film struggling to get out. Critics have tended to discover such underlying themes in McKellen's films, sometimes, it seems, simply because of the publicly proclaimed sexuality of the actor himself. But here it is too clear to ignore. The subtext surfaces most obviously late in the film in the character of the tramp who thinks Dussander is picking him up for gay sex, but in fact ends up getting murdered in the kitchen. At the very end it's back again in a wholly unconvincing sequence in which David Schwimmer's moustachioed school councillor is scared off by Todd with threats of sexual allegations. But it's also there in the way that Brad Renfro is shot – naked in the showers, bare torsoed in bed and, more oddly, on the basketball court. Then there's some very strange dialogue in one of Renfro and McKellen's scenes as they debate who is manipulating whom: 'You're f***ing me,' says Renfro. 'We're f***ing each other,' is McKellen's reply.

The shower sequence actually generated legal controversy after parents of the extras playing the other high-school students alleged that Singer had bullied their boys, aged between fourteen and seventeen, into appearing nude. A civil suit, alleging false imprisonment, unlawful sexual harassment and intentional infliction of emotional distress, was filed, though the authorities eventually found no basis for prosecution. The scene was reshot using other actors before release.

Apt Pupil is not a great film, nor did it do too well at the box office, though with a budget of just $14 m there wasn't too much riding on its success, but it was another very significant step for McKellen the screen actor. This wasn't Laurence Olivier doing his guest spot as an old Nazi in a Dustin Hoffman picture (*Marathon Man*); this was a McKellen picture – his was the leading role. And in his first Hollywood leading role, he had proved that he could now carry a movie. Less than two weeks after *Apt Pupil* opened in the US, McKellen had another movie on general release, which would raise his profile still further and start people talking about Oscars again.

Gods and Monsters was actually filmed before *Apt Pupil*, but despite rave reviews at the 1998 Sundance Festival, it then struggled through most of the year to find a distributor, and was within hours of disappearing into the 'release straight to video' pile when director Bill Condon finally found a buyer.

A philosophy graduate who moved to LA from New York in 1983, Condon had been doing time in what he called in an *Independent* interview 'filmmaker's jail', directing cable movies, when he was approached by British horror writer Clive Barker about making a film of Christopher Bram's 1985 novel *Gods and Monsters*, a fictionalised account of the last days in the life of film director James Whale. Born in a one-up one-down back-to-back in working class Dudley in the Midlands, Whale had discovered acting as a prisoner of war during World War I. After the war he appeared on stage with John Gielgud and Noel Coward before directing the original production in 1929 of R C Sherriff's classic drama of trench warfare *Journey's End*. The following year he went to Hollywood to turn it into a film, and stayed to invent Hollywood horror movies in the 1930s, directing among others *Frankenstein* (1930), *The Old Dark House* (1932), *The Invisible Man* (1933) and *The Bride of Frankenstein* (1935). But in 1940 he retired from filmmaking and became a virtual recluse in his house in Pacific Pallisades, eventually committing suicide in 1957 at the age of 67 by drowning himself in his swimming pool.

Christopher Bram's novel focuses on the end of Whale's life, building a story about a relationship between Whale and his young gardener. It also centres on the fact that he was homosexual, living more or less openly for over two decades with film producer David Lewis. Hailing from the north(ish) of England? A stage actor in London before coming to Hollywood to make movies? Gay? Christopher Bram claimed to have been thinking of McKellen as he wrote the book. Bill Condon certainly had him in mind as he wrote the screenplay.

Condon sent the finished script to McKellen in London, but was met with silence. Unwilling to give up, Condon pestered his agent to pursue the actor, to persuade him at least to read the script. When McKellen finally did get round to it, he immediately realised the part was made for him.

This was a low budget film, to be shot for $3 m in just 24 days, so McKellen and Condon decided to do their preparation carefully. McKellen flew out to Hollywood to talk to people who had known James Whale. He spoke to TV director Curtis Harrington and Gavin Lambert, screenwriter on *The Roman Spring of Mrs Stone* (1961). He met the 97-year-old actor David Manners who had taken over from Laurence Olivier in the original stage version of *Journey's End* and gone on to make the film. But no one could agree on what sort of man Whale had really been. There were photographs, showing a carefully dressed, slightly dandified character, but no film and no recording of his voice.

Still looking for clues, they drove out to Pacific Pallisades to look at the house where Whale had died. Goldie Hawn had done a complete makeover when she owned the place and there was little to be learned there. Then the current owner dropped a little titbit into the conversation, saying she had had trouble with a poltergeist when she first moved in. The exorcist she got in claimed it was James Whale himself throwing things around, and dealt with the problem. 'She said this,' McKellen observed wryly in an interview with Demetrios Matheou, 'to a group of people who would have given part of their body to come in contact with his ghost.'

Condon, meanwhile, was feeling somewhat intimidated by his star, as much for the directors he had worked with as for his acting talents. 'It was like being the new lover of someone who has been in bed with many of the greatest filmmakers of all time,' was how he put it to Liese Spencer of the *Independent*.

With research inconclusive, McKellen was thrown back on the script – which is where he prefers to be anyway – and on himself. And of all his screen roles to date this is the one that is closest to himself, which is perhaps why it is arguably his best. McKellen's James Whale is a finely judged performance, full of variety: there is the naughtiness and sly humour of the scene where he persuades an enthusiastic interviewer to remove an article of clothing for each question he answers; there is desire, bitterness and pain. The script wants to fit in more back story than is really good for the film, and the flashback sequences are a little uneasy, featuring cheap war footage. But McKellen copes well with all the memory close-ups, eyes widening and lips twitching with great subtlety, as he slips into nightmare memories of the trenches. Condon builds interesting and highly unusual relationships between Whale and the other two main characters, his Teutonic housekeeper, a grotesque drawn consciously from Whale's own movies and played with relish by Lynn Redgrave, and Clay, the gardener, played by Brendan Fraser.

Only at the beginning of the final act – much the same place as *Apt Pupil* goes off the rails – does *Gods and Monsters* really falter. The climax of the plot turns on the hoary old Hollywood cliché of getting all wet in a rainstorm, prompting the shedding of clothes and a final consummation of Whale's desire for his previously heterosexual gardener. At this point Condon unwisely slips into the *grand guignol* of Whale's monster movies with thunder and lightning and naked men in gas masks. Condon told *The Times*, 'I thought there was a chance to make a film about Whale in the style of him.' But Whale's campy humour is out of place. The strength of *Gods and Monsters* is in the meticulous detail, subtlety and absolute believability of McKellen's performance.

So what had happened since *Priest of Love*? Where had all the fidgeting and rushing gone? For one thing, there was the coming out factor: 'If I can be Gandalf or James Whale in front of the camera, it's because I can be Ian McKellen away from the camera.' There's also the fact that he'd had a lot more practice, doing all those bits during the 90s. McKellen puts a great deal of the change down to confidence. Actors like Peter O'Toole or Kenneth Branagh look as if they were born with absolute self-confidence, but McKellen had to learn his. He learned it first with Tyrone Guthrie on stage. Now he had learned it on screen. He wasn't frightened of the camera any more. He had come to realise that all those technicians peering at him from the dark, people who had once seemed so threatening, were not there to judge. They were there to help. They wanted him to be good. It's the same breakthrough many actors have about auditions: the people behind the table don't want you to fail – they want you to be good; they want you to succeed.

After *Apt Pupil* opened, a senior figure in the film industry whom McKellen didn't know telephoned to congratulate him on his performance as Kurt Dussander. He was particularly impressed with the way McKellen even smoked in character, holding his cigarette the way people of that generation tended to hold them. That kind of detail had been fundamental to a McKellen stage performance for years – one has only to think of Iago and his roll-ups – now he was taking the time to build that kind of detail into his film acting. On stage the details can turn into studied 'business', leading to the accusations of striving for external effects which continue to dog McKellen. But, as director Richard Lester (*Superman II* and *Superman III*) has said, film making is not like a performance, it's more like a rehearsal with the camera rolling. The actors try out different things on different takes, and the director chooses which one works best. There is no repetition, so there is no time for a performance to become mannered or over-studied.

One other thing to note about Kurt Dussander and James Whale: both characters are considerably older than the actor. There is a pleasing symmetry to the fact that McKellen's first national review was for his ancient Justice Shallow back at Cambridge: it was part of what made him go into the theatre in the first place. Now it was as two old men that he had found himself as a screen actor. But Justice Shallow and the other 'make-up' parts McKellen so relished in his early days as a stage actor had been all about disguise, hiding from the audience the real self that he was not yet ready to reveal. Dussander and especially James Whale are not about disguise – they are about revealing something from inside. What the age of the characters does is to force McKellen to slow down, to play, as the acting coaches would have it, in a slower tempo-rhythm. And that in turn helps to draw the camera and therefore the viewer with him. He's learned John Hurt's trick.

McKellen's greatest strength as a stage actor had been his greatest weakness on film. Alan Cohen, assistant to Peter Hall on *Coriolanus*, had been on stage with McKellen and noted his ability to reach out to individual members of the audience. Robert Chetwyn, director of McKellen's *Hamlet* and *Bent*, as well as countless parts in rep at Ipswich, describes it as 'sending out massive waves all around the theatre'. But try that on camera and you're sunk. On screen he had learned to make the audience come to him, not to go looking for them, and that is the fundamental change in McKellen the film actor.

The shoot of *Gods and Monsters* ran two days over schedule. McKellen completed his last shot at four in the afternoon, made it to the airport for a flight at eight, and was in rehearsal at the National Theatre for Trevor Nunn's *An Enemy of the People* the following day. But his focus was very much still in Hollywood. The film made it into American cinemas in time for the Oscars deadline, and in February 1999 came the announcement everyone had been predicting: McKellen was nominated for the Best Actor Oscar up against Tom Hanks in *Saving Private Ryan*, Nick Nolte in *Affliction*, Edward Norton in *American History X* and Roberto Benigni in *Life is Beautiful*. Lynn Redgrave was also nominated and Bill Condon was up for Best Adapted Screenplay.

McKellen was the first openly gay actor to be nominated for an Oscar. He embarked on the kind of campaign of TV appearances that is thought obligatory if you're going to win. 'I must say,' he admitted quite freely to Amanda Mitchison, 'if I don't win, I shall be very disappointed.'

He didn't. Bill Condon won the Oscar for his screenplay, but Roberto Benigni was the surprise winner of the Best Actor Oscar that year.

But McKellen did pick up some fifteen other acting awards for the film, and the momentum that was now gathering in his film career showed no sign of slackening in 1999. In fact, this was the year he got the two parts which finally made his name internationally famous.

Plans for a movie based on the *X-Men* comics started in 1995. But when Tom Desanto, co-producer of *Apt Pupil*, approached Bryan Singer with his script ideas, the director was not initially keen. Desanto convinced Singer the film could be more than popcorn, selling the basic scenario as an allegory for human prejudice. Singer in turn would use the same line to sell it to Ian McKellen. Created by Marvel Comics, the *X-Men* are human mutants with superpowers, who are treated with suspicion and sometimes downright hostility by the authorities and ordinary people. The stories turn on the conflict between the two mutant leaders, Professor Xavier, who wants mutants to be a force for good in the world, and Magneto, who believes they must fight for their right to exist.

Almost as soon as news of the planned movie reached the Internet, *X-Men* fans were demanding that Patrick Stewart should play Xavier. One year younger than McKellen and born just the other side of the Pennines in Mirfield, Yorkshire, Stewart was a stalwart of the RSC for twenty years before metamorphosing in 1987 into Captain Jean-Luc Picard in *Star Trek: The Next Generation*. Trading in the gravitas of the classical actor at an initial $100,000 an episode, by 1999 Stewart's combination of warmth and authority did indeed make him the obvious choice for the god-like Xavier. No wonder that for his nemesis, the evil genius Magneto, Singer wanted another British classical actor, who could stand up to Stewart in the film's pivotal debate.

McKellen said Bryan Singer's initial pitch for *X-Men* was as an allegory of black American civil rights, with Xavier as the non-violent Martin Luther King figure and Magneto as the more extremist Malcolm X. A veteran of the schisms of gay politics, McKellen might have been more inclined to see the mutant leaders as, say, himself and Peter Tatchell. 'It's true,' he told David Thompson, 'that each civil rights movement splits between the integrationists and the separatists, the proponents of non-violence versus violent activism. Any member of a minority facing discrimination can relate to the mutants' dilemma.' So, cast as Magneto, he got to be Peter Tatchell – on screen at least!

Both McKellen and Stewart were eager to stress the fundamental seriousness of *X-Men*, and to counter suggestions that comic-book heroes might be beneath the dignity of a Shakespearean actor. As far as McKellen was concerned, Shakespeare's heroes were thinkers and men of action and so was Magneto. Neither actor claimed ever to have read the original comic-book stories, though they had both been fans of Dan Dare in the *Eagle* as boys. McKellen had particularly liked the fact that Dan Dare's sidekick Digby came from Wigan.

Filming on *X-Men* was due to start in July 1999 but, following delays, McKellen was not needed until September. Singer had promised he would be finished by the end of the year. The timing was crucial.

Earlier in the year a film director from New Zealand had turned up with his wife at the house in Narrow Street with a script and some designs. McKellen had been taken with the eccentricity and enthusiasm of the pair, though they were planning to make a film of a book widely regarded as unfilmable. The woman dressed as a Goth and the large man with hair everywhere wore flip-flops. It was Peter Jackson and Fran Walsh, director and screenwriter of *Heavenly Creatures*, the film which made Kate Winslet a star. They were planning a movie of J R R Tolkien's *The Lord of the Rings*. Jackson and Walsh seemed eager to persuade McKellen to take part in their film. But there was no follow-up; no call to the agent; no offer. Had someone else got the part? Was Gandalf to be another Ned Kelly?

Anthony Hopkins was mentioned. So was ex-Dr Who Tom Baker. But Sean Connery was frontrunner for Gandalf. Connery ultimately baulked at the year-long shoot in New Zealand that was being proposed, and in the end they came back to McKellen. Then came the delay which pushed *X-Men* back to September, and McKellen had to phone Jackson to say he couldn't be in his film after all. That same evening he found himself having dinner in the same London restaurant as New Line Cinema boss Bob Shaye, the man who was putting up the money for *The Lord of the Rings*. He gave Shaye the bad news in person. Shaye was adamant that he could fix it.

High-level discussions followed between New Line and Fox. These were most definitely not low-budget, low-risk projects. *X-Men* was costing $75 m and Bob Shaye was financing Jackson to shoot all three parts of *The Lord of the Rings* at the same time over a full year at a cost of $130 m. The last thing either of the companies could afford was a hold-up caused by an actor being busy elsewhere. In similar circumstances, Dougray Scott had already been forced to withdraw from *X-Men* because of conflicting dates with *Mission Impossible II*. Hugh Jackman was the lucky actor that time, grabbing his chance as Wolverine. But this time a deal was struck. Magneto would be in the can by the end of the year. The shooting schedule for *The Lord of the Rings* would be adjusted to start with sections of the story which did not involve Gandalf – McKellen could do both. The only thing was he still hadn't read the book.

McKellen's casting was announced on 24 July 1999. To many he was the obvious choice. He would bring a classical actor's authority to the part. Connery could have done Gandalf's warmth, wit and wisdom just as well; he would have made just as convincing a warrior; he might even have been better at the grumpiness, which Christine Crawshaw, chair of the Tolkien Society, acknowledged some thought missing from McKellen's Gandalf. But if Connery had done it, it might have been a Connery picture, and the balance of 'the fellowship', populated with relative unknowns, might have been completely upset. Later in the year there were complaints on one fansite about the prospect of 'a gay Gandalf', but by then McKellen was cooling his heels in Canada.

The open-air part of Magneto's Lair had been built in Hamilton, seventy minutes north of Toronto. There, through the increasing chill of the oncoming Canadian winter, *X-Men* shot through the night. McKellen, in tights and knee-length boots, had some protection from the elements. The unfortunate Rebecca Romijn-Stamos as Mystique was naked in her blue make-up apart from a few carefully positioned plastic scales. McKellen and Stewart reminisced about the British theatre in the long breaks between shots. With one of them from Lancashire and the other a Yorkshireman, McKellen joked that Xavier and Magneto were still fighting the fifteenth-century Wars of the Roses. But the director was having trouble keeping their performances down to the scale he wanted. He wanted a low-key, conversational tone for both characters but, especially in their scenes together, McKellen and Stewart's first instinct was to give it the full Shakespearian power.

Meanwhile, there was trouble on the X-Men Internet fansites. Both *The Lord of the Rings* and the *X-Men* comics had huge followings. Many fans felt as if their personal property was being taken over by the movie makers. This time it was costume designs leaking out, and the fans were not happy. There were complaints about the modernisations. Others had the temerity to find McKellen's physique inadequate for the muscle-bound torso of Magneto, the comic-strip villain. Singer himself wrote in dialogue in which Wolverine complains about the X-Men outfits, only to be asked by Cyclops, 'What would you prefer? Yellow spandex?' It was a direct response to fans of the original comic book in which yellow spandex is exactly what they do wear. There were also rumours of trouble on the set that were later found to be untrue: that the release date had been delayed; that Bryan Singer had been sacked.

X-Men opened on 14 July 2000, taking nearly $55 m in its opening weekend and going on to gross nearly $300 m worldwide. And that is the terms in which a big budget blockbuster is judged. Because, despite the best efforts of McKellen and Stewart and the best intentions of Desanto and Singer, the film only gestures at metaphorical seriousness. Taken as a comic-book romp, it's quite fun, but there are some very serious miscalculations. If the use of the concentration camps as background worried some in *Bent* and more in *Apt Pupil*, the opening of *X-Men*, in which a young boy discovers his mutant powers while being separated from his parents at the entrance to a death camp, will try the strongest stomachs. The boy turns into Magneto, which provides McKellen with some token psychology, which is not followed through.

McKellen walks effortlessly through the whole proceedings, lending tone, but unable to raise the material from essential silliness. Aided by some blue side-lighting he casts a certain chill. But the quick cutting, usually thought essential in a movie aimed at a young audience, prevents any of the scenes, including his famous confrontation with Professor Xavier, from developing. Someone seems to have asked him to adopt a mid-Atlantic accent. But he does almost entirely avoid camp, into which the exhibition of effortless power could easily have degenerated. Only when levitating does he permit himself just a hint of archness. In any event, the main interest of the movie lies not with Xavier and Magneto, but with Hugh Jackman's Wolverine and Rogue, played by Anna Paquin, who had proved she could act when she won a Best Supporting Actress Oscar at the age of eleven as Holly Hunter's daughter in *The Piano* (1993).

True to his word, Singer released McKellen from *X-Men* in time for Christmas 1999. With just ten days at home, McKellen threw an all-night party to welcome in the new millennium. From his perch overlooking the Thames he and his friends watched the Queen go past by boat on her way to the ill-fated Millennium Dome at Greenwich. In the aftermath of the party McKellen swore off the booze for a spell. He wanted clear eyes for all those close-ups because, within a week, leaving the house to the builders, he was en route for Wellington, New Zealand to begin work on *The Lord of the Rings*. Give or take the odd zero on the fee, it would be more or less the ultimate rep job.

On a film you just don't get the sense of family that McKellen has always relished so much in the theatre. A film is all over in a few weeks at the most, and people come and go – actors playing small parts may only be there for a day. But *The Lord of the Rings* wasn't like that. On *The Lord of the Rings* McKellen did all the things you're supposed to do on tour or in rep: he made friends; he explored the countryside; he even fell in love. But then *The Lord of the Rings* was different in a lot of ways.

There had been attempts to make a movie of Tolkien's fantasy epic before. The Beatles had been desperate to do it with Paul as Frodo, Ringo as Sam Gamgee, John as Gollum and George playing Gandalf. Then in 1978 Saul Zaentz bought the screen rights and produced an animated version of half the story. Directed by Ralph Bakshi, the film bombed at the box office, and plans to film the second half were rapidly dropped. It had always been received wisdom that the book was unfilmable with live actors. That was until Peter Jackson came along.

Jackson made his first film at the age of twelve. It was set in World War II and shot in his back garden. With a day job as a photo-engraver at a Wellington newspaper, at the weekends Jackson went on making films. At the age of 22, after four years' work, he completed a movie called *Bad Taste*, in which he directed, produced, operated the camera and acted. What followed was the stuff of pure fairy-tale. The chairman of the New Zealand Film Commission took Jackson's home-made movie to the Cannes Film Festival of 1988. The critics loved it, and it was eventually seen in thirty countries.

Bad Taste is a science fiction comedy about aliens who abduct humans, process them into food and serve them up in an outer-space fast food restaurant. *Meet the Feebles*, often described as 'the Muppet show on drugs' and *Braindead*, Jackson's follow-ups, led to him being known as the first Kiwi King of Splatter and certainly didn't suggest that Tolkien's epic, voted Britain's favourite book in a BBC poll in 2003, was safe in his hands. Indeed, with Jackson announced as director of the film, a petition on a Tolkien fan site gathered 16,000 signatures begging him not to violate the integrity of the books. *Heavenly Creatures* (1994), however, a sensitive telling of a famous New Zealand murder case, showed him capable of handling both complex character relationships and fantasy sequences. It was the success of this movie, with Oscar nominations for Jackson and his partner Fran Walsh for their original screenplay, that got the New Zealander a shot at making *The Lord of the Rings*.

Then came the Hollywood wheeler-dealing with some real high-risk gambling thrown in. In January 1997 Miramax optioned the rights to the book with Jackson as director. At that stage the plan was to make two films. After eighteen months' development Miramax got cold feet and said they would only finance one film. Jackson and Walsh refused to compromise. Hawking the project around the Hollywood studios, they reached Bob Shaye at New Line Cinema, part of the AOL-Time Warner conglomerate and previously best known for the *Nightmare on Elm Street* series. Shaye's response was, 'It's three books. Why not three films?' And that's how Jackson's *The Lord of the Rings* came to be a trilogy.

There was more. After his success with *Heavenly Creatures*, Jackson had taken the unprecedented step of refusing to move to Hollywood, developing instead his Wellington special effects studio, Weta, named after a New Zealand grasshopper. Now he wanted to do principal photography on all three films at once in New Zealand, using local technicians and casting the films largely with non-American actors. Shaye went for it, ultimately committing a total of some $310 m to the project. Based in his studio in an old paint factory next door to Wellington Airport, Jackson directed the whole thing like a military operation, filming up to seven scenes at once, linked by video camera to his assistant directors. Sound was a nightmare. 'Every take was preceded by a conversation between the assistant director and air traffic control, letting us know we had three minutes to get the shot,' remembered McKellen in an *Observer* interview. Despite the precautions, Jackson was still unhappy with the sound in the end, and almost every line of dialogue had to be redubbed in the studio later.

It was not immediately obvious to McKellen that they were making a movie classic or anything like it. For one thing much of the time the actors were being shot in front of a blue or green screen, so they had little idea of what the finished article would look like once the effects department had done their work. For this process a flatly lit coloured screen is placed behind the actors. Blue or green is used, because those colours don't occur in human flesh tones. Once the shot is in the can, it is scanned into a computer, and all the blue or green is digitally removed and replaced with another image, which might be an army of orcs on the march or the Balrog, the demon Gandalf battles in the mines of Moria. There can't be any blue in the actors' costumes in front of a blue screen or green in front of a green screen, otherwise there will be digital holes in the composite image.

It sounds tough on the actors, but for a stage actor who had done some of his best work talking to an invisible dagger in a tin hut, it was nothing new to be imagining the scenery or even some of his fellow performers. For his fight with the Balrog, for instance, McKellen battled thin air, while a tennis ball was held up to give him an eye-line. So much for high technology! The problem was that looking at the first versions of the effects in the screening room at Weta, McKellen was less than impressed. He began to wonder if they weren't just making the most expensive home movie in history.

Brought up on the patrician grandeur of Tyrone Guthrie, McKellen admitted later that he initially underestimated the very unusual general who was conducting this particular military campaign. Dressed in his trademark scruffy shorts, with no shoes, apparently a stranger to the hairbrush, and the owner of only two shirts – both the same colour – Jackson cut a less then Guthriesque figure, slumped in his specially reinforced armchair. Elijah Wood felt Jackson had a wildness about him unlike any director he'd worked with. But McKellen found that, despite the exterior, Jackson's approach was methodical and thoroughly organised. Gradually the Kiwi director won his respect. He liked the calm, unhurried approach. He liked the way Jackson always made sure everyone else on the set was happy with the shot before he gave his own approval. This was movie making as a collaborative enterprise. It had to be.

The sheer statistics of the shoot were staggering. It lasted 274 days over fifteen months from October 1999 to December 2000. That's against 24 days for *Gods and Monsters*. Twenty-one cameras were used in five studios, exposing 4.5 m feet of film. 350 sets were built, including Helm's Deep, scene of one of the climactic battles, which was as large as a city block. Making huge savings on time and money, many of the sets were carved out of polystyrene, which can be sprayed to look like ancient wood or stone. The Prancing Pony Inn and the stone sculptures at the gates of Minas Tirith were constructed in this way. Three hundred and thirty vehicles were used. Two thousand crew members were involved. Thirty kilometres of roads and forty-eight thousand props were built. Hobbiton was built and fully planted up a year in advance so that flowers and crops could have a chance to establish themselves. Only the oak tree under which Bilbo Baggins has his birthday party was artificial. Standing in concrete and supported with wire guy ropes, the enormous structure was covered with a quarter of a million hand-painted leaves and acorns.

The film became one of New Zealand's major employers, but at times the whole enterprise had the air of a cottage industry. Armour for 15,000 extras, for instance, was knitted out of string by the old ladies of the Wellington Knitting Club. Then there were the effects. Every single frame of film was logged into a computer for digital manipulation in post production, so that, for example, the green grass of the Shire could be made just a little greener and all the colour could be drained from the landscape of Mordor. These were New Zealand locations, but New Zealand subtly morphed into Middle Earth. Weta developed a completely new computer program called Massive, which generated 'intelligent' armies of orcs, elves and humans, so that individual tiny figures would behave unpredictably on screen, giving a more realistic dimension to the most spectacular battles cinema had ever seen.

But what about the actors? Jackson believed that the key was to approach the whole project not as a fantasy movie but as if they were making an historical film. That meant that for all its expense, the technical wizardry was secondary; what came first was the human wizardry called acting.

A lot of names came and went. Daniel Day-Lewis turned down Aragorn. David Bowie was said to be interested in playing the Elf Lord Elrond. At one time Timothy Spall was cast as Gimli the dwarf. Irish actor Stuart Townsend actually started filming as Aragorn but left after a fortnight, when Jackson decided he was too young. Jackson originally wanted to use only British actors as hobbits, but on 12 July 1999, eighteen-year-old Elijah Wood and 28-year-old Sean Astin were announced as Frodo and Sam. Dominic Monaghan and Billy Boyd, English and Scottish respectively, were instructed to introduce their American co-stars to the ways of British pubs, while dialect coach Andrew Jack got to work on their English accents. Elijah Wood claims his British co-stars also taught him to swear.

But arguably the most crucial casting for the film's success was the two English Sir Ians – McKellen and Holm. Jackson and his two fellow screenwriters agonised long and hard over how to start *The Fellowship of the Ring*, the first movie of the trilogy, the one which would make or break the entire project. Finally they wisely settled for a brief explanatory prologue, followed by the way Tolkien starts his book, with the wizard, Gandalf, and the old hobbit, Bilbo. It is these scenes between McKellen and Holm which really set the tone of the entire trilogy, focusing on unhurried character development and the creation of a believable environment, rather than crash-bang effects.

The two highly experienced actors were battling difficult circumstances. In order to achieve the impression that Bilbo is only three foot six tall, a number of tricks were employed. Two complete versions of Bilbo's house, Bag End, were constructed. One was hobbit-sized, so that Gandalf would look too big for it, one was human-sized so that Bilbo would look small. 'Scale doubles' were then employed to play Bilbo in the small set and Gandalf in the normal-sized set. Kiran Shah stood in for both Bilbo and Frodo, while McKellen's double was a seven foot four local man named Paul Webster, who towered convincingly over Holm and Elijah Wood, both just five foot six tall.

But Jackson was well aware that he could not expect his actors to create believable relationships if they were never actually in a shot together, so he used the old movie trick of forced perspective. If, say, Bilbo and Gandalf were to talk to each other across the kitchen table – a table incidentally which reminded McKellen of his childhood home – McKellen was placed near the camera, while Holm was placed at the diagonally opposite corner. In the finished shot, with both actors in focus, they look as if they are facing each other, but Holm looks much smaller because he's further away. This still means that the actors can't actually look at each other in a two-shot. They have to fake an eye-line directly in front of them.

Amidst these difficulties, McKellen and Holm set up the entire film in those first crucial twenty minutes, giving the whole enterprise weight, and steering the film away from feyness. The serenity and prelapsarian innocence of the Shire is generated as much in the twinkle in McKellen's eye as in the computer-enhanced, drenched greens of the fields. He is everybody's favourite uncle, shifting effortlessly between magisterial wisdom, gentle irony and playfulness. A Pied Piper figure, spreading merriment everywhere he goes, he can also bring to bear his full Shakespearian power for 'One ring to rule them all and in the darkness bind them.' And, in extreme close-up, just a shift of the gaze and tiny flickers of expression convey Gandalf's knowledge of the terrible, unspeakable evil which threatens this Eden. And only McKellen manages to give the Celtic 'r' in Mordor the shiver it really needs. His pronunciation conveys all his knowledge of the terrible power of the Dark Lord. There's Cicely Berry's work at the RSC being transmuted into big bucks.

Holm meanwhile, walking stoop-shouldered with a half waddle, has a hint of Mrs Tiggy-Winkle, but also captures wonderfully the ambiguity of Bilbo, who retains energy and optimism but has been terribly damaged by keeping Sauron's ring of power so long. Indeed, the power and evil of the ring is conveyed much more strongly in Holm's depiction of the corrupting effect it has had on him than it ever is again, despite all the CGI and agonised close-ups of Elijah Wood.

Always eager to learn, McKellen was struck by Ian Holm's improvisatory method of filming, so akin to the way McKellen himself had tried to keep fresh his stage performances since his formative encounter with Mike Alfreds at the National Theatre in 1985. Bilbo was different on every take. Jackson averaged around ten takes on every set-up throughout the shoot. Holm would give him something totally different on each one, never repeating a successful moment, leaving a range of choices for the director in the cutting room later.

The film hurries on to Gandalf's encounter with Saruman. McKellen shifts to low status for his encounter with Christopher Lee, subtly showing us Saruman the White's authority and the respect Gandalf the Grey accords him, while Lee deploys a wonderful menace. The special effects, which then send these two mature, venerable actors spinning on their backs and flying through the air like Ninjas, come as a horrible anticlimax. For one terrible moment it looks as if the whole film is about to descend into a fairground attraction.

But it doesn't.

The Fellowship of the Ring, to many the best of the trilogy, has wonderful pace, and shifts tone effortlessly from comedy to mystery to horror to sword and sorcery to Arthurian-style legend and back again. The plot helps. This is the simplest and most focused section of the books with a clear linear narrative of a journey, a catastrophe with the apparent loss of Gandalf in the Mines of Moria and even a tragically flawed hero in Sean Bean's Boromir who really does die. His death and Gandalf's apparent defeat mean the heroes don't look so obviously invincible in this film as they do later, when whole armies of orcs are effortlessly mowed down single-handed. There is more sense of risk therefore. More excitement. More emotional impact. And McKellen's Gandalf the Grey is at the centre of the film. His most successful stage performances have almost all been of characters who are at best morally questionable. Gandalf draws on a side of Ian McKellen that hasn't so often been seen. Brian Cox wrote in *The Lear Diaries* about the way McKellen played Kent to his King Lear in Deborah Warner's 1990 production at the National Theatre: 'You could see some of his extraordinary goodness which is clear to anybody who meets him, but which isn't always apparent on stage.' The real success of McKellen's Gandalf was to make that 'goodness' apparent on screen.

Not every member of the cast warmed to the experience of being stuck in New Zealand for a year. Liv Tyler (Arwen) initially called it an honour to be one of the few women in the picture, but made no bones of her homesickness once the shoot got under way. Part of her problem was that while Peter Jackson was sure he wanted to beef up her role as Arwen, as well as that of Miranda Otto as Eowyn, she remained stubbornly where Tolkien had put her – peripheral. Women did not feature prominently in the old Oxford don's mythological world.

But McKellen loved it. He rented a house five minutes from the studio in Seatoun, not far from Peter Jackson's own family home. Rather like the Shire itself, he found New Zealand to be both England and not England. The Queen was on the banknotes. Marmite and Cadbury's chocolate were on sale in the shops. But the dramatically beautiful mountain landscapes were genuinely empty in a way that his beloved Lake District simply isn't, and though the language was the same, the familiar English reserve seemed to be missing. He found New Zealand's natural, untouched wilderness a breath of fresh air – metaphorically as well as literally. He noted what he called in the *Observer* a 'relaxed and liberal' attitude to alternative lifestyles and 'the most forward-looking and easy partnerships – two men, even three men, bringing up children together'.

With all the principal actors far away from home a camaraderie, familiar from touring days, developed. McKellen may have shied away from the bungee jumping and surfing that some of the younger actors went in for, but he certainly joined in at the Good Luck bar in downtown Wellington, even if he found dancing to hip-hop a shade tricky. A fellow Brit from the same generation of actors, Bernard Hill, playing Théoden, became a particular friend, making him laugh with his endless stories. He also admired the modesty with which Viggo Mortensen dealt with the fuss that came with his rugged good looks. Sean Bean, finally meeting up with McKellen professionally after that false start on *Coriolanus* at the National Theatre, felt the friendship between the actors was reflected in the finished product they created. It's exactly what they'd said in the Actors' Company back in Wimbledon in the 1970s.

On New Year's Day 2001 McKellen was on his way home – by no means unchanged by his year in New Zealand. For one thing he had a tattoo on his right shoulder. Billy Boyd is sure it was Dominic Monaghan's idea, and that Viggo Mortensen came up with the design of a number nine as a Celtic numeral. McKellen and Sean Astin (Sam) think it was probably Elijah Wood's idea. But whoever thought of it first, the actors of the original fellowship of the ring had been to a downtown Wellington tattoo parlour on a Sunday morning and done the deed. Sean Bean wasn't there, because he'd finished filming, but he got the tattoo done later in New York. Jonathan Rhys Davies who played Gimli the dwarf wasn't there either. He sent his stunt double instead.

But more significantly, he wasn't leaving New Zealand alone. McKellen had met an art student named Nick Cuthell on the street in Wellington. Though high school friends seem to remember Cuthell as having been attracted to women, the two men started an affair. Some fourteen years since Sean Mathias moved out, McKellen was taking Cuthell back to England to share his Narrow Street home. He knew there would be comment. He was approaching his 62nd birthday. Nick Cuthell, six foot two tall and dramatically handsome with long, flowing black hair, was forty years his junior.

10. FAME

Walking down Chorley New Road in Bolton on his way from the bus stop to a school dress rehearsal, the young Ian McKellen had a fantasy – he was opening in a play in the West End; BBC radio was interviewing him. To the surprise of other pedestrians he would practise some modest answers under his breath. The only fantasy better than that one was to be appearing in a hit play and a successful film at the same time. It was the double Albert Finney had achieved way back in 1963 with *Luther* and *Tom Jones*, while McKellen was playing Luther at Ipswich rep. In December 2001, at the age of 62, Ian McKellen finally matched Finney, and fulfilled his ultimate childhood dream.

Since he had got his first real chance at the National Theatre with Uncle Vanya in 1992, Sean Mathias's career as a director had prospered. Now he had been asked by the all-powerful Shubert Organisation to mount a production on Broadway of *The Dance of Death*, August Strindberg's savage tale of marital disharmony. McKellen had wanted to play the part of the Captain ever since seeing Laurence Olivier's memorable performance in 1967. *The Fellowship of the Ring* was due to open in December. Could they find a theatre for the same period? Naturally, given his immense success there in *Amadeus*, the Broadhurst was McKellen's top choice. So the Broadhurst it was. Helen Mirren was persuaded to take on the role of Alice, the other half of a married couple widely thought to have inspired Edward Albee to write *Who's Afraid of Virginia Woolf?*

Then history took a hand. They were doing a final run-through in a studio on 42nd Street on the morning of 11 September 2001. In a break, the cast came out onto Times Square. There, on a live relay on a giant screen, they watched the twin towers of the World Trade Center collapse following the Al-Qaeda attack. Rehearsals continued later that day. It was not just the way of the theatre, it was the British way.

In the days that followed McKellen reminded American friends of the British experience of bombing in the Second World War and the IRA's long campaign of terror. 'I was slow to see the scale of the impact on Manhattan,' he admitted in an *Evening Standard* interview later.

The fact that from then on there were no tourists in New York, and Broadway shows were closing right and left was a relatively minor matter in the great scale of things. But for McKellen and Mathias and the rest of the cast it meant an uneasy opening just a week after the attack. To everyone's surprise they were a hit. Reviews were excellent and, for some reason, this seemed to be the moment for Strindberg's bleakly funny vision.

They were playing Tuesday to Sunday at the Broadhurst with Monday off, so on Monday 10 December McKellen boarded Concorde at JFK and was in London in time for the very first premiere of *The Lord of the Rings: The Fellowship of the Ring* at the Leicester Square Odeon.

The newspapers had hyped the occasion as J R R Tolkien versus J K Rowling. The first of the Harry Potter films had opened almost exactly a month earlier in London and was now on worldwide release, having racked up ticket sales of over $90 m in its opening weekend in the US. The New Line Cinema publicity machine was selling their film as independent cinema against Warner's big studio, Disneyesque treatment of Harry Potter – which showed some nerve, given *The Fellowship of the Ring*'s monstrous production budget and the worldwide publicity drive that was accompanying its release. Still, the ramshackle figure of Peter Jackson in an open-necked shirt for what the press inevitably called 'a glittering occasion' did retain a suggestion of the independent filmmaker. 'It has been an all-consuming, exhausting experience,' the director muttered to the *Daily Telegraph* reporter. 'At times I was almost driven insane.'

McKellen arrived in his rented Mercedes. He signed autographs. He posed for the cameras. Inside the cinema, the speeches over, he settled down in the front row of the circle with his cousin's grandchildren, Andrew, sixteen, and Robin, fourteen. Next to them was Christopher Lee. Just behind sat Ian Holm.

McKellen had already seen a preview in New York. So after Gandalf disappeared into the depths beneath the mines of Moria with the Balrog, he nipped out for a cigarette. Everyone was nervous. There was $310 m of New Line Cinema's money riding on this one. For McKellen it was fifteen years since he'd said he thought he was too old to make it in the movies. This was the one which everyone said could turn his screen career and his whole life upside down.

The screening finished at around eleven p.m. and they all decamped to Tobacco Dock for the party – just upriver from McKellen's home. New Line had gone to town with ten different areas under one roof, each 'themed' for a different part of Middle Earth. There was a hobbit area and a Rivendell area and so on, each with appropriate food being served. There was a good feeling in the air, but no one yet knew what the public response would be.

The aim had been to make a film that would please the Tolkien fans, who would form the core audience, but also draw in people who had never even heard of *The Lord of the Rings*. The danger as far as the marketing people were concerned was that they would fall between two stools and please no one. Shooting all three films in one go had been an economy of scale, but it did make the risk all the bigger – particularly at the opening of the first film. If *The Fellowship of the Ring* had failed it would have been impossible to market the two sequels.

As it was, the financial statistics that followed were as awesome as the statistics of the shoot. The first film alone trebled New Line Cinema's original investment. As of the time of writing all three films were in the top ten highest grossing movies of all time, with a combined worldwide gross of almost $3,000 m – and that's before you start counting all the videos, DVDs, Gandalf goblets and Frodo figures.

The film did get good notices, but there were dissenters, and some critics saw McKellen as following in a long and dishonourable tradition of top British actors who have sold their theatrical souls for the American dollar. Like the ageing Olivier's Zeus in *Clash of the Titans* and Alec Guinness in *Star Wars*, McKellen's Gandalf was judged by some as just another classical actor hamming it up for Hollywood. The Academy disagreed. Among the thirteen Oscar nominations the film received, McKellen was there for Best Supporting Actor. He was the only actor in the film to be nominated.

Three years earlier he had done the rounds of the talk shows promoting himself for *Gods and Monsters*, but he had been in Leeds at the West Yorkshire Playhouse when the actual awards were handed out. This time he was determined to give it the full treatment. On 16 March he even presented American TV's *Saturday Night Live*, appearing in drag as Maggie Smith and, on Sunday 24 March 2002, he was in the audience for the Oscars Ceremony with Nick Cuthell as the Oscar for Best Supporting Actor was announced. ABC Television got a shot of McKellen holding his boyfriend's hand. He would have known the cameras were on him – it must have been deliberate. There was to be no repeat of the airbrushing of Sean Mathias from the 1981 Tonys. There were plenty of people on the edge of their seats, hoping for a barnstorming acceptance speech, packed with references to closeted Hollywood actors.

Jim Broadbent got it for his role in *Iris*. Buckingham had stolen Richard III's crown. 'Ian should have got this. He really wanted it,' Broadbent told Fiona Maddocks later. But later that night, partying at Morton's on Melrose Avenue, McKellen looked anything but depressed, still dancing in the Veranda Room with Nick at three a.m., as the crowds thinned out and the bartenders packed up, and Hollywood's biggest night finally came to a close for another year.

The Lord of the Rings: The Fellowship of the Ring won Oscars for cinematography, visual effects, make-up and music. The top awards all went elsewhere. The film was a hit, but director, actors and technicians still had something to prove. Plus they had to make sure the two sequels were bigger hits. So the next two years turned into a regular schedule of publicity tours and post-production work for McKellen. The special effects for the second two films had not been done before *The Fellowship of the Ring* opened, so Peter Jackson was kept busy largely with his technicians at the Weta studios. But, although in theory all the principal photography had been done at one go in the original shoot, Jackson and his co-scriptwriters Fran Walsh and Philippa Boyens continued to refine the storytelling of the second two films, adding new scenes to clarify the plot or some important character point. So in the summers of 2002 and 2003 McKellen was reunited with other members of the cast in Wellington to make minor adjustments. For instance, in *The Return of the King* a scene was added in which Merry and Pippin dance on the table in the Great Hall at Edoras, and Aragorn and Gandalf discuss whether Frodo and Sam are still alive.

It was an opportunity for McKellen to add a more human dimension to the warrior wizard, Gandalf the White, into whom he metamorphoses in *The Two Towers* – which was no bad thing, for his character is much less interesting in the second film, and he has noticeably less screen time. And although *The Two Towers* was a bigger hit at the box office than the first film, some felt it was not nearly such a good movie. Jackson turns the orcs, monstrous and silent through most of the first movie, into a bunch of south London bovver boys, and he has trouble handling the split focus of the plot. Even the special effects department struggles with Treebeard and his fellow Ents, who never look like anything but animated models.

The bandwagon rolled on. As premiere time approached for the final film in the trilogy, *The Return of the King*, Jackson and his team were still hard at work putting the finishing touches to their magnum opus. With an upfront fee of $10 m and a share of the massive profits, Jackson had already made a fortune out of the films, but this one had to be the biggest and the best, the one which would ensure a classic status for the trilogy, the one that would give them a shot at the Oscars which had largely eluded them so far. Just days before the film was to be 'locked off' with no possibility of further changes, McKellen found himself called into a dubbing studio in London to re-record Gandalf the White shouting instructions to the troops of Minas Tirith as he rallies them for the great battle against Saruman's armies.

For the final film it had been decided the world premiere should be in Wellington in New Zealand. The city responded in style, closing down for the day with a crowd of 100,000 on the streets to join in the tickertape parade for the stars. McKellen was there as always, tireless in his promotion of the films which were turning him into an international celebrity. Back when *The Fellowship of the Ring* opened, the Wellington authorities had changed the name of the city to Middle-earth for the day. McKellen as Gandalf was put on the stamps and on a coin. This time Air New Zealand had painted the Tolkien characters on the side of the planes for the publicity tour. Everyone knew there was money to be made. The films, together with McKellen's constant boosting of the country in every interview, were turning New Zealand into the tourist destination of the decade.

As they prepared for the big event, emotions were running high among those involved in the making of the trilogy. Liv Tyler, already with a reputation among the rest of the cast for bursting into tears at the drop of a hat, was said to have cried for the entire last hour at a screening a few days earlier. Peter Jackson described himself as sick with nerves. They had nothing to worry about. *The Return of the King* seemed to break down all resistance to the *Lord of the Rings* phenomenon. Even those who hadn't liked the first two films declared this one a masterpiece, and the entire trilogy was soon being hailed as the stuff of movie legend.

The film certainly handles its multiple storylines more deftly than *The Two Towers* and the opening flashback to the corrupting of Sméagol by the ring is a clever touch, moving us again from the innocence of Sméagol's hobbit-like world to the scorched earth of Mordor, like a recapitulation in miniature of the first two films. The dual climax of the massive battle outside the gates of Mordor and Frodo and Sam's slow-motion struggle up the sides of Mount Doom is gripping. But there still isn't the variety of the first film; with Saruman excised from the final cut, it lacks a decent baddie; and Jackson's struggle to end the film becomes interminable.

As for McKellen: he was offered the part of God shortly after the film came out and it is easy to see why. In his white robes, white hair and beard blowing in the breeze, his words of comfort to Pippin, delivered in extreme close-up in a lull in the battle for Minas Tirith, sound like a promise of salvation to come. The film gives him much more scope than *The Two Towers*, ranging from caring god to Shakespearian warlord on the battlefield to a quasi-parental anxiety for the absent Frodo. And, as ever in the trilogy, the play of expression across his face, suggesting thought process and an emotional journey, draws the viewer in and makes them care for these mythic people.

This time the Academy couldn't resist either. The first two films had managed Oscars only on the technical side. *The Return of the King* swept the board, winning Best Picture, Best Director and nine other Oscars. Only the actors still came away with nothing. McKellen was at the ceremony again, making a little speech before presenting the extract from *The Return of the King*. But Sean Mathias was his date for the evening – Nick Cuthell was no more.

According to a friend who spoke to the *Daily Telegraph*, it was not the age difference which had been the problem: 'The fact that Ian is almost three times as old as Nick was never much of an issue for them – more for everybody else.' The reason for the break-up was altogether more prosaic: 'They broke up because Nick was modelling in New York, while Ian is based in London.'

Most unusually for a man who, though he will talk at great length about his own sexuality, never discusses his sexual relationships, McKellen had talked about this relationship publicly on a couple of occasions. He never named Nick Cuthell, but in December 2001 in an interview with Chip Crews he described himself as 'rewarded with a relationship of a year's standing'. While in February 2003, with the affair at an end, he told Bryan Appleyard, 'It was another attempt to get in touch with real life. It didn't continue, and there are reasons why it shouldn't.'

He wouldn't say what those 'reasons' were. Perhaps he was simply referring to the literal ocean between them. But the language is interesting: 'another attempt to get in touch with real life . . .' McKellen once said of his years at Cambridge, 'I found I could only be confident when acting, because it's a wilful escape from life.' As a gay man when homosexuality was still illegal, the stage was a place of escape for him, a place of safety where he felt absolutely at home, where, as he put it, 'Nothing can go wrong.' The theatre became the family that accepted him as he was, when he was losing his own family one by one, and had anyway never revealed to them who he really was. But he'd come to despise the man who had taken refuge in that way. 'I think what I despised in myself,' he told the *Washington Post* in December 2001, 'was not entering the real world.' Real life. The real world. For McKellen, relationships, whether with an actor or a non-actor, are part of the 'real world', the dangerous place he calls 'real life', outside the safety of the theatre family.

In November 2003, after an eighteen-month battle with cancer of the eyes, the last member of his boyhood family, his sister Jean, died following a stroke. Almost to the end she had been a cornerstone of amateur theatre in the town of Colchester. Stepmother Gladys, now 97 years old, was still alive, and he went north for regular visits, calling on old family friends like the Bulloughs in Wigan, next door to the family home on Parson's Walk. In London he withdrew to what he knows best, living alone in Narrow Street, Limehouse. 'I'm not unhappy living on my own,' he told *The Times* in February 2003. 'Living on your own is an appropriate thing for a human being to do.'

And then there was work, because for all the round of interviews, premieres and publicity junkets, *The Lord of the Rings* was by no means the only thing occupying the time of McKellen the actor in the new millennium. 'I move from job to job,' he explained to journalist Kenneth Plume, 'from family to family, from group of friends to group of friends.'

In June 2002 he had been back in Canada for *X2*, Bryan Singer's follow-up to *X-Men*. Staying in a villa in Vancouver throughout a fifteen-week shoot in which he was only needed for fifteen days, the job was pretty close to a holiday. With a personal trainer in tow, and having given up cigarettes – temporarily – he was on a keep-fit regime of running on the beach, massage, Jacuzzi and home-cooked vegetarian food. For Patrick Stewart's 62nd birthday on 13 July he even did his party piece, George Formby's 'I'm leaning on a lamp-post' with voice coach Jesse Platt on the piano. Never renowned for his singing, he nevertheless doesn't seem to have thought much of Brian Cox's contribution to the festivities, Robert Burns's 'My love is like a red red rose'.

Cox had joined them for the sequel to play William Stryker, the villain who causes Magneto and Xavier to join forces, albeit temporarily, to thwart this greater menace. Much more plot driven and packed with more visceral thrills than the first movie, there's less room for character in *X2*. McKellen becomes even more understated, adopting an almost throwaway delivery to suggest immense power. But if McKellen's Gandalf goes well beyond the terms of Alec Guinness's Obi-Wan Kenobi, there is a fair argument for saying that McKellen as Magneto really is no more than another in a long line of smoothie British baddies from Claude Rains and James Mason to Alan Rickman and Jeremy Irons.

McKellen completed principal photography on *X2* on 19 November 2002. While in Canada, he had been approached by a young independent filmmaker called Carl Bessai, who wanted him to consider a film he was planning to script, produce, direct and photograph called *Emile*. Based on Ingmar Bergman's *Wild Strawberries*, the script McKellen read told the story of a Canadian professor who returns to his hometown to receive an honorary degree. Perhaps envisaging problems with the accent, McKellen turned it down. But when the director offered to make the main character English, he changed his mind. Having spent three and a half months getting paid a great deal of money for doing not a great deal, he felt he should put something back into the Canadian film industry. *Emile* was shot on a shoestring budget, and McKellen worked for fifteen days in three weeks instead of fifteen days in fifteen weeks.

The finished article has its moments, particularly in the awkward first scenes between McKellen and Deborah Unger, playing a long-lost niece, abandoned by Emile to an orphanage after her parents died. Elsewhere, Carl Bessai is fatally attracted to slow motion, and the whole thing is underpowered emotionally. The inevitable reconciliation between McKellen and Unger doesn't really seem to cost either of them enough.

With shooting on *Emile* completed a week before Christmas 2002, McKellen was back in London, putting *The Dance of Death* into rehearsal for the West End. There had been talk on Broadway that he and Helen Mirren hadn't got on. Certainly she didn't want to adopt the Mike Alfreds approach to the play, leaving the blocking unfixed, allowing for total spontaneity each night. At any rate, when they opened at the Lyric on 4 March 2003, it was Frances de la Tour playing Alice, not Helen Mirren.

McKellen was aiming for a more conversational style than he had brought to the play in New York but, though the production garnered some good reviews, some of McKellen's fellow actors who attended the first night and the party afterwards at the Swedish Embassy thought it a less than glorious return to the London stage. It was the first time he had been seen in the West End since he had gone off to the West Yorkshire Playhouse back in 1998, declaring that he might never work in London again. One colleague comments, 'I'd like to see Ian come back to the stage and work with Trevor Nunn or Adrian Noble or Howard Davies or someone – someone who won't let him get away with stuff.'

The production closed on 7 June.

The next day McKellen was on a plane to New Zealand to put the finishing touches to *The Return of the King*. Interviews around this time suggested he was working less, taking time out that he never had before to cook dinners for his friends, visit London landmarks like Tate Modern and the British Library, enjoy the fruits of his new fame and financial security. But McKellen's work schedule doesn't really bear out the image of a theatrical knight enjoying the twilight of his years.

Back from the Antipodes, he was in Yorkshire and Ireland in October, working on young Scottish film director David Mackenzie's *Asylum*, set in a fictional version of Broadmoor. McKellen plays a psychiatrist, Peter Cleave, who tries to warn Natasha Richardson against falling in love with one of his patients. Billed as 'a very dark romance', the film also stars Hugh Bonneville and Marton Csokas, Celeborn in *The Lord of the Rings*. The movie got a limited release in the US on 29 October 2004.

In December 2003 he received what for some is the ultimate accolade, featuring in an episode of *The Simpsons*, entitled 'The Regina Monologues', alongside cartoon versions of Tony Blair, J K Rowling and Eric Idle. McKellen meets the Simpsons while starring in *Macbeth*. He is then soaked with water, struck by lightning and has an anvil fall on his foot, before the theatre billboard collapses on top of him – all because the Simpsons keep saying the unlucky name of the play. Still, at least they recognise him. Tony Blair is mistaken for Mr Bean.

McKellen seemed intentionally to work less in 2004. He took *The Dance of Death* to Australia's Sydney Arts Festival for a month at the beginning of the year, before flying out to the Oscars in Los Angeles to bask in the deluge of accolades falling at last on the final part of *The Lord of the Rings*. Bypassing his agent, by now McKellen seemed to be arranging his own work through the press and TV. Repeated declarations that his one remaining ambition was to appear as a pantomime dame finally produced results in an offer from the Old Vic to play Widow Twankey in *Aladdin* for Christmas 2004, with who else but Sean Mathias directing. Some sixteen years after he moved out of the house in Narrow Street, and despite the fact that Mathias now has a home in Cape Town, he and McKellen are still friends and working colleagues. 'I'm a person who likes to stay friends with people I've had relationships with,' explained Mathias to Chip Crews of the *Washington Post*. 'Ian and I . . . have been lovers, we've been not-friends, we've been friends. I love working with him now. It's a real privilege.'

For his part, McKellen immediately sounded typically serious about the entire project, commenting to Catherine Shoard with a professorial air, 'Lately the form has been awfully debased. But we're going to pull it out of the drain, get back to the story.' And then comes the political sting in the tail that he can't quite resist. 'And Aladdin is born in Baghdad! Think of that!'

Because, despite reaching the statutory retirement age in May 2004, McKellen the activist has not gone away. His direct involvement with Stonewall has diminished. For nine years in a row through the 1990s he either directed or cast the annual fundraiser at the Albert Hall, his job basically to trawl through his phone book and assemble as starry a line-up for the Equality Show as he could. People like Elton John, Sting,

Boy George, Robbie Williams and Julian Clary appeared and, with Stephen Fry and Sandi Toksvig presenting, the show raised in the region of £100,000 a year. Sick with nerves before the show in 1996, having just come out, Toksvig remembers McKellen, the old pro, hugging her in the wings to boost her confidence. But Stonewall has grown into a professional lobbying group, run by lawyers, journalists and politicians, who only need the showbiz front men once a year.

Tending still to confine his political pronouncements to gay rights, the Iraq war of 2003 tempted McKellen, the militant pacifist, out of the closet. He cancelled rehearsals of *The Dance of Death* on Saturday 15 February to join the massive anti-war march through London. 'War is a sign of failure,' he fulminated in the *Evening Standard*. 'A putative war leader is someone who has failed. Failed at compromise, failed at diplomacy, failed to persuade. Failed!'

McKellen's love affair with New Labour was over anyway. Both his parents had been life-long Labour voters. As far back as 1969, he had described himself as 'committed in a vague sort of way', and Antony Sher persuaded him to campaign for Labour at the disastrous 1992 General Election, when the party snatched defeat from the jaws of victory. But by 2001 McKellen was no longer a Labour voter. He feels the many advances in gay rights in recent years have come more from the European Court of Human Rights than the Labour government. The equalisation of the age of consent, lifting the ban on gays in the military, anti-discrimination legislation specifically banning discrimination on the grounds of sexual orientation – at every turn it has been the European Court pushing the British government. 'And to think I voted against Europe all those years ago,' he told Fiona Maddocks.

As for divisions within the gay rights community, everyone likes everyone these days. Even Peter Tatchell, the wild man of gay politics who attempted a sensational citizen's arrest on Robert Mugabe in 1999, now says he gets on well with McKellen. And the clash with Derek Jarman has also been airbrushed. 'I don't think the criticism of his visit to Downing Street was intended as a personal attack,' Tatchell told *Gay Times*. 'I know Derek Jarman didn't mean it like that. He said the things he said to provoke a debate, rather than to marginalise the efforts made by Ian.' And McKellen claimed in a *Sunday Times* interview to have received a message from the filmmaker before he died, 'saying that everything I was doing was wonderful'.

But McKellen, raised in a school of intense moral seriousness by Christian nonconformist parents and educated in the school of F R Leavis who taught above all else the moral worth of art, retains high ambitions for the impact of his own example on young lives. 'It would be nice,' he told Kenneth Plume in July 2000, 'to think that I'd changed some people's lives. I know that [some] people coming out now have said to their parents, "Ian McKellen is gay, you know." '

Similarly his ambition for his work as an actor goes well beyond entertainment. Firstly, in the tradition of Leavis and Stanislavski, he sees drama as having a moral function in broadening people's ability to empathise with others. 'If you can imagine how other people would feel in any situation,' he wrote once in *The Times*, 'you are more likely to be a balanced person and to lead a good life than if you single-mindedly follow your own interests.' But he also wants the intellectual, even political impact of Bertolt Brecht, believing that drama should stimulate an audience intellectually, and change their perception of the world. As a boy brought up on the last of the great Music Hall acts, it's no surprise that he goes to that world for an example: 'The famous English comic, Ken Dodd, goes on for three or four hours if necessary,' he explained to Kenneth Plume, 'and what's necessary for him is that he does not want anybody to leave the theatre unless he feels that their minds have shifted.'

That kind of seriousness implies looking for scripts which avoid pandering to prejudices and existing attitudes. 'I'm interested,' he said in the same interview, 'in the radical, and the possibility that, having seen a film or watched a television show or been to the theatre, you could be enlightened in some way.' That's ambitious. Widow Twankey sounds like fun, but doesn't exactly measure up to such exacting criteria.

Before *Aladdin* he fitted in a play for BBC Radio and another independent film called *Neverwas*, with screenwriter Joshua Michael Stern making his directorial debut. It was another one set in a lunatic asylum, with McKellen as patient rather than psychiatrist this time. Maybe that's one way he could go. Appearing in relatively few new plays, he has not been a great patron of young playwrights. Perhaps he could be a patron of young filmmakers. *X-Men 3* is already announced and scheduled for release in 2006. Will that be radical and enlightening? Patrick Stewart is already on board; so are Halle Berry, Hugh Jackman and James Marsden. At the time of writing the name of Ian McKellen was still notable by its absence, but it had been announced that he would be providing the voice of Zebedee in an animated film of the old British children's TV show, *The Magic Roundabout*.

Being in more *X-Men* movies doesn't seem to fit in with the other thing McKellen says about how he chooses his jobs these days. It's not parts he knows he can do that he wants. It's parts he thinks he can't do

– parts to puzzle over, to make him ask questions, think, work, seek advice. 'The achievement,' he told Kenneth Plume, 'if you've managed to pull it off to your own satisfaction, or the director's, or the audience's, or the critics' – well, that's why it's the best job in the world for me.'

Robert Chetwyn, who directed McKellen in Ipswich as a young actor, and then in *Hamlet* and *Bent*, declares himself 'slightly disappointed that Ian so much wanted a film career. If he'd been born a generation before, we'd have seen him do every Shakespearian role and every classical play.'

'I still hope he comes back and takes on the great classical roles in the theatre,' agrees Tim McInnerny who appeared alongside McKellen in the film of *Richard III*. 'You wouldn't want to be in the situation like Richard Burton, where just before he died he was finally coming back to do *The Tempest* at the Old Vic, and then he died. Ian hasn't got anything to prove but I think he might have things to prove to himself. Nobody lies on their deathbed saying, "God, I wish I'd done *X-Men 26*", but Lear . . .'

King Lear is the one the theatre world is waiting for. There have been hints – some positive, some not. In December 2003 he described the part as 'looming' in an *Independent* interview, and even mentioned Trevor Nunn as possible director. But questioned by Michael Parkinson about Lear or Falstaff two months later, he was back-pedalling: 'They're very difficult plays and others have done them wonderfully well.'

So maybe Lear or maybe not. One dilemma for his audience is when to go and see it, or any other McKellen stage performance for that matter. As McKellen himself wrote in *The Times* in 1976 about the way he develops the part in a performance: 'At best each performance is a recreation, not a repetition, of ideas developed in rehearsal and since amended through the experience of varying audience response. Any performance is therefore a step along the never-ending journey toward definition, clarity, unambiguity of expression.' It implies the perfectibility of a theatrical performance; that he will go on working on the part throughout the run, refining and improving. Critics and fellow actors agree that he does this. So perhaps the time to go is towards the end of the run – assuming you can still get a ticket. Zoë Wanamaker, a memorable Emilia to McKellen's Iago, disagrees entirely: 'I like seeing Ian very early on in a run when he's still finding his feet, because it all comes very freshly to him then. In *Othello* by the time we got to the Young Vic he was much more polished and he got more and more clever with his props so that sometimes the props started to take over and interfered with him doing it as if it's just happening rather than as something you've rehearsed.'

On 25 May 2004, Sir Ian McKellen turned 65, and promptly posted a piece on his website, thanking everyone who had e-mailed birthday wishes from around the world. Five years earlier his PA, Louise Hardy, and Mig Kimpton, a long-time associate who had produced the UK tour of *Acting Shakespeare* back in 1988, had thrown him a mammoth sixtieth birthday party, inviting showbiz luminaries from every part of McKellen's life, as well as other friends and family. McKellen looks delighted in the photographs, smiling with Francesca Annis, Susan Hampshire, Derek Jacobi, Sting, Trevor Nunn, Steven Berkoff, Jane Asher, Dawn French, David Hockney, Monica Lewinsky, Geri Halliwell . . . the list goes on and on. He may have been less delighted when the photographs featured so prominently in *Hello* Magazine. For his sixty-fifth birthday there was no party, just a trip to the theatre and dinner.

In *Emile*, McKellen's character is asked how old he feels. He replies, 'About ten.' McKellen himself says he doesn't feel old at 65. 'I feel like everything's to come, like I'm just over halfway,' he told the *Daily Telegraph* in May 2004. 'I'm aware of the end, but it's not in sight.' He had an AIDS test several years ago at a time when many of his friends were getting the disease. Almost certain that his lifestyle had left him safe from the virus, he nevertheless spent an uneasy day awaiting the result. It was negative. Twenty years ago he was already saying that he wanted to end in glory and in harness. He has no regrets at having no children to give him immortality, claiming in a *Times* interview he would have made a dreadful father, 'as most people are, of course'. Perhaps there is a trace there still of residual feelings about Denis McKellen.

Actors aren't supposed to get old, any more than politicians, and McKellen has a little trick he uses now, picked up from meeting Ronald Reagan not long after John Hinckley shot him in 1981. At the White House for a celebration of Shakespeare's birthday, McKellen watched the seventy-year-old president run into the room to prove how fit he was. 'Now I tend to run a lot at premieres!' he told James Rampton. What is utterly disarming is that he admits to the trick perfectly happily. It's what keeps him an actor and not a celebrity.

At smaller-scale events with the public he's different again. The London opening of his film *Emile* was an extremely low-key event in a small cinema on Shaftesbury Avenue. There were no movie stars, no massed phalanx of TV cameras and photojournalists, no red carpet. McKellen talks quietly after the screening to anyone who's bothered to show up. He's in jeans and a pair of blue clogs with an incipient beard. It's Sunday. He's spent the afternoon with a young filmmaker named Josh Stern, and he's happy to announce working with him as his next project to this group of ordinary folk. Stern is in the audience. 'What did we decide my character was going to be called, Josh? Oh, yes. Gabriel.'

The publicity man, who thinks this should be a staged event, is priming him with typical showbiz questions: 'Do you like meeting the public, Ian?' There's a hint of a pause, and then, 'Well, I'm a member of the public.' He's too quick to be caught off guard by this kind of rubbish. 'Isn't the point of *The Lord of the Rings* that people will discover your other work through it, Ian?' A short laugh. 'Well, I don't think that's the point of *The Lord of the Rings* at all.' He's not being awkward. He's just avoiding any hint of grandness, of starriness.

He treats every question seriously. He'd like to work with Woody Allen and Steven Spielberg. His favourite performances of his own are Macbeth, Richard III, Iago, James Whale. A gay subtext in *The Lord of the Rings*? Sam and Frodo? He becomes playful, teasing: 'What are they doing up that mountain? Getting away from it all . . .?'

Some of the answers are formulaic. He tells a story about a girl coming up to him during the run of *Hamlet*, which he's told in the press a dozen times before. '. . . she was breathless, panting with excitement, "I thought Laertes was going to kill you!"' then he realises he must have got the story wrong. Laertes *does* kill Hamlet. He improvises his way out of trouble: 'Well, anyway, she'd just seen an awful lot of deaths!' And then he makes his point about the audience he likes to reach – the kind who haven't seen the play a hundred times before.

His air is more professor than actor – this could be a Cambridge seminar, rather than a publicity event. But then again, his character in the film was a professor. So, having watched his own performance, is he still in character? Is it an act after all? That's the mark of a great actor – it's impossible to tell the difference.

At 65, McKellen has perfected a whole range of public personae. There's the professor we've just met; there's the sixty-year-old smiling public man among school children in LA's Koreatown; there's the serious actor of the movie junket interview; there's caring and concerned for gay causes persona. There's ironic-amused, modest-bemused, waspish-impatient and mischievous-camp. And there's a line in intense self-deprecation to deal with the fame Gandalf has brought. If he's sharing a chat show with some loud-mouthed comedian, he'll say he's always wanted to do stand-up. If he's talking to Parky, it's, 'I wanted to be what you are, Michael.'

Asked to be themselves in public, actors don't know what to do; they need a character and a script.

*   *   *

So what do his friends say? What's the real Ian McKellen like? Is he the secular saint of gay rights? No. 'He's not a saint,' Richard Eyre told Robert Cheshyre for the *Sunday Telegraph* magazine. 'He can be incredibly difficult, moody.' Is the humility an act? Maybe not. 'He doesn't stand on his dignity,' Angela Mason, ex-executive director of Stonewall, told *Gay Times*. 'The first time I met him he was changing and taking off his trousers and shirt in our grubby little office. I felt embarrassed and he was completely nonplussed, because, as he said, actors are taking their clothes off all the time.'

A lot can be found out about a star actor by talking to other people in the cast – especially those well down the cast list. Actors will soon tell you if someone likes to pull star stuff. About Ian McKellen people are likely to comment: 'Very amenable'; 'Very approachable'; 'No airs and graces'. David Ashton, carrying a spear at the Cambridge Theatre in McKellen's *Hamlet* in 1971, said, 'He had a kind of knack although he was a star – of being very easily with you and you didn't feel there was any condescension. He was an actor in a company of actors.' Margery Mason of the Actors' Company says, 'He hasn't got star mannerisms.' 'It's like Ralph Fiennes,' says Emily Richard, veteran of the RSC small scale tour of 1978 and married to one of McKellen's oldest friends, Edward Petherbridge. 'He looks at you as though he means it. He doesn't look at you as though he's trying to look for someone more interesting.'

'Very loyal.' That's the way old friends like Sean Mathias and Zoë Wanamaker describe McKellen. Gawn Grainger, a mate from Ipswich days, remains a close friend. Many have stories to tell of how he has put himself out for them and particularly for their children. 'He was very kind to our older boy when he was ill in hospital, gave him loads of presents,' recalls Geoffrey Banks. Faith Brook, Gertrude to McKellen's Hamlet, remembers her son, Brook Horowitz, was only nine when the tour opened in Nottingham. McKellen went out of his way to be friendly, to the point where Brook began to refer to him as his brother. 'After that Ian would always say, "How's my baby brother?"' Trevor Peacock's eight-year-old daughter used to make him jelly on the Cambridge Theatre Company tour, and watch while he ate it up in his dressing room.

Critics have complained that there's a lack of tenderness in McKellen, the actor – and he would need it for the second half of *Lear* – yet there is tenderness in the man. Emily Richard tells this story of going with Edward Petherbridge to a party in Narrow Street at the end of 2003: 'I thought it was going to be rather stuffed full of celebrities. But it wasn't. They were just actors that you'd worked with and that you know and you like and you respect. And I just remember seeing Ian standing in a corner at one point, stroking Edward's head – both of them are grey haired now – and I just thought, Well that's really nice. It's nothing that I'm afraid of. They're just friends. And I like that.'

But it's also been said that it's not easy to become McKellen's friend. Clive Swift found him reticent at Cambridge, rarely talking about himself or his family. 'I think it was very difficult to get to know him,' says Richard Digby Day, assistant director up in Nottingham, when McKellen was first making his name. 'I never got terribly close to Ian,' Lucy Fleming, who played his Queen on the *Richard II* tour which made him a star, says. 'I never really knew whether he thought I was any good or not.' The anxiety is still there, more than thirty years on.

Tim McInnerny was Catesby in the film of *Richard III*. He offers an interesting picture of what it takes to be accepted into the McKellen circle. 'He doesn't suffer fools gladly. You go through quite a rigorous testing process as to whether you're worth having as a friend or whether you are going to be a total bore. Ian is so intelligent and such a fast thinker, that anyone who can't keep up with him, I imagine, he would find very dull. I quite relished being tested. You could tell when you were being tested: there'd be a slight arching of the eyebrow to see if you were going to rise to some intellectual prodding. If you could wield the rapier in conversation, then you might be worth talking to the next day.'

Acting and politics go hand in hand in many people's summing up of Ian McKellen. 'Everyone, including people at Outrage!, has a great deal of respect for him, because of his coming out and the stature of the man being prepared to put himself on the line in that way,' says David Allison, spokesman of rival gay rights organisation Outrage! 'I think he's been very brave,' offers his school contemporary Michael Shipley. 'I don't think anybody disrespects him for it in Bolton.' 'I'm Scottish,' says Alan Cohen, 'and you would say of him, "He's a good man." And that's a big testament in Scottish.'

'There is another side,' offers one old friend, and that comes out in a certain inflexibility in rehearsal. 'He has to do his own version. It's not up for grabs.' That led to clashes with Alan Ayckbourn during *Henceforward* in 1988. Some say it led to the recasting of *The Dance of Death*. McKellen himself admitted to Amanda Mitchison in the *Sunday Telegraph* back in 1998, 'I do get impatient with theatrical practitioners who settle for second best or for doing what they've done before.'

Richard Eyre, director of the stage *Richard III*, admires McKellen as an actor and a political activist. He tells the story of McKellen performing his one-man show one evening in his sitting room and being overwhelmed at getting the full force of the actor's virtuosity at such close range. Yet he also wrote in his *Diary*, 'He dominates rehearsals often at the expense of other actors.' Eyre explains, '. . . all strong actors radiate an energy that has an almost physical heat, and they draw the heat like poultices from the actors around them. Being combative, impatient, irascible and frustrating is often an implicit demand to be challenged and stimulated, to be given competition by their fellow actors.'

Everybody says that McKellen wanted to be a film star for years before success on-screen finally came. Now, without doubt, he is professionally happy in a way that he has probably never been before. 'I saw him just after the 2004 Oscars,' comments Nigel Havers, 'and he seemed really really pleased. Because he's worked bloody hard at it. And if you do crack Hollywood at that age with a classical background, they worship you. They deify you. You are the god of acting.'

At the same time, to retain the respect of fellow professionals – at least in the UK – an actor can't be seen to take it all too seriously. That's why McKellen treads his fine, ironic line through the hype and the merchandising, declaring Burger King's Gandalf goblet his favourite drinking ware these days, saying of the latest Magneto action toy that it looks like his father without his teeth in. It's for the theatre world, as well as the public. 'I think he's taken his ridiculous fame very graciously,' says Margery Mason.

London docklands has transformed itself around him since McKellen moved to his house in Limehouse in 1981. The Docklands Light Railway has come almost to his door. The riverbank opposite is lined with bijou 1980s developments, which he hates – 'They haven't even got a cupboard to put the Hoover,' he complained in the *Sunday Times*. This is New Town London, where the old warehouses have become apartments and smart offices, the Ragged School is a museum and Canary Wharf looms at the end of the street just like the chimney of the old bleach works at the end of Barrow Bridge Road outside Bolton. Limehouse is all marinas and new housing. Only the Commercial Road remains forever the Commercial Road, as rough as the proverbial badger's bottom. Limehouse has changed around him; McKellen has stayed where he is. In some ways that's true of McKellen the actor too.

Antony Sher tells a story about McKellen in his autobiography *Beside Myself*. The two actors were having dinner one night, when the conversation turned to Laurence Olivier. 'We can't match him – none of us can – ever,' said McKellen gloomily. Sher was surprised. He'd come to think of McKellen as a better actor than Olivier, more truthful, more dangerous. McKellen changed the subject brusquely, and would say no more. It's a game the critics have been playing since *Richard II* in 1969. Is McKellen as good as Olivier? The question is meaningless – much like asking: which is the better mode of transport – a barouche-landau or a Jaguar XJS? But Sher's story suggests it's a question McKellen asks himself.

Faith Brook thinks he always had a sense of himself in the great tradition of classical actors. Zoë Wanamaker thinks as an actor, 'He's of another era in a lot of ways – in a sense of penny plain tuppence coloured.' Cicely Berry agrees, but goes further. She thinks McKellen's reverence for Olivier and the whole tradition of British classical acting has been a hindrance to him. 'I'm not sure that he's entirely of now,' is how she puts it. 'Maybe there's a certain sense of style which interferes. There's an over-reverence for that style. Sometimes I wish he would just let it go and be him.' But then maybe McKellen always was a bit of a throw-back with his grand gestures, his soaringly theatrical voice and those endless Shakespearian tours of the provinces.

The stage and the movie set are places of attention but also of threat – the staring eyes of the audience, the staring camera lens. For a few actors they are places where anything is possible, nothing can go wrong: change everything every night; take your clothes off unrehearsed. For the British, notoriously a nation whose greatest fear is embarrassment, it's exhibitionism, and almost incomprehensible. So we protect ourselves from actors behind derision, calling them luvvies and worse. As long ago as 1976 in an article in *Plays and Players* McKellen made his response in typically measured language: 'At its most rewarding acting involves an intense combination of intellect, imagination and hard work, belying the popular image of dressing up, booming voices and shrieking exhibitionism.'

So he's a hard grafting professional who's learned his trade and worked his way up from the bottom. Someone a bit like Denis McKellen, in fact. Maybe not. With his wit and his air of mild detachment from the processes of stardom, McKellen retains something of the old-fashioned amateur – the actor who didn't go to drama school; the actor who brushes past Antony Sher who is genuinely breathless and sweating in the wings of the Cottesloe Theatre, ready for his first entrance as Astrov who must look as if he's galloped miles across country. 'Oh, darling,' drawls McKellen, 'you're such a Method actor, there is an easier way, y'know.' And he dabs a little spit from tongue to forehead – 'Like so!'

CREDITS

THEATRE:
A Man for All Seasons, *When We Are Married*, *You Never Can Tell*, *Black Coffee*, *Celebration*, *End of Conflict*, *Mr Pickwick*, *Toad of Toad Hall*, *The Seagull*, *The Bride Comes Back*, *Much Ado About Nothing*, *Happy Returns*, *Ten Little Niggers*, *Irregular Verb to Love*, *Semi-Detached*, *Noah* (Belgrade Theatre, Coventry), 1961–2; *Beckett*, *The Gazebo*, *Caste*, *The Big Killing*, *The Amorous Prawn*, *The Keep*, *David Copperfield*, *Aladdin*, *How Dare We!*, *Henry V*, *Under Milk Wood*, *Arsenic and Old Lace*, *Luther* (Arts Theatre, Ipswich), 1962–3; *The Big Contract* (Belgrade Theatre, Coventry), 1963; *A Long Day's Journey into Night*, *To Dorothy a Son*, *I, John Brown*, *Salad Days*, *The Corn is Green*, *The Public Eye*, *Sergeant Musgrave's Dance*, *All in Good Time* (Arts Theatre, Ipswich), 1963; *Coriolanus*, *The Life in My Hands*, *The Bashful Genius*, *The Mayor of Zalamea*, *Saturday Night and Sunday Morning*, *Sir Thomas More* (Nottingham Playhouse), 1963–4; *A Scent of Flowers* (Duke of York's), 1964; *Much Ado About Nothing*, *Armstrong's Last Goodnight*, *Trelawney of the Wells* (National Theatre: Old Vic, London; Chichester; UK Tour),1965; *A Lily in Little India* (Hampstead Theatre; St Martin's Theatre, London), 1965–6; *Their Very Own and Golden City* (Royal Court Theatre, London), 1966; *O'Flaherty, V.C./The Man of Destiny* (Mermaid Theatre, London), 1966; *The Promise* (Oxford Playhouse; Fortune Theatre, London; Henry Miller Theatre, New York), 1966–7; *White Liars/Black Comedy* (Lyric Theatre, London), 1968; *Richard II* (Prospect Theatre Company: UK Tour), 1968; *The Bacchae*, *The Prime of Miss Jean Brodie* [dir.], *Three Months Gone* [dir.] (Liverpool Playhouse), 1969; *Richard II/Edward II* (Prospect Theatre Company: UK & European Tour; Mermaid & Piccadilly Theatres, London), 1969–70; *Billy's Last Stand* (Royal Court Theatre Upstairs, London), 1970; *The Recruiting Officer*, *Chips with Everything* (Cambridge Theatre Company: Arts Theatre, Cambridge; UK Tour), 1970; *Hamlet* (Prospect Theatre Company: UK & European Tour), 1971; *Swan Song* (Crucible Theatre, Sheffield), 1971; *The Real Inspector Hound* [dir.] (Phoenix Theatre, Leicester), 1972; *Erpingham Camp* [dir.] (Watford Palace Theatre), 1972; *Ruling the Roost*, *'Tis Pity She's a Whore*, *The Three Arrows* (Actors' Company: UK Tour), 1972; *A Private Matter* [dir.] (Vaudeville Theatre, London), 1973; *The Wood Demon*, *The Way of the World*, *Knots*, *King Lear*, *Ruling the Roost*, *'Tis Pity She's a Whore* (Actors' Company: UK Tour; Shaw Theatre, London; Brooklyn Academy, New

York; Wimbledon Theatre), 1973–4; *Dr Faustus*, *The Marquis of Keith*, *King John* (RSC: Aldwych Theatre), 1974–5; *The Clandestine Marriage* [dir.] (Savoy Theatre), 1975; *Ashes* (Young Vic), 1975; *Too True to Be Good* (RSC: Aldwych & Globe Theatres), 1975; *Romeo and Juliet*, *The Winter's Tale*, *Words, Words, Words*, *Macbeth*, *The Alchemist*, *Every Good Boy Deserves Favour*, *Pillars of the Community*, *Acting Shakespeare*, *Days of the Commune*, *A Miserable and Lonely Death* (RSC: Stratford, Newcastle, London), 1976–7; *Twelfth Night*, *Three Sisters*, *Is there honey still for tea?* (RSC: UK Tour), 1978; *Bent* (Royal Court and Criterion Theatre, London), 1979; *Acting Shakespeare* (British Council European Tour), 1980; *Amadeus* (Broadhurst Theatre, New York), 1980–1; *Acting Shakespeare* (Tour – Europe, Israel, USA), 1982–4; *Short List* (Hampstead Theatre), 1983; *Cowardice* (Tour & Ambassadors Theatre, London), 1983; *Venice Preserv'd*, *Wild Honey*, *Coriolanus*, *The Duchess of Malfi*, *The Real Inspector Hound*, *The Critic*, *The Cherry Orchard* (National Theatre and Chicago) 1984–6; *Wild Honey* (Virginia Theatre, New York), 1986; *Acting Shakespeare* (US tour; Playhouse Theatre, London; UK tour), 1987–8; *Henceforward* (Vaudeville Theatre, London), 1988; *Bent* (Adelphi Theatre, London), 1989; *Othello* (RSC: Stratford & London), 1989; *Bent* (National & Garrick Theatre, London), 1990; *Chip in the Sugar* (Haymarket Theatre, London), 1990; *King Lear*, *Richard III* (National Theatre World Tour), 1990–2; *Napoli Milionaria* (National Theatre), 1991; *Uncle Vanya* (National Theatre), 1992; *A Knight Out* (US, S Africa, UK, Europe), 1994–7; *An Enemy of the People*, *Peter Pan* (National Theatre), 1997–8; *An Enemy of the People* (Ahmanson Theatre, Los Angeles), 1998; *The Seagull*, *Present Laughter*, *The Tempest* (West Yorkshire Playhouse), 1998–9; *Dance of Death* (Broadhurst Theatre, New York), 2001; *Dance of Death* (Lyric Theatre, London; Theatre Royal Sidney), 2003–4; *Aladdin* (Old Vic, London), 2004–5

TELEVISION:

Kipling (BBC), 1964; *Sunday out of Season* (ATV), 1965; *The Trial and Torture of Sir John Ramplayne* (BBC), 1965; *David Copperfield* (BBC), 1966; *What if it's just Green Cheese?* (BBC), 1969; *John Keats* (BBC), 1970; *Richard II* (BBC), 1970; *Edward II* (BBC), 1970; *Ross* (BBC), 1970; *The Last Journey* (Granada), 1971; *Hamlet* (UK/CBS Cable), 1972; *Craven Arms* (Granada), 1973; *The Recruiting Officer* (BBC), 1973; *Graceless Go I* (BBC), 1973; *Hedda Gabler* (BBC), 1974; *Every Good Boy Deserves Favour* (BBC), 1978; *Macbeth* (Thames), 1979; *Dying Day* (ITV/PBS), 1980; *Acting Shakespeare* (PBS), 1982; *The Scarlet Pimpernel* (London Films/CBS), 1982; *Walter, Walter and June* [aka *Loving Walter*] (Channel

4), 1982; *Ian McKellen's Diary of a Year* (South Bank Show), 1985; *Ian McKellen Acting Shakespeare* (PBS), 1985; *The Witches* (BBC), 1986; *Suleiman the Magnificent* [narration only] (PBS), 1987; *Windmill of the Gods* (CBS), 1988; *Othello* (RSC), 1989; *Countdown to War* (Granada), 1989; *Mister Shaw's Missing Millions* (Channel 4), 1993; *Tales of the City* (Channel 4/PBS), 1993; *And the Band Played On* (HBO), 1993; *Cold Comfort Farm* (BBC), 1994; *Anglia at War* [narration only], 1995; *National Poetry Day* (BBC), 1995; *Rasputin* (HBO), 1996; *David Copperfield* (BBC), 1999; *The Oliviers in Love* [narration only] (Channel 4), 2001; *Everest – View from the Top* [narration only] (Channel 4), 2002; *Churchill* [narration only] (TW1/Carlton), 2003; *The Simpsons* (Fox), 2003; *A Year in the Life of Ian McKellen* (South Bank Show), 2004

FILMS:

The Bells of Hell Go Ting-a-ling-a-ling, 1966 [unfinished]; *A Touch Of Love* [aka *Thank You All Very Much*], 1969; *Alfred the Great*, 1968; *The Promise*, 1969; *Priest of Love*, 1979; *The Keep*, 1983; *Zina*, 1985; *Plenty*, 1986; *Scandal*, 1988; *The Ballad of Little Jo*, 1992; *I'll Do Anything*, 1992; *Last Action Hero*, 1993; *Six Degrees of Separation*, 1993; *The Shadow*, 1994; *Jack and Sarah*, 1994; *Restoration*, 1995; *Thin Ice*, 1995; *Richard III*, 1996; *Surviving Friendly Fire* [narration only], 1997; *Bent*, 1997; *Swept from the Sea* 1997; *Apt Pupil*, 1998; *Gods and Monsters*, 1998; *Cirque du Soleil: Journey of Man* [narration only], 2000; *X-Men*, 2000; *The Lord of the Rings: The Fellowship of the Ring*, 2001; *The Lord of the Rings: The Two Towers*, 2002; *X2*, 2003; *The Lord of the Rings: The Return of the King*, 2003; *Emile*, 2004; *Asylum*, 2004; *Neverwas*, 2005; *The Magic Roundabout Movie* [voice], 2005

BIBLIOGRAPHY

Alan, Paul. *Alan Ayckbourn – Grinning at the Edge* (Methuen, 2001)

Barton, John. *Playing Shakespeare* (Methuen, 1984)

Berkoff, Steven. *Free Association – An Autobiography* (Faber and Faber, 1996)

Cox, Brian. *The Lear Diaries* (Methuen, 1992)

Cox, Murray (ed.). *Shakespeare Comes to Broadmoor* [foreword by Ian McKellen] (Jessica Kingsley, 1992)

Eyre, Richard. *National Service: Diary of a Decade at the National Theatre* (Bloomsbury, 2003)

Fay, Stephen. *Power Play – The Life and Times of Peter Hall* (Hodder & Stoughton, 1995)

Frost, David. *David Frost – An Autobiography Part One – From Congregations to Audiences* (Harper Collins, 1993)

Goodwin, John (ed.). *Peter Hall's Diaries – The Story of a Dramatic Battle* (Hamish Hamilton, 1983)

Hall, Peter. *Exposed by the Mask* (TCC, 2000)

Hancock, Sheila. *Ramblings of an Actress* (Hutchinson, 1987)

Hill, Susan (ed.). *People: Essays and Poems* (Chatto and Windus, 1983)

Hoare, Philip. *Noel Coward – A Biography* (Sinclair Stevenson, 1995)

Various. *For Ian Charleson: A Tribute* (Constable, 1990)

Jarman, Derek. *At Your Own Risk: A Saint's Testament* (Hutchinson, 1992)

Jarman, Derek, [ed. Collins, Kevin]. *Smiling in Slow Motion* (Century, 2000)

Kott, Jan. *Shakespeare Our Contemporary* (Methuen, 1964)

Laing, R D. *Knots* (Penguin Books, 1971)

Major, John. *John Major – The Autobiography* (Harper Collins, 1999)

McKellen, Ian. 'Before, Now and In Between' from *Stonewall 25: The Making of the Lesbian and Gay Community in Britain* [eds. Healey, Emma and Mason, Angela] (Virago, 1994)

McKellen, Ian; Loncraine, Richard. *Richard III: A Screenplay* (Doubleday, 1996)

Miller, John. *Judi Dench: With a Crack in Her Voice* (Weidenfeld and Nicholson, 1998)

Miller, John. *Peter Ustinov: The Gift of Laughter* (Weidenfeld and Nicholson, 2002)

Nadel, Ira. *Double Act: A Life of Tom Stoppard* (Methuen, 2002)

Olivier, Laurence. *On Acting* (Simon & Schuster, 1986)

Orwell, George. *The Road to Wigan Pier* (Penguin, 1962)

Peake, Tony. *Derek Jarman* (Little Brown & Co., 1999)

Robinson, Ian. 'FR Leavis The Cambridge Don' (Paper delivered to the University College Swansea English Society, 1992)

Rowell, George; Jackson, Anthony. *The Repertory Movement – A History of Regional Theatre in Britain* (CUP, 1984)

Sher, Antony. *Beside Myself – An Autobiography* (Hutchinson, 2001)

Sher, Antony. *The Year of the King* (Methuen, 1985)

West, Timothy. *A Moment Towards the End of the Play: An Autobiography* (Nick Hern Books, 2001)

INDEX